Women in STEM Careers

For

Marisha, Hillary and Kelly,

Nigel, Nick and Kate

Women in STEM Careers

International Perspectives on Increasing Workforce Participation, Advancement and Leadership

---

Edited by

Diana Bilimoria

KeyBank Professor and Professor and Chair of Organizational Behavior, Weatherhead School of Management, Case Western Reserve University, USA

Linley Lord

Associate Professor and Director, Maureen Bickley Centre for Women in Leadership, Curtin University, Australia

Edward Elgar

Cheltenham, UK • Northampton, MA, USA

Published by
Edward Elgar Publishing Limited
The Lypiatts
15 Lansdown Road
Cheltenham
Glos GL50 2JA
UK

Edward Elgar Publishing, Inc.
William Pratt House
9 Dewey Court
Northampton
Massachusetts 01060
USA

A catalogue record for this book
is available from the British Library

Library of Congress Control Number: 2014938764

This book is available electronically in the ElgarOnline.com Business Subject Collection, E-ISBN 978 1 78195 407 2

ISBN 978 1 78195 406 5

Typeset by Columns Design XML Ltd, Reading
Printed and bound in Great Britain by T.J. International Ltd, Padstow

Contents

Figures

Tables

Contributors

Mary Ayre has recently retired from a senior lectureship at the University of Glamorgan in Wales, UK, and is currently completing her PhD on women in the engineering profession at the University of South Australia (UNiSA). She has been active in women-in-engineering education, research, and advocacy for 30 years in the UK and Australia. In 1998 she received a national award from Engineers Australia for her work on gender inclusive curriculum with the Engineering Schools at UNiSA, and in 2010 she co-authored the book *Gender Inclusive Engineering Education* with the other authors of her chapter in this book.

Diana Bilimoria, PhD is KeyBank Professor and Chair and Professor of Organizational Behavior at the Weatherhead School of Management at Case Western Reserve University. She is co-author of *Gender Equity in Science and Engineering: Advancing Change in Higher Education*; *Women on Corporate Boards of Directors: International Research and Practice*; and *Handbook on Women in Business and Management*. She has published several journal articles and chapters in edited volumes. She has served as the chair of the Gender and Diversity in Organizations Division of the Academy of Management and as editor of the *Journal of Management Education*. She has been internationally recognized for her scholarship, leadership, and service.

Inge L. Bleijenbergh, PhD is Assistant Professor at Radboud University Nijmegen, The Netherlands. Her research involves gender in organizations, participatory research methods and policy change. She received European Union 7th framework research grants for the projects STAGES (Structural Transformation to Achieve Gender Equality in Science) and EGERA (Effective Gender Equality in Research and Academia). She is associate editor of *Gender, Work and Organization* and has published in journals such as *Social Politics*, *European Journal of Industrial Relations*, *Quality and Quantity*, *Equality, Diversity and Inclusion*, *Marriage & Family Review* and *European Journal of Employment Relations*.

Dede Bonner, EdD was awarded her doctorate degree in Executive Leadership from George Washington University. Dr. Bonner is an internationally known consultant, author, speaker and educator. As a part-time professor at Curtin University in Australia, George Washington University in Washington, DC and other US universities, Dr. Bonner has taught diverse business and leadership courses for graduate students. She is the co-editor of the pioneering bestseller on knowledge management *In Action: Leading Knowledge Management and Learning* (2000). She was the member chief editor for ASTD's acclaimed journal *T+D*, and her work has been presented in many international books, journals, keynote addresses, conference presentation and workshops.

Kathleen Buse, PhD, having started her career as an engineer, has worked in various technical and management roles for more than 25 years. Kathleen obtained her PhD in Management from Case Western Reserve University. Her research has been framed by her practical experience and has focused on women who persist in the STEM professions and includes professional and leadership development, women in leadership and women's careers. Today Kathleen has faculty positions in the Leadership Lab for Women in STEM, the Weatherhead School of Management and the Case School of Engineering.

Erin L. Cadwalader, PhD is the Phoebe S. Leboy Public Policy Fellow at the Association for Women in Science (AWIS). She works to execute the organization's mission of improving the professional ecosystem to help women in STEM achieve their full potential. Previously Dr. Cadwalader worked as a science policy fellow at Research!America, an advocate for the Utah Health Policy Project, and as a freelance science writer. She earned a PhD in Neurobiology and Anatomy from the University of Utah and a BS in Biochemistry from the University of Wisconsin-Madison.

Wen Hsin Chang is a third year Educational Psychology doctoral student at the University of Wisconsin-Milwaukee. She has a bachelor's degree in Educational Psychology and Counseling, and a master's degree in Educational, School and Counseling Psychology, with a specific focus on occupational counseling. Wen Hsin's research interests include vocational psychology and multicultural counseling. She is interested in the effects of micro-aggression on individuals' career decision making.

Catia Figueiredo is a third year Educational Psychology doctoral student at the University of Wisconsin-Milwaukee. She has a bachelor's degree in Psychology, and a master's degree in Educational and Developmental Psychology, with a specific focus on positive interventions in communities. Catia's research interests include work in identity development, well-being promotion, and vocational psychology. She is interested in the effects of creativity on learning and adjustment processes, as well as contextual approaches to work adjustment.

Mary Fitzpatrick, PhD holds a doctorate in Educational Psychology with a special emphasis on vocational and career psychology from the University of Wisconsin-Milwaukee, and is a licensed psychologist. She currently serves as a Director for Diversity Research and Initiatives in the College of Engineering at the University of Wisconsin-Madison. Prior to becoming a psychologist, Dr. Fitzpatrick was a practicing engineer and program manager in new product development for leading companies such as GE Healthcare and Microsoft. She holds an undergraduate degree in Biomedical Engineering and a master's in Electrical Engineering. Her research interests include occupational sex and racial segregation, retention of underrepresented groups in science, technology and engineering and math (STEM) fields, workplace bullying and multicultural issues in the workplace.

Nadya A. Fouad, PhD received her doctorate from the University of Minnesota in Counseling Psychology. She is currently Distinguished Professor and Chair of the Department of Educational Psychology at the University of Wisconsin-Milwaukee and faculty member in the Counseling Psychology program. She was editor of *The Counseling Psychologist* and is on the editorial boards of the *Journal of Vocational Behavior* and the *Journal of Career Assessment*. Her work on cross-cultural vocational assessment and counseling, career development of women and racial/ethnic minorities, and interest management has earned her several awards. She is currently working with her colleague, Romila Singh, on two large NSF-funded studies to examine the persistence and engagement of men and women in engineering careers.

Judith Gill is an Adjunct Associate Professor in Education at the University of South Australia. Her previous research interests have included gender in educational contexts, girls and mathematics and comparisons between single sex schooling and coeducation. More recently she has led investigations into aspects of women and work and citizenship education. She has authored, co-authored and edited seven books on these and related topics along with many research publications. Her most recent publication is *Challenging Knowledge, Sex and Power: Gender, Work and Engineering* (2013).

Joan M. Herbers, PhD is Professor of Evolution, Ecology and Organismal Biology and of Women's, Gender, and Sexuality Studies at the Ohio State University. Trained as an ecologist, she studied the inner working of ant colonies for most of her academic life, and recently has developed expertise in gender equity issues. She is currently Principal Investigator of Comprehensive Equity at Ohio State (CEOS), an NSF-funded ADVANCE Institutional Transformation Award, and is Past President of the Association for Women in Science.

Channah Herschberg is a PhD candidate at the Institute for Management Research, Radboud University Nijmegen, The Netherlands. She did a BSc in Psychology and an MSc in Human Resource Management and Organisational Analysis. Her research interests include gender and diversity, academic careers, sustainable careers, and organizational norms. Channah has been involved in a research project on gender in the career paths of ERC applicants. Her PhD project focuses on gender and precarious workers in academia in seven countries. This project, Gendering the Academy and Research: Combating Career Instability and Asymmetries (GARCIA), is part of the EU 7th framework program.

Charlotte Holgersson, PhD is a researcher at the Department of Industrial Economics and Management at KTH Royal Institute of Technology, Sweden. Her research is located in the intersection between organization and management studies and gender studies. She defended her doctoral thesis in 2003 at the Stockholm School of Economics. One of her main empirical concerns has been the perpetuation of men's dominance of top positions in organizations but she is also interested in processes of change and several of her research projects focus on both gender equality and diversity practices in organizations.

Pia Höök, PhD has been the global diversity manager at Skanska Group since 2012. Prior to that, she was diversity director at Volvo Group. She has a PhD in Business Administration from Stockholm School of Economics and she became an associate professor of organization, management and gender at the Royal Institute of Technology in 2010. She has been a visiting scholar at Stanford University twice, and she has been an expert contributor to several governmental studies and delegations on gender equality. The main focus of her research is gender equality work in organizations.

Xiangfen Liang, PhD holds a PhD in Organization Behavior from City University of Hong Kong and a BS and MS in Psychology from Beijing Normal University. Xiangfen has worked in industry in marketing research and strategy consulting, and at Case Western Reserve University as a research staff member. She is co-author of *Gender Equity in Science and Engineering: Advancing Change in Higher Education*, published in 2012. She has written several articles in the areas of employee turnover behaviors, gender diversity, and organizational transformation.

Linley Lord, DBA is an Associate Professor and the Chair of the Academic Board at Curtin University. She is the Academic Director for the Curtin Leadership Centre and the Director of the Maureen Bickley Centre for Women in Leadership (MBC) at Curtin's Graduate School of Business. Dr. Lord has presented her research on women in non-traditional areas of employment, women's experience in leadership roles, new models of leadership, and women on corporate and university boards at key international conferences in Europe, the UK and the US. Dr. Lord is a member of the Chamber of Minerals and Energy (WA) Women in Resources Reference Group, and has been a sessional member of the Western Australian State Administrative Tribunal since its inception in 2005.

Sally Male, PhD undertakes research on engineering education and women in engineering at the University of Western Australia (http://uwa.academia.edu/SallyMale). Current projects include: industry engagement in engineering degrees; and gender inclusivity of engineering students' experiences of workplace learning. Sally has honors in electrical engineering and a PhD in engineering education. Sally previously worked at Curtin University and has served on the State and National Women in Engineering Committees of Engineers Australia. Sally is a Fellow of Engineers Australia and is the Western Australian Convenor of the Women in Science Enquiry Network.

Melissa Marinelli is a final year doctoral researcher and Research Associate at Maureen Bickley Centre for Women in Leadership at Curtin University. She holds bachelor and postgraduate engineering degrees from the University of Western Australia and has worked primarily in the oil and gas industry, in technical and managerial roles. She was the Chair of Engineers Australia Women in Engineering group in Western Australia from 2008 to 2010. Melissa is passionate about engineering careers for women, and is committed to increasing the representation of women in engineering and non-traditional industries through research, advocacy, education and example.

Julie Mills, PhD is Professor and Head of Civil Engineering at the University of South Australia. Prior to entering academia she worked for 15 years as a structural engineer in private industry. Julie has received several national and university teaching grants and awards and co-authored a book on *Gender Inclusive Engineering Education* (2010). She was convenor of Australia's Women in Engineering Committee from 2004–06 and co-authored *Challenging Knowledge, Sex and Power:*

Gender, Work and Engineering (2013) based on a decade of research on women in the engineering workplace.

Margaret Nowak, PhD is an Emeritus Professor at the Curtin Graduate School of Business. Professor Nowak was the founding Director and Head of School of the Curtin Graduate School of Business from 1993 to 2003. Since then, she has continued to undertake research and doctoral supervision in the areas of governance, leadership, corporate social responsibility and labor market economics. Recent research programs have included collaboration in research on nursing leadership and a project on issues around the return to work following maternity leave. Professor Nowak gained her PhD from Murdoch University. She is a Fellow of the Australian Institute of Company Directors, with extensive board experience.

Alice B. Popejoy is a PhD student at the Institute for Public Health Genetics (IPHG) at the University of Washington, Seattle and a National Science Foundation (NSF) Graduate Research Fellow. She was previously the inaugural Phoebe S. Leboy Public Policy Fellow at the Association for Women in Science (AWIS) in Washington, DC. Alice is committed to keeping the lines of communication between science and policy-makers as open and accessible as possible, while pursuing her academic interests in gender equity, the evolution of gene families, bioinformatics, and access to genetic information.

Romila Singh, PhD received her doctorate in Organizational Sciences from Drexel University. She is an Associate Professor at the University of Wisconsin-Milwaukee Lubar School of Business. She is currently a representative-at-large at the Careers Division of the US Academy of Management. Romila's research focuses on understanding career management issues related to career choices, work–life relationships, retention and turnover decisions of women and people of color. Her research has appeared in leading journals in management and vocational behavior and in several book chapters. With her colleague Nadya Fouad, she is working on two large National Science Foundation (NSF) grants to investigate engineers' engagement, persistence, and turnover decisions.

Lineke Stobbe is a senior lecturer and curriculum coordinator at the Windesheim Honours College, Windesheim University of Applied Sciences, Zwolle, the Netherlands. She has done research on gender and work, mainly in male dominated organisational contexts, in the 1990s and the beginning of the 2000s. Currently, she educates talented and motivated students to become excellent international project and change managers and she is developing a research programme for the Honours College.

Marieke van den Brink, PhD is Associate Professor in Strategic Human Resource Management at the Radboud University Nijmegen. She researches the place and functioning of gender and diversity in organizations and the possibilities for change. Her PhD research, 'Behind the Scenes of Science', focused on the various gender practices tied in with professorial recruitment and selection, such as gatekeeping, micropolitics and the construction of scientific excellence. She is currently working on a large-scale case study research on diversity, organizational learning and change, and a comparative research on gender and precarious workers in European universities.

Marloes L. van Engen, PhD works at the Department of Human Resource Studies, Tilburg University. Marloes is also Gender Policy Advisor for Tilburg University. Her research interests are in the areas of sustainability in career and care, work–family issues in organizations, diversity, inequality and inclusion in organizations, gender in academia, stereotypes and status in teams. She has published in *Psychological Bulletin*, *Leadership Quarterly*, *Organizational Behavior and Human Decision Processes*, *Journal of Organizational and Occupational Psychology*, *Journal of Social Issues*, and *International Journal of Human Research Management.*

Claartje J. Vinkenburg, PhD is Associate Professor of Organizational Behavior and managing director of the Amsterdam Center for Career Research (ACCR) at VU University Amsterdam. Her PhD (VU, 1997) concerned gender in managerial behavior and effectiveness. She has been a visiting scholar at Northwestern University, USA and is a visiting professor at ESADE, Barcelona. Claartje's research relates to gender, diversity, leadership, and careers in organizations including professional service firms and in science. As principal investigator, Claartje studies gender in the career paths of ERC applicants, on a CSA-grant commissioned by the ERC (2012–14). She has written for and edited various academic and professional publications.

Anna Wahl, PhD is Professor of Gender, Organisation and Management at the Royal Institute of Technology (KTH), Stockholm, and guest professor at Tema Genus, Linköping University. Her current research interests are the gendering of management in different contexts, work for change and the impact of gender equality in organizations. Recent publications include articles in *Leadership through the Gender Lens*

(2010); Husu, Hearn, Lämsä and Vanhala (eds), *On the Shoulders of Giants* (2011); Jenssen and Wilson (eds) and NORA (*Nordic Journal of Feminists and Gender*), *Male Managers Challenging and Reinforcing the Male Norm in Management* (2014).

Acknowledgements

The idea for this book emerged from a series of conversations about the career development of women in the science, technology, engineering and mathematics (STEM) fields at an Academy of Management Conference we attended. During and since those early conversations, we have benefited greatly from numerous interactions with colleagues, scholars, mentors, supporters, and friends. Melissa Marinelli has been our most valuable ally throughout; this book simply would not have happened without her tremendous assistance and support. Melissa has shepherded and coordinated the entire writing process with the contributors to this volume as well as with our publishers, and she has provided keen insight into the shape and purpose of this volume.

Diana's passion for studying and facilitating the careers of women in STEM continues from the National Science Foundation's ADVANCE grants at Case Western Reserve University that she has been part of for the past 12 years. Deputy Provost Lynn Singer at Case Western Reserve University, the lead Principal Investigator (PI) on these awards, remains an inspiration and much admired colleague and friend. Diana also thanks the PIs, Co-PIs, research scholars and project team members of the extended ADVANCE family for the important change work collectively undertaken to create improved institutions of higher education for the enhanced recruitment, advancement, career development, retention and leadership of women in STEM.

Linley has had a long interest in women in STEM having completed an undergraduate degree in science then worked for many years as an equity practitioner, which included a focus on career opportunities for women in non-traditional areas. The strong resources sector in Western Australia has provided ongoing opportunity to continue this interest, most recently through the Maureen Bickley Centre for Women in Leadership at Curtin University, which has encouraged a number of research projects that relate to women in STEM careers. Linley would like to also thank Melissa Marinelli not only for her outstanding contribution to this book but for her ongoing passion regarding career opportunities for women in engineering.

We thank Francine O'Sullivan of Edward Elgar Publishing for being most encouraging of the creation of this book and extremely supportive throughout our writing and editing process.

Finally and most importantly, our love and gratitude goes to all our families and friends in the US, India, and Australia, for their wholehearted encouragement of our work. This book is the result of their unreserved support.

PART I

Women's individual experiences in STEM careers

1. An introduction to women in STEM careers: International perspectives on increasing workforce participation, advancement and leadership

Diana Bilimoria, Linley Lord and Melissa Marinelli

The fields of science, technology, engineering and mathematics (STEM) continually bring innovation and improvement to our daily lives as well as offer the potential for expansion of business and employment. Science and technology are applied to discover new opportunities and solve problems, and shape the formation, design, and development of new products and innovative production processes. An advanced science and technology enterprise offers distinctive national advantages to compete and win in today's fast-paced global business environment. With this increasing importance of science and technology for global economic competitiveness and growth, considerable attention is being paid to these industries as career choices for women and men. Individuals with STEM expertise have become critical for the success of both industry and academe sectors as their talents are conducive to an increased capacity for innovation.

Clearly, the full participation of women and men in STEM workforces is necessary to solidify and grow competitive advantage in the coming years and decades, yielding long-term benefits to national economies. Not surprisingly, in recent years there has been considerable focus in the United States, the United Kingdom, Europe and Australia on increasing the number of women in STEM fields. Over the past 40 years, initiatives implemented and supported by government, industry, academic institutions, and companies have aimed to attract and retain women into these professions (National Academies, 2007; Australian Academy of Science, 2013). Governments have committed considerable resources to attract women into STEM programs and equal opportunity legislation has resulted in changes in organizational practice with an aim to improve the workforce participation and advancement to leadership of women in STEM. Concurrently, there has been a spate of research on the lack of women in STEM areas including a number of recommendations for increasing attraction and retention rates (e.g., Bell, 2009; genSet, 2010; National Science Foundation, 2010). Despite this focus, women's participation in science and technology based careers remains disappointingly low in the industrialized world and their progress into senior roles can be best described as slow (Bell, 2009). Indeed, there are suggestions that progress may have stalled (Mills et al., 2010). Much of the previous research has explored the reasons why women leave or fail to succeed long term in STEM careers. Well documented are the lack of a critical mass of women in STEM at all ranks and in leadership, a leaky pipeline (the systematic loss of women at key career transition points), unequal employment opportunities and sex based occupational segregation (e.g., disproportionately large numbers of women in certain STEM fields and disproportionately few in others), inequitable treatment and valuing of women employees (for example, through stereotyping, excessive scrutiny, biased evaluations, and unequal access to resources and compensation), and differential effects of conflicts between work and life/family demands for women and men employees. We believe that it is timely now to focus also on success stories, as they may provide insights and new ways to address the issue at individual and systemic levels.

Thus, the aim of this volume is to bring together current research that spans both industry and academic sectors to examine the reasons for women's low participation in STEM and offer examples of successful ameliorative strategies at individual and systemic (organizational and profession/industry) levels. The research presented in this volume focuses on the barriers that women continue to face in STEM fields, the nature of STEM careers as experienced by women, individual career success strategies, and successful organizational and institutional initiatives related to appreciating, advancing and developing the contributions and careers of women in STEM.

Adopting an international perspective, we draw on research from the United States, Europe and Australia not only to explore the reasons for women's low participation in STEM fields but also to draw attention to the places where progress has occurred. We present the latest research spanning industry and academe, focusing on individual career success stories and successful organizational, institutional and educational initiatives related to women in STEM careers. Our focus in this volume is a shift from previous work, building on and complementing existing knowledge that pertains to the barriers and issues that women in these professions continue to face.

WHAT DO WE KNOW ABOUT WOMEN IN STEM CAREERS?

The dearth of women in STEM professions is a persistent puzzle that intrigues researchers and practitioners alike. This lack is a common phenomenon across the industrialized world (Hewlett et al., 2008; Bell, 2009; genSet, 2010). Those interested in how and why the proportion of women in these professions remains low and unchanging have produced a substantive body of work exploring the attraction, retention and attrition of women in STEM studies, in academia and in professional STEM careers (see for example McIlwee and Robinson, 1992; Burke and Mattis, 2007; National Research Council, 2007; European Parliament, 2008; Hewlett et al., 2008; Mills et al., 2008; Fouad et al., 2011; Fouad and Singh, 2011).

Yet despite increases in the numbers of women obtaining university qualifications in STEM fields including through to doctoral level, women remain underrepresented in the sciences both academically and professionally (Valian, 1998; Bilimoria, Joy and Liang, 2008; Bell, 2009; Bilimoria and Liang, 2012). Issues that have been identified that impact on women's under-representation include the lack of role models; assessment, recruitment and promotion systems that favor men; and under-representation that can lead to token status and to excessive commitments in order to meet the organization's gender equity commitments (genSet, 2010). Hostile work environments and extreme job pressures have also been identified as major factors regarding why women leave the sciences (Hewlett et al., 2008). In this regard, Fouad and Singh (2011) found in their survey that nearly half of the 3700 women respondents who had graduated with an engineering degree said they left because of working conditions, too much travel, and lack of advancement or low salary and a third of the women left because they did not like the workplace climate, their boss or the organization's culture.

In academic settings, women are less likely to have doctoral degrees and are more likely to be employed in non-tenure track positions (Long, 2001; Bilimoria and Liang, 2012). Goulden, Frasch and Mason (2009) found that family formation – most importantly marriage and childbirth – accounts for the largest leaks in the pipeline between PhD receipt and the acquisition of tenure for women in the sciences. Blickenstaff (2005, pp. 371–2) noted nine factors used to explain women's absence in STEM.

In addition to the factors already identified above were certain biological differences between men and women; girls' lack of preparation for science studies and careers; girls' attitudes toward science; irrelevant curricula; pedagogical approaches that favor male students; a "chilly" climate towards girls and women in science; pressure on girls and women to undertake traditional gender roles; and an inherently masculine world-view in scientific epistemology.

STEM CAREERS

Careers in the STEM areas tend to follow traditional career models that favor men more than women. Based on perceptions that the *ideal worker* is a man, STEM work and career expectations include long hours, face time, and uninterrupted career paths (cf. Acker, 1990, Bailyn, 2003, Benschop and Brouns, 2003; Dean and Fleckenstein, 2007). O'Neil and Bilimoria (2005) have argued for the need for women's careers to be examined separately from men's careers. They suggest that there is a gap between organizational rhetoric and practice in relation to actions aimed at retaining women.

In STEM areas, women are more likely to report that they are not taken as seriously nor does their work receive the same respect as their male counterparts (Fox, 2001). Fox (2001, p. 661) has noted that "women's educational attainments do not translate into scientific career attainments, especially advancement in rank, on a par with men's". Women's lack of progress to senior roles in organizations has been attributed to glass ceilings, sticky floors, maternal walls (Shellenbarger, 2007) and concrete walls (Burke and Vinnicombe, 2005) – all barriers to women's careers. More recent metaphors have described women's labyrinth-like career pathways through organizations (Eagly and Carli, 2007) and the high risk, glass cliff leadership positions into which women are disproportionately appointed (Ryan and Haslam, 2005, 2007).

De Welde and Laursen (2011, p. 571) suggest that a more useful metaphor is that of a "glass obstacle course" as this more appropriately captures the unequal nature of the gendered processes that operate in relation to women's careers in STEM. They identify these processes as including exclusion from the "old boys club", sexism, insufficient number of women as role models and work–life balance. These barriers impact on women's choices and their satisfaction with their careers in the STEM fields in a range of ways. Faulkner (2009), for example, has noted the impact of being excluded from the old boy's network and how this can reduce women's power and influence as well as their access to knowledge on how work gets done and how the promotion systems operate. For De Welde and Laursen, the barriers women face are not static and can appear and reappear at any stage regardless of whether or not these challenges have already been "conquered". The authors contend that viewing women's career development as advancement through a glass obstacle course helps explain why some women advance further than others even when working under the same conditions.

Pipelines

Women's representation in senior roles has been explained in terms of pipelines. Firstly, there is a talent pipeline that women must negotiate. The talent pipeline proposes that with the right education, training and experience it is only a matter of time before women make it to senior positions in organizations (Fox, 2001). However, a recent report *Pipeline's Broken Promise* suggests otherwise (Carter and Silva, 2010). The talent pipeline is not as promising for women as had been expected and despite equivalent qualifications and experience women lag behind men in terms of their advancement and salary (Carter and Silva, 2010). The leaky pipeline metaphor has been used to explain women leaving organizations at various stages of career trajectory (Blickenstaff, 2005; Hewlett and Luce, 2005; Bilimoria and Liang, 2012). There are a variety of reasons that women leave organizations, some of which have been noted above. Women academics, for example, are less satisfied with academic workplaces and are more likely to leave unwelcoming cultures at earlier stages than their male counterparts (Hill et al., 2010). The usefulness of the leaky pipeline metaphor has been questioned, being seen by some as oversimplifying the reasons why women leave STEM studies and careers (e.g., Herzig, 2004; Mattis, 2007; Banning and Folkstead, 2012).

OUR RESEARCH FOCUS

As noted earlier, much of the research to date has looked at why women leave and why they appear to be less successful than their male counterparts in pursuing careers in STEM. The adequacies of the metaphors that are in use to describe women's careers generally and women in STEM in particular have been questioned. Thus it is timely to move beyond the question of "Why do they leave?" and to instead move the focus to why women stay, what organizations are doing to facilitate the career development of women in STEM areas, and challenging organizational discourse and practice to further encourage the recruitment, advancement and retention of women in STEM careers.

The research on women's careers in STEM presented in this edited volume can be broadly grouped into three areas, focused at the individual, organizational, and praxis levels. The first section focuses on individual perspectives relating to women's experiences and decisions to stay in or leave their STEM careers. In other words, the research presented in this section addresses why women persist in STEM careers, how they advance their STEM careers, and how they navigate caring- and family-related decisions in the context of their work and performance demands. The second section of this volume focuses on organizational initiatives and describes how such changes make a positive difference for women's careers in STEM. This research looks at how gender change projects can be designed and implemented within feminist frameworks and what this might mean for participants and gender equity, diversity and inclusion in the organization. Successful initiatives are examined and key lessons highlighted in this section. The third section, addressing praxis, focuses on the need to reframe organizational discourse and practice. Areas highlighted include critical reflection on the norms relating to what makes a successful STEM worker, how caring and family responsibilities are described and enacted, extant discourse and practice relating to gender based organizational initiatives, and the changes needed within university education so that gender becomes a visible part of STEM curricula. These themes are explained in more detail in the next section.

ORGANIZATION OF THIS VOLUME

This book presents 11 research studies about women in academic and professional occupations within STEM. There are five chapters in the first section that focus on women's experiences.

Part I: Women's Individual Experiences in STEM Careers

In Chapter 2, Kathleen Buse and Diana Bilimoria qualitatively examine factors at the individual level that differentiate women who remain or have "persisted" in engineering careers and those who have not. Interviews with 31 women with engineering qualifications and careers from the United States of America reveal differences between those who stay and those who leave in areas that include engineering identity, self-efficacy and outlook and in their interpretations of deriving meaning, purpose and challenge from their engineering work. Through the theoretical concepts of the ideal self and work engagement, the authors explain their observations and make suggestions for practices enhancing persistence in the careers of women in engineering.

The theme of career persistence is continued in Chapter 3. In this chapter Romila Singh, Nadya Fouad, Mary Fitzpatrick, Catia Figueiredo and Wen Hsin Chang explore the drivers behind the career choices made by women engineers. Using social cognitive career management theory and turnover theory, they establish the key differences between women who have left technical workplaces and those who remain. Factors such as perceived organizational support, workplace barriers related to undermining behavior and incivility, support from co-workers and supervisors, career satisfaction, and commitment to the engineering profession were identified as differentiating the women engineers who persisted in their careers versus those who did not.

In Chapter 4, Margaret Nowak, Melissa Marinelli, Linley Lord and Dede Bonner examine the career attitudes and motivations of women working in professional technical and scientific roles in the mining industry in Australia. Using a career anchors questionnaire supported by in-depth interviews, the authors provide insights regarding the career decisions of these women. A desire for lifestyle, constant challenge and stimulation from work, job security and stability, and a desire to build their careers are revealed as key career influences. The authors suggest that the combination of the career anchors questionnaire with a career focused discussion on key motivators may help organizations develop more appropriate and targeted retention strategies for women in science and technology careers.

The challenges of work and family responsibilities for women in STEM careers are explored in Chapter 5. In their Australian based study, authors Mary Ayre, Julie Mills and Judith Gill examine the family issues that affect women engineers and the ways they resolve these issues. Utilizing a similar approach to a larger Australian study, the Careers Review of Engineering Women (CREW), this study explores the career experiences of women from a single Australian technical university who graduated between 1974 and 2008. This group had a remarkably high retention rate and were more likely to have caring and family responsibilities. The authors found that the selection of an employer with family-friendly policies as well as joint responsibility for parenting by both parents were key contributing factors to women's decisions to remain in engineering careers.

In Chapter 6, the focus moves to the advancement of women in the engineering profession. Melissa Marinelli and Linley Lord examine the successful transitions of women engineers into managerial and leadership roles within the engineering profession. From interviews with Australian women engineers occupying senior roles, the authors provide insight into the nature of the roles these women have chosen to pursue as they advance their careers, and the aspects of these roles that are most important to them. The factors influencing movement to manager/leader roles are presented, revealing the combination of individual, structural, and interpersonal or relational elements vital to successful transition to senior roles.

Part II: Organizational Initiatives Advancing Women in STEM Careers

The three chapters in the second part of this book focus on organizations that employ and represent women in STEM careers and the initiatives that create change in women's workforce participation and advancement in these fields.

In Chapter 7, Charlotte Holgersson, Pia Höök and Anna Wahl describe the design and implementation of a women-only change project involving women engineers in two technical organizations in Sweden. The purpose of the project, which drew on the concept of "women as a power resource", was to engage the participants to work toward improving gender equity within their organization. Changes were realized in both organizations studied, and individuals reported increased knowledge, awareness and empowerment, and advancement of careers in many cases. Within the organizations, the creation of women's networks and the prioritization of diversity as a strategic objective were realized. The authors conclude by reflecting on the implementation of the project and share lessons learned.

The exploration of initiatives to increase the number of women in STEM careers continues in Chapter 8. Focusing on the academic sector, Diana Bilimoria and Xiangfen Liang discuss the National Science Foundation's ADVANCE program to address gender equity issues and the leaky pipeline in academic STEM in colleges and universities in the United States. Analysis of the effectiveness of a variety of initiatives broadly grouped as pipeline initiatives and cultural initiatives was undertaken. Results showed a positive change in the number of women faculty in STEM at involved universities, but that women continue to be under-represented particularly at associate professor and professor ranks. The authors conclude that a portfolio of varied and multi-targeted gender equity initiatives is most effective in achieving gender equity transformation.

The role of institutional and representative bodies is addressed in Chapter 9. In this chapter, Erin Cadwalader, Joan Herbers and Alice Popejoy highlight the issue of gender disparity in scholarly recognition as an important influence on the attrition of women from academic STEM careers. The authors detail the development and outcomes of a particular initiative – the Advancing Ways of Awarding Recognition in Disciplinary Societies (AWARDS) project. This project was implemented by the Association for Women in Science (AWIS) with the purpose of working with scientific disciplinary societies on the elimination of gender bias from their awards selection processes. Although it is too early to know if long-lasting change has been achieved, the authors point to early successes in raising awareness of implicit bias and strategies for overcoming it.

Part III: Praxis: Changing Extant Discourse and Practice about Women in STEM Careers

The final three chapters of Part III focus on exploring and challenging the norms, discourse and practice surrounding gender and gender equity in STEM careers.

In Chapter 10, Marieke van den Brink and Lineke Stobbe examine the perceptions surrounding gender equality interventions in The Netherlands aimed at encouraging women to stay in the scientific STEM community and increasing the number of female STEM professors. Using material related to two formal equality interventions discourse analysis reveals a contradiction – termed the "getting help" dilemma – in which such programs are perceived by scientists to be both helpful and harmful to women's scientific careers. To explain this contradiction, the authors challenge the assumption that meritocracy is gender neutral and exposes the invisible privilege that male scientists enjoy. The "getting help" dilemma is proposed as an instrument for reflection and questioning of current gender equality practice.

The organizational norms relating to combining career and care responsibilities are explored in Chapter 11 by Channah Herschberg, Claartje Vinkenburg, Inge Bleijenbergh and Marloes van Engen. The authors present findings from an action research project conducted within the engineering faculty of a technical university in The Netherlands. Interviews and a focus group conducted with male and female academics reveal that whilst care issues are important for both male and female engineering academics, the recognized norm is that care is not a topic of conversation within the faculty. However, in some situations this norm is negotiated and challenged. The authors show that actively negotiating norms is a potential source of change and present a suite of suggestions for enacting this change within academe.

Our edited collection closes with Chapter 12 by Sally Male. In this chapter, the author proposes that the idea that "engineering is gendered" is a threshold concept. The gendered nature of engineering – or the influence of stereotypically masculine attributes – limits the effectiveness of engineering education, practice, and the inclusivity of the profession. Threshold concept theory defines threshold concepts as transformative and troublesome. The author argues that recognizing the gendered nature of engineering as a threshold concept can open new ways of thinking and understanding for engineers, but that assistance is needed in becoming comfortable with the concept. The chapter concludes with the suggestion that this threshold concept be taught to engineering students, academics and professionals, and approaches to its teaching are also recommended.

CONCLUSION

Drawing on research conducted in the United States, Australia and Europe, this volume examines the reasons for women's low participation in STEM and offers examples of successful ameliorative strategies at individual, organizational, and normative discourse and practice levels. The research presented here spans industry and academe, and focuses on the nature of STEM careers, individual career success strategies, successful organizational initiatives relating to women in STEM careers, and recommendations for praxis – changing the normative structure of extant discourse and practice. We hope that this volume will be interesting and relevant to researchers and practitioners seeking to increase women's participation and success in the STEM fields and transform organizations and institutions to better facilitate the advancement and development of women in STEM careers.

REFERENCES

Acker, J. (1990), 'Hierarchies, jobs, bodies: A theory of gendered organizations', *Gender and Society*, **4**(2), 139–58.

Australian Academy of Science (2013), *Gender Equity: Current Issues, Best Practice and New Ideas*, Canberra, Australia, Australian Academy of Science, accessed December 15, 2013 from http://science.org.au/policy/documents/GenderEquityEMCRForum.pdf.

Bailyn, L. (2003), 'Academic careers and gender equity: Lessons learned from MIT', *Gender, Work, and Organizations*, **10**, 137–53.

Banning, J. and J. Folkstead (2012), 'STEM education related dissertation abstracts: A bounded qualitative meta-study', *Journal of Science Education and Technology*, **21**(6), 730–41.

Bell, S. (2009), *Women in Science in Australia: Maximising Productivity, Diversity and Innovation*, Canberra, Australia, accessed from http://www.lhmartininstitute.edu.au/publications/3-prof-sharon-bell.

Benschop, Y. and M. Brouns (2003), 'Crumbling ivory towers: Academic organizing and its gender effects', *Gender, Work and Organization*, **10**(2), 194–212.

Bilimoria, D., S. Joy and X. Liang (2008), 'Breaking barriers and creating inclusiveness: Lessons of organizational transformation to advance women faculty in academic science and engineering', *Human Resource Management*, **47**(3), 423–41.

Bilimoria, D. and X. Liang (2012), *Gender Equity in Science and Engineering: Advancing Change in Higher Education*, New York: Routledge.

Blickenstaff, J.C. (2005), 'Women and science careers: Leaky pipeline or gender filter?', *Gender and Education*, **17**(4), 369–86.

Burke, R.J. and M.C. Mattis (2007), *Women and Minorities in Science, Technology, Engineering and Mathematics: Upping the Numbers*, Cheltenham, UK and Northampton, MA: Edward Elgar.

Burke, R.J. and S. Vinnicombe (2005), 'Advancing women's careers', *Career Development International*, **10**(3), 165–7.

Carter, N. and C. Silva (2010), *Pipeline's Broken Promise*, New York: Catalyst.

Dean, D.J., and A. Fleckenstein (2007), 'Keys to success for women in science', in R.J. Burke and M.C. Mattis (eds), *Women and Minorities in Science, Technology, Engineering and Mathematics*, Cheltenham, UK and Northampton, MA: Edward Elgar, pp. 28–46.

De Welde, K. and S. Laursen (2011), 'The glass obstacle course: Informal and formal barriers for women Ph.D. students in STEM Fields', *International Journal of Gender Science and Technology*, **3**(3), 571–95.

Eagly, A.H. and L.L. Carli (2007), 'Women and the Labyrinth of Leadership', *Harvard Business Review*, **85**(9), 63–71.

European Parliament (2008), 'European Parliament resolution of 21 May 2008 on women and science', accessed December 15, 2013 from http://www.europarl.europa.eu/sides/getDoc.do?type=TA&language=EN&reference=P6-TA-2008-0221.

Faulkner, W. (2009), 'Doing gender in engineering workplace cultures: I. Observations from the field', *Engineering Studies*, **1**(1), 3–18.

Fouad, N., M. Fitzpatrick and J. Liu (2011), 'Persistence of women in engineering careers: A qualitative study of current and former female engineers', *Journal of Women and Minorities in Science and Engineering*, **17**(1), 69–96.

Fouad, N. and R. Singh (2011), *Stemming the Tide: Why Women Leave Engineering*, accessed December 15, 2013 from http://studyofwork.com/files/2011/03/NSF_Women-Full-Report-0314.pdf.

Fox, M. (2001), 'Women, science and academia: Graduate education and careers', *Gender and Society*, **15**(5), 654–66.

genSet (2010), *Recommendations for Action on the Gender Dimension in Science*, Science in Society Programme of the European Commission, accessed December 15, 2013 from http://www.google.com/url?sa=t&rct=j&q=&esrc=s&frm=1&source=web&cd=1&ved=0CCwQFjAA&url=http%3A%2F%2Fwww.genderinscience.org%2Findex.php%2Fdownloads%2Fdoc_download%2F18-genset-consensus-report-recommendations-for-action-on-the-gender-dimension-in-science&ei=ZAevUtPZA4ngqQHrvICwBQ&usg=AFQjCNFqpv1e1tMSAWuEBG_sYgbt0rNnlg&sig2=BuMkTCB0zhz0bI2wKpRMlA&bvm=bv.57967247,d.aWM.

Goulden, M., K. Frasch and M.A. Mason (2009), *Staying Competitive: Patching America's Leaky Pipeline in the Sciences*, accessed December 15, 2013 from http://www.americanprogress.org/issues/2009/11/women_and_sciences.html.

Herzig, A.H. (2004), 'Becoming mathematicians: Women and students of color choosing and leaving doctoral mathematics', *Review of Educational Research*, **74**(2), 171–214.

Hewlett, S. and C. Luce (2005), 'Off-ramps and on-ramps: Keeping talented women on the road to success', *Harvard Business Review*, **83**(3), 43–54.

Hewlett, S., C.B. Luce, L.J. Servon, L. Sherbin, P. Shiller and E. Sosnovich (2008), *The Athena Factor: Reversing the Brain Drain in Science, Engineering and Technology*, Boston, MA: Harvard Business Review.

Hill, C., C. Corbett and A.S. Rose (2010), *Why So Few? Women in Science, Technology, Engineering and Mathematics*, Washington, DC, USA, AAUW, acessed December 15, 2013 from http://www.aauw.org/research/why-so-few/.

Long, J.S. (ed.) (2001), *Scarcity to Visibility: Gender Differences in the Careers of Doctoral Scientists and Engineers*, Washington, DC: National Academies Press.

Mattis, M.C. (2007), 'Upstream and downstream in the engineering pipeline: What's blocking US women from pursuing engineering careers? in R.J. Burke and M.C. Mattis (eds), *Women and Minorities in Science, Technology, Engineering, and Mathematics: Upping the Numbers*, Cheltenham, UK and Northampton, MA: Edward Elgar, p. 334.

McIlwee, J. and J. Robinson (1992), *Women in Engineering: Gender, Power and Workplace Culture*, Albany, NY: State University of New York Press.

Mills, J., M. Ayre and J. Gill (2010), *Gender Inclusive Engineering Education*, New York: Routledge.

Mills, J., V. Mehrtens, E. Smith and V. Adams (2008), *CREW Revisited in 2007: The Year of Women in Engineering:- An Update on Women's Progress in the Australian Engineering Workforce*, Barton, Engineers Australia, acessed December 15, 2013 from http://www.engineersaustralia.org.au/shadomx/apps/fms/fmsdownload.cfm?file_uuid=7DA323DA-E3CC-A6FB-8DB3-4D97EFFBBEEF&siteName=ieaust.

National Academies (2007), *Rising Above the Gathering Storm: Energizing and Employing America for a Brighter Economic Future*, Washington, DC: National Academies Press.

National Research Council (2007), *Beyond Bias and Barriers: Fulfilling the Potential of Women in Academic Science and Engineering*, Washington, DC: National Academies Press.

National Science Foundation (2010), 'Science and Engineering Indicators 2010', accessed December 15, 2013 from www.nsf.gov/statistics/seind10/start.htm.

O'Neil, D.A. and D. Bilimoria (2005), 'Women's career development phases: Idealism, endurance and reinvention', *Career Development International*, **10**(3), 168–9.

Ryan, M.K. and S.A. Haslam (2005), 'The glass cliff: Evidence that women are over-represented in precarious leadership positions', *British Journal of Management*, **16**, 81–90.

Ryan, M.K. and S.A. Haslam (2007), 'The glass cliff: Exploring the dynamics surrounding the appointment of women to precarious leadership positions', *Academy of Management Review*, **32**(2), 549–72.

Shellenbarger, S. (2007), 'Government eases path for parents to sue employers', *Wall Street Journal Online*.

Valian, V. (1998), *Why So Slow: The Advancement of Women*, Cambridge, MA: MIT Press.

2. Women persisting in the engineering profession: The role of the ideal self and engagement

Kathleen Buse and Diana Bilimoria

Women continue to be under-represented in the engineering profession comprising only 10 percent of employed engineers in 2010 in the United States. At the same time women comprised 47 percent of the total workforce and more than 50 percent of all professionals and managers (Bureau of Labor Statistics, U.S. Department of Labor, 2011). Although the number of women graduating with engineering degrees, both graduate and undergraduate, has steadily increased from 5 percent in 1980 to 22 percent (National Science Foundation, 2010) the retention of women employed as engineers has not kept pace as the percentage of women employed across the various engineering disciplines has not changed since the mid-1990s (Bureau of Labor Statistics, U.S. Department of Labor, 2012).

In this study we present findings from new analyses conducted on data previously reported (Buse, Bilimoria and Perelli, 2013) wherein we interviewed women with engineering degrees, 21 who persisted in the profession and ten others who left the profession. From the voices of these women engineers we learn about the complicated factors driving their decision to persist or opt-out of the engineering profession. Thorough analysis of these stories resulted in grounded theory to answer our research question "What individual-level factors explain women's persistence in the engineering profession in US corporations?" where persistence is defined as continuing in the engineering profession and/or advancing to a position that would normally be achieved by successful engineers. The findings from this study aid in developing programs to retain women in the engineering profession and contribute to the development of theories related to engagement, intentional change and careers.

WOMEN AND ENGINEERING CAREERS

The US in particular needs to aggressively address the retention problem of women not just in engineering but also in other STEM (science, technology, engineering and math) professions to maintain global leadership (National Research Council, 2007). A deficit of one million STEM workers in the next decade has been projected for the US (President's Council of Advisors on Science and Technology, 2012). Drawing on a large body of scientific evidence both the National Academies (National Research Council, 2007) and the American Association of University Women (Hill, Corbett and St. Rose, 2010) conclude that women have the ability and the motivation to succeed in the STEM fields but leave at high rates owing to barriers and biases that uniquely disadvantage women. Discrimination manifests itself in the workplace with women receiving lower pay than their male peers for the same work and with men more likely to be promoted or obtain leadership roles. In a study specifically addressing gender bias in science (Moss-Racusin, Dovidio, Brescoll, Graham and Handelsman, 2012) university professors were asked to evaluate candidates for a laboratory manager position. The researchers changed only the first name on the submitted documents. The documents with "John" as the applicant received higher ratings on competence, hire-ability and willingness to mentor as compared to "Jennifer's" application. Further, John was offered on average a 14 percent higher starting salary than Jennifer and the bias was demonstrated by both male and female faculty members.

The Moss-Racusin et al. study joins the growing body of research that has focused on the broader problem and impact of gender bias in society (Rouse, 2000; Heilman, Wallen, Fuchs and Tamkins, 2004; Ely, Ibarra and Kolb, 2011) and specifically as this bias relates to the under-representation of STEM women in academia (National Science Foundation, 2012). However, only 6 percent of all engineers are employed by educational institutions whereas 83 percent are employed in business and industry with the remaining 11 percent in government employment (National Science Foundation, 2011). Few studies concentrate on women employed in the private sector (Hewlett et al., 2008) and for those that are available a difficult work environment is portrayed (Gill, Sharp, Mills and Franzway, 2008; Jorgenson, 2002; Miller, 2004; Powers, Bagilhole and Dainty, 2009; Watts, 2009) explaining why women leave (Frehill, 2008; Hewlett et al., 2008; Fouad and Singh, 2011).

From a purely economic standpoint more women should consider the engineering profession as the number of jobs is expected to grow and salaries are relatively high. Of the 20 highest paying occupations in the US in 2010 three are engineering-related: engineering managers, computer managers and petroleum engineers. Engineering and other STEM careers not only provide economic benefits to women but also benefit organizations, institutions and society as a whole. Organizations and society benefit from the broadened perspective and diversified talent women bring to the field (Margolis, Fisher and Miller, 1999/2000) as well as from their contributions in leadership positions. However, empirical studies focused on women in engineering are rare as compared to research on women in other professions (Jorgenson, 2002) and many of those available are based on samples of engineering students (Cech, Rubineau, Silbey and Seron, 2011; Hartman and Hartman, 2009; Betz and O'Connell, 1992; Betz and Hackett, 1981; Betz and Schifano, 2000; Blum, 2001; Chiu, Chiu, Chiu and Chiu, 2002) or women in academic engineering careers (Bagilhole, 2002; Bilimoria, Joy and Liang, 2008; Stout, Dasqupta, Hunsinger and McManus, 2011; Glass and Minnotte, 2010). The few studies that are available on women in the non-academic engineering profession focus on the difficult work environment that causes women to leave the profession but do not address the complexities related to the interplay between individual, institutional, social and cultural factors (National Research Council, 2007).

Despite the bias, the barriers, the discrimination and the difficult work environment in the engineering profession many women do persist. Here our goal is to provide empirical evidence of the individual-level factors impacting women's persistence in the engineering profession. Semi-structured interviews were conducted with women who persisted on average 21 years in the engineering profession with a goal of generating a grounded theory describing women's persistence in the profession. Informed by prior research and preliminary interviews with professionals knowledgable about the problem of practice, we expected that both individual and organizational factors might influence career persistence, but remained open to discovering if, how and why they did. The results reflect assessment of the beliefs, attitudes and behaviors of the persistent engineers as compared to a second group of ten women with an average of 12 years of engineering practice who had left the engineering profession. Comparing and contrasting evocative personal narratives from both groups enriched our understanding of the research question. Understanding those women who persist not only aids in developing practical interventions to support the retention of women in engineering and other STEM professions but also adds to theory development related to women's careers.

METHODS

Methodological Approach

Qualitative research as described by Glaser and Strauss (1967) is most suited to efforts to understand the process by which participants take meaning from their experience. The strengths of qualitative research according to Maxwell (2005) derive from its inductive approach, its focus on specific situations or people, and its emphasis on words. Use of grounded theory is appropriate when a researcher wants to make knowledge claims about how individuals understand reality (Suddaby, 2006) as in this study that has explored the realities of women in engineering careers.[1]

The sample consisted of 31 women aged 34 to 60, all of whom had some experience as an engineer or as a technical manager in a corporation located in the US (see Table 2.1). The respondents were identified through the personal network of the first author. All were college graduates with the following engineering degrees: biomedical (one), chemical (12), civil (four), industrial (four), electrical (two) material/metallurgical (two), or mechanical (five). More than half of the women had master's degrees, nine in engineering, seven MBAs, one master's of education, and one master's in counseling. Three had doctorate degrees; two in engineering, one in business and two others were in the process of obtaining doctorate degrees. A little more than half of the women received their degrees from private universities. One woman was educated in the former Soviet Republic.

At the time of the interviews, 21 of the women continued to work in an engineering role and had between 13 and 30 years of experience, averaging about 21 years. The remaining ten women had left an engineering career prior to the time of the study after an average of 12 years of experience that ranged from eight to 17 years in engineering. Of the ten women who left engineering, six were currently employed in a career that was not at all related to engineering and four were self-described as homemakers or stay-at-home mothers.

At the time of the interviews the average age of the women who persisted was 44 and of those who opted out was 43 years. Of the women who persisted 17 were or had been married and two mentioned they were currently in a long-term relationship with men for 16 and 25 years. Nine of the ten women who opted out were or had been married. The women who persisted had on average 1.1 children ranging from none to three. Women who opted out had on average 1.9 children with a range of none to four children.

Table 2.1 Summary of respondents

	Engineering Degree(s)	Year of 1st Eng Degree	Graduate Degree	Years of Engineering Experience	Age	Still Engineer?	Industry Type	Married	Children
1	Civil Engineering	1979		30	60	Yes	Automotive	Formerly	1
2	Mechanical Engineering	1979	MS	28	52	Yes	Communication	No	1
3	Electrical and Computer Engineering	1981	MS	28	50	Yes	Defense	Yes	2
4	Biomedical and Electrical Engineering	1985	DM, MS	24	48	Yes	Utility	No	0
5	Electrical Engineering	1988	MS	8	43	No	Communication	Yes	4
6	Industrial Engineering	1988	MBA	12	43	No	Automotive	Yes	3
7	Industrial Engineering	1988		14	43	No	Manufacturing	Yes	3
8	Chemical Engineering and Packaging Engineering	1991		16	38	Yes	Paints & Coatings	Yes	3

9	Chemical Engineering and Engineering and Public Policy	1985		24	46	Yes	Consumer Products	Yes	2
10	Chemical Engineering	1990	MBA	18	40	Yes	Paints & Coatings	Yes	2
11	Chemical Engineering	1979		30	52	Yes	Consumer Products	Yes	0
12	Materials Engineering	1994	PhD MS	15	42	Yes	Fluid System Technology	Yes	2
13	Chemical Engineering	1979	MS	25	52	Yes	Food Manufacturing	Yes	2
14	Chemical Engineering	1987	MBA	22	42	Yes	Paints & Coatings	Yes	0
15	Mechanical Engineering	1996	MBA	13	34	No	Automotive	Yes	1
16	Mechanical Engineering	1977	MBA	11	54	No	Electrical Eqpt	Yes	1
17	Industrial Engineering	2007	PhD	15	35	Yes	Entertainment	Formerly	0
18	Mechanical Engineering	1994		15	36	Yes	Systems	Yes	0
19	Chemical Engineering	1990	MBA, ME	17	42	No	Chemical Mfg	Yes	3
20	Chemical Engineering	1992		17	40	Yes	Chemical Mfg	Formerly	1

	Engineering Degree(s)	Year of 1st Eng Degree	Graduate Degree	Years of Engineering Experience	Age	Still Engineer?	Industry Type	Married	Children
21	Mechanical Engineering	1983	MS	15	50	No	Auto Supplier	Yes	2
22	Chemical Engineering	1986	MS	21	45	Yes	Chemical Mfg	Yes	2
23	Industrial Engineering	1989		20	42	Yes	Entertainment	Yes	3
24	Metallurgical Engineering	1990		19	41	Yes	Consumer Products	Yes	2
25	Chemical Engineering and Business	1981	MBA	28	50	Yes	Air Separation	No	0
26	Civil Engineering	1983		10	48	No	Petroleum	Yes	0
27	Civil Engineering	1992	MA in Counseling	8	39	No	Consulting	Yes	2
28	Chemical Engineering	1996		11	35	No	Chemical Mfg	No	0
29	Chemical Engineering	1996		13	35	Yes	Pharmaceuticals	Yes	0
30	Civil Engineering	1996		13	35	Yes	Consulting	Yes	1
31	Telecommunications	1989	MS	20	42	Yes	Entertainment	No	0

An interview protocol designed a priori was used to guide the interviews but, consistent with the semi-structured approach to interviewing, allowed respondents freedom of expression. The key interview questions focused on personal and career histories, examples of fulfilling and non-fulfilling career experiences, early and current career expectations, and beliefs about the pros and cons of an engineering career for a woman. Women currently employed in engineering were also asked to explain their reasons for staying in the field and women who left engineering were asked why they exited.

FINDINGS

The data analysis identified two areas that clearly divided persisting women engineers from out-opting engineer: individual characteristics and accounts of their work as an engineer. The individual characteristics of persistent women engineers include: identity as an engineer, self-efficacy, and a positive outlook. When discussing their job or career persistent women engineers describe meaning and purpose in the work, ongoing challenges, novelty and feelings of value and worth.

Identity

Women who persisted in engineering discussed themselves in terms of their identity as an engineer, as for example:

> I'm a hopeless geek. I love solving problems. I love working with users. My husband tells me that I am so analytical about everything that he just wants to run from the room screaming sometimes. I love to solve problems (consultant with 28 years' experience).

The persistent engineers sought out work opportunities that enabled them to express their identity as an engineer. For example:

> I really enjoy technical things. With two kids in college I need to be working and I want to be working. One of the things I really felt when I wasn't working after France (a move with her family for her husband's job) was I felt like there was a part of me that was dying. I like technical challenges. I like thinking about things. I like working in spreadsheets and dealing with technical issues. That part of me wasn't being tapped into at all, and I really missed it. I did enjoy some of the other things I was doing, but I think my bigger passion is for technical things (manufacturing manager with 28 years' experience).

Women who opted out of engineering professed identities inconsistent with engineering. For example:

> I think I was always just not sure that I had chosen the right thing. I looked at people who seemed to be in the right job, like my family members, and I thought I'm just not in the right job (14-year engineering career, now a stay-at-home mom).

> It [engineering] really wasn't what I wanted to do. It was just something to get out of mom's house…I always knew I would leave. Because my mom worked, so that was something I'd always planned to stay home with my child (12-year engineering career, now a stay-at-home mom).

Self-Efficacy

Persistent engineers demonstrated greater levels of self-efficacy and confidence than out-opting engineers. All 21 of the respondents still working in engineering careers narrated experiences in which they demonstrated initiative and/or manipulated difficult situations. Self-efficacy was expressed in relation to finding new assignments, dealing with difficult work situations, or tackling tough technical problems. Specific examples involved managing conflict with superiors or co-workers and effecting formal job changes, as follows.

> And I think with women, in particular, feeling credible and having credibility behind you can really help your career, and I think having that technical expertise gives you that confidence and that credibility that helps you move your career forward (industrial engineer with 20 years' experience).

> My confidence has increased because of the experience. You do some stuff and you have a success, and then you do a little bit more and you have a bit more success. The more wins that you have – and also, you start to see the same problem over and over, so it's like, oh, I had this problem, or this is how we fixed it, or I've seen this before, this is how we dealt with it (process engineer with 16 years' experience).

> I happen to believe in myself even when no one else does. And I think that if I believe I can do something then I can do it. And just because somebody tries to stop me, it's usually not enough (technical manager with 30 years' experience).

In contrast, nine of the ten engineers who had exited the field told stories in which uncertainty, confusion, and self-doubt predominated. For example:

> I really was low on confidence even though I had this great engineering degree and all this stuff, it was still tough for me to have the confidence to go and interview (12 years in engineering career, now a stay-at-home mom aged 43).

> I think I had very little confidence, and I kind of waited for the other shoe to drop that somebody was going to find out that I really didn't know what was going on, and so if I had a boss who wasn't confident in me, who treated me with no respect, then I got into that completely (11 year engineering career, now a college professor).

Positive Outlook

Persistent women engineers, even after many years on the job, exuded enthusiasm, energy and commitment to their work. For example:

> I have options to steer my way towards one thing or another towards something I enjoy more … I got into a large company that had a lot of opportunity for someone with an engineering background to a lot of different things. … I want to work on something that's important. I want to get satisfaction out of what I do. I want people to value me and want to include me in things that are important (technical manager with 24 years' experience).

> … having had the opportunity to do a number of different things keeps you from getting bored with it because having the growth, being able to come in every day … and I'd learn something every day (technical manager with 22 years' experience).

> You can do so many different things. You do not have to work in this field or that field or this field or that field. You can be an engineer in just about every field. Every field needs an engineer somehow, someway, whether it's medical or manufacturing or aeronautical or whatever. So there's variety. There's – it opens doors (manufacturing engineering with 19 years' experience).

The women who opted out of engineering described their experience as engineers as "not happy," "didn't feel I was giving back," "had accomplished nothing," and felt "detached."

Meaning and Purpose

In direct response to our question about why they stayed in their engineering career, 19 out of 21 persistent engineers described meaning and purpose as an engineer. Further they discussed challenging work, novelty, and continuous learning opportunities. Many of the women explained that within the scope of their careers they were able to find opportunities to work on new technologies, new projects, or new products. The novelty coupled with the ability to continuously learn provided the motivation for them to continue to work in technical careers. We found that these women were stimulated by the challenges associated with the new technologies. They sought out these challenges, some within the scope of their organization, others moving into different industries in their quest for challenges, novelty, and the ability to continue to learn. Examples of quotes related to meaning and purpose within a work role follow.

> So I felt like God gave me a little snippet into the difference you can make if you don't care who gets the credit and you do the right thing … I can keep doing this. I can put up with all the crap. And then it sort of hit me that everybody is somebody's brother or father or son or cousin or whatever. And every single one of these guys and gals is there. Whatever it is that I can help bring to the fight to make sure that they're coming home to their three little toddlers or whatever. But I mean, it just – it hit me in a huge, huge way (consultant with 28 years' experience).

> I can feel like I did something that made a difference. Now, we can say that making XX that goes in paints and plastic is only so exciting, but it's something that I can look around and go, yeah, I impacted the world a little bit. So I think that's it (technical manager with 17 years' experience).

In contrast, women who left engineering for a career as a business professor described the absence of meaning and purpose in her work as an engineer. For example:

> I wanted to leave a legacy, and all I saw was stock prices going up and down, but because I was so detached from how what I did was affecting the world in any way, it just – that's why my soul hurt. [Now] I've got this ability to make an impact (11 year engineering career, now a college business professor).

Challenge and Novelty

The persistent engineers described the challenges and novelty of their work along with continued opportunities for learning in a number of different ways as described below.

> Well, I think because the good times have definitely outweighed the bad ones, and it really is a very good group of people. I think having had the opportunity to do a number of different things keeps you from getting bored with it because just having the growth, being able to come in every day, and I'd learn something every day. Sometimes I'd learn a lot; sometimes I'd learn a little; sometimes I'd learn things I really didn't want to know. But at the end of the day, there's something new that you've taken back (retired engineer with more than 30 years' experience).

> I stay in engineering because I just really love it. I love it! I love the challenge. I love coming in and having different things to do every single day. I love the people that I work with; I have a great support team, the maintenance guys are excellent (process engineer with 16 years' experience).

> I enjoy what I do. I enjoy the challenges. I enjoy the people. I like the fact I can travel and see something new. … So I couldn't imagine doing something else. I can't imagine anything else that would be this much fun on a regular basis (technical manager with 22 years' experience).

> They were giving me assignments that were brand new. You know, Greenfield, nobody had done before. … It was the carrot from the job. I always got to do something. And my whole career has been that. I mean the water supply to the hazardous waste site worked; I mean I just kept cutting edge stuff, brand new. So, that's – yeah, I think it's finding out what the carrot is for the stay, 'cause as I hear myself talk about it, I think it was the new stuff that kept me (technical manager with more than 30 years' experience).

Feeling Worthwhile, Valuable and Fulfilled

The work described by the persistent engineers led to feelings of worthiness and value, as described for example below.

> I feel needed. I feel like if I didn't show up to work – maybe not one day; maybe not a week, but if I was gone for a month, I would be missed. There are a lot of things that I can do, that I'm the only person who can do those things. The controls, I did the programming (to control a new machine) all on my own, I was really proud of that (process engineer with 16 years' experience).

In contrast, women engineers who left were more likely to describe feeling unfulfilled as an engineer, as for example:

> There are certain things that kind of trigger it in life; I think you reflect upon really doing what you should be doing, and my dad passed away suddenly in May of 2005. What am I doing with my kids? … What do I want to be, and I really didn't feel like I was giving back enough because so much of your time is spent at work and not really concerned in serving the community. … I realized I wasn't happy anymore (17 year engineering career, now a grade school teacher).

Women who remained as engineers conflated career and personal achievement, revealing that career accomplishments provided personal fulfillment. For example:

> I had my first child … I began to work part-time, which I recognized could slow down my rate of progress within the working world for my career, but I

> made the conscious decision that I didn't want to do everything, and I did want to have time to be with my child (production manager with 25 years' experience).

> One of the things that I wanted to do was to get more of a research position because I wanted to be able to balance my work life and my home life. So I applied at Company Y and I've been here for almost ten years (research manager with 18 years' experience).

Women who left the engineering field articulated a tension between work-related and personal goals, often citing the need to fulfill personal aspirations not satisfied by work as the motivation for leaving their jobs. For example:

> And now I have a baby I was like I have to breast feed exclusively no formula, make my own baby food and everything. So I remember like missing work and thinking how could I possibly juggle. There's no way I could have juggled them (eight year engineering career, now an office manager in family business).

DISCUSSION

The findings from this study suggest there are two important theoretical concepts that play a role in women who persist in an engineering career: (1) women who persist in the engineering profession realize their ideal self through their identity as an engineer, self-efficacy within their work role and a positive outlook to future career opportunities; and (2) women who persist in the engineering profession are highly engaged in their work as they find meaning and purpose, challenge and novelty, subsequently feeling valued, worthwhile and fulfilled in their work. A framework is proposed that integrates these findings into a model that explains persistence for women in the engineering profession (shown in Figure 2.1).

Ideal self. Persistent engineers, but not those that had voluntarily exited the profession, seem to realize in their careers what Boyatzis and Akrivou (2006) have described as one's ideal self. The ideal is the intrinsic motivator for one's behavior, emotions, perceptions and attitudes. It comprises: (1) one's identity, (2) hope as a function of self-efficacy and optimism, and (3) one's dreams and aspirations. The concept of the ideal self is rooted in the psychology literature specifically in work on motivation. Higgins (1987), promoting self-discrepancy theory, distinguished between two guiding end states, the ideal self and the ought self with the former guided by the individual's hopes, wishes

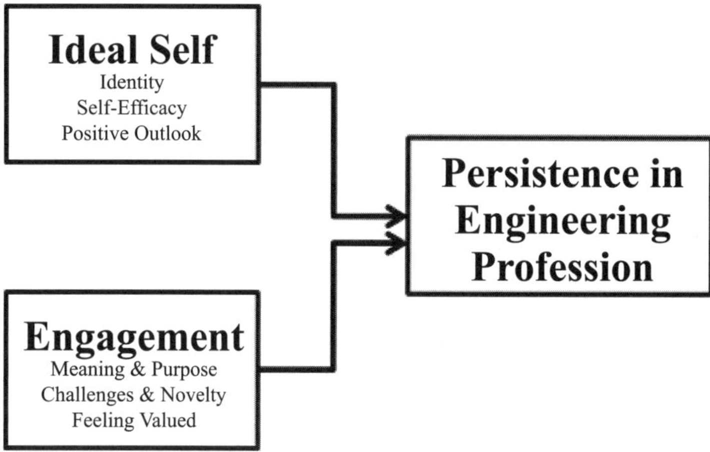

Figure 2.1 Hypothesized model of women's persistence in the engineering profession

and aspirations, and the latter by demands regarding duties, obligations and responsibilities. Since the ideal self engages in behavior consistent with one's desired end state, sacrifices are sometimes made in the short term to accomplish more important longer-term goals (Boyatzis and Akrivou, 2006).

Hope, defined as the feeling that something desirable is likely to happen, is proposed by Boyatzis as constituted by self-efficacy and optimism. Self-efficacy determines how much effort will be expended and how long one will persist when facing difficult circumstances (Bandura, 1982). Those with a strong sense of self-efficacy will exert greater effort to master challenges and overcome obstacles. The higher levels of self-efficacy demonstrated by persistent women engineers and their ideal self provided the means and motivation for overcoming difficult work situations and aids in explaining persistence.

Both persistent and out-opting engineers acknowledged the male-dominated culture of many engineering environments as an obstacle to career persistence. Boyatzis (2008) argues that people who produce alternative routes when facing obstacles to goals are said to have high hope. Persistent women engineers not only recognized that they needed to be creative in handling situations in the context of their work culture but were able to cleverly manipulate situations to ensure positive outcomes for themselves. The persistent engineers saw unrelenting opportunity in their professional futures, assured, despite decades in the field, that they would continue to find novelty in their work. Persistent engineers also described on-going challenges and the desire to learn continuously. This same level of optimism, the preoccupation with novelty and the desire to continue to learn was not discovered in the out-opting engineers.

The image of the desired future is explained by Boyatzis and Akrivou (2006) to be influenced by one's values and philosophy, life stage, and calling in life. Important identity groups such as the family, as well as one's history and enduring dispositions, create and nurture values and philosophy. Awareness of one's passion, according to Boyatzis, makes one feel as if life is worth living by fulfilling a calling in life. The sustained passion for their jobs expressed by women engineers more than 20 years into their careers surprised us – as did their certainty about the fit between their careers, values and callings in life.

The third component of Boyatzis' notion of the ideal self is core identity, or one's strengths, context and resources. Core identity is relatively stable and is a compilation of a person's enduring dispositions, involving a set of individual characteristics. Motives and roles taken in group settings are described by Boyatzis and Akrivou (2006) as part of core identity and related to one's social identity groups. Our persistent engineers repeatedly self-identified as engineers, demonstrating an embracement of the profession as part of their identity.

Using complexity theory to illustrate the discontinuous nature of change, Boyatzis argues that discontinuities may jolt one out of equilibrium. Gladwell (2000) described this jolt as a tipping point. All of the women in our sample who had left engineering described a tipping point that forced a realization that their engineering careers were not aligned with their personal and/or professional aspirations. These tipping points included: the birth of a child, the death of a parent, a new manager, a company-wide reorganization, or the effects of a hostile work environment. In each case the tipping point resulted in an exit from the profession to pursue another, presumably more ideal self. Contrarily, although there is evidence of personal and professional discontinuities in the narratives of our persistent engineers, these did not jolt incumbents to reconsider their careers.

Engagement. Our interviewees discussed difficulties in their jobs and how at times they questioned their career choices; however, those who persisted overcame the difficulties because they found meaning, felt needed, overcame challenges, had autonomy and were able to leverage their unique capabilities within the scope of their job. Kahn (1990) theorized that work could provide a sense of meaning when employees felt worthwhile, useful and valuable. Tasks within a role that provide challenge or autonomy and have clear goals influence engagement, as do roles that carry status or influence. Work interactions that provide employees respect and a sense of worthwhileness promote what Kahn described as personal engagement or the connection one brings to a work role where one employs and expresses themselves physically, cognitively, and emotionally. There is a dynamic process in which the person drives individual energies into the work role while showing one's self within that work. Kahn goes on to describe how those engaged in work become physically involved, thoughtfully aware, and empathically connected to others enabling them to express their beliefs and values.

Kahn described meaningfulness as a dimension of engagement where meaningfulness is having a purpose or that one is making a difference resulting in feelings of usefulness and value. Organizations that can create work that is challenging, clearly delineated, varied and somewhat autonomous provide the opportunity for individuals to experience meaningfulness in these roles. Task and role characteristics as well as work interactions can lead to meaningfulness. Kahn's description of meaningfulness is exactly how the engineers described why they persisted including stories of meaningfulness, unrelenting opportunities, novelty, challenge and the alignment between personal and professional aspirations leading to feelings of worthiness and value.

Schaufeli and Bakker (2004) discuss engagement as the opposite of job burn-out where engagement is characterized by vigor, dedication and absorption. An aspect of vigor important to the present study is the willingness to invest effort in one's work and to persist in the face of difficulties. Dedication is described as a sense of significance and challenge while absorption is characterized by being fully and happily focused in one's work. Schaufeli and Bakker did find a moderate negative relationship between engagement and burnout: they concluded that these psychological states play similar roles in different processes, specifically that burnout mediates effort based energetic processes driven by high job demands and can lead to health problems and intention to quit, where engagement is part of the motivational process that is negatively related to intention to quit. Additionally Saks (2006) hypothesized and showed empirically that work engagement impacts organizational commitment and is negatively related to intention to quit.

Engagement is a key mechanism that explains relationships between individual factors and benefits to organizations according to Rich, Lepine and Crawford (2010). Engagement is explained as a motivational concept and emphasizes relationships with behavioral consequences. Women engineers who persisted in their careers as compared with those that did not showed higher levels of personal engagement with their work roles, primarily by finding meaning and purpose in their work, positively dealing with novelty in the work and overcoming challenges and barriers, and finding a sense of personal fulfillment, worth and value.

Limitations

Several limitations to this study should be noted. Our sample is small and non-random and thus may not broadly represent all women in engineering. We focused only on women engineers with corporate experience and our results may not be generalizable to women engineers in government, academia or other non-corporate engineering venues. As Corbin and Strauss (2008) discuss, researchers must be self-reflective about how the research process is influenced by the researcher. The first author in this study has worked both as an engineer and a technical manager in several US corporations for more than 25 years. While every effort was made to remain self-reflective and to avoid the imposition of personal values on the data, we acknowledge the potential effect on them of our experience and knowledge. Finally, in this analysis we focused on the individual-level differences between women engineers who persisted in their careers and those who did not; we focused less on differences in the organizational circumstances facing women engineers who persisted or not.

Implications for Practice

The findings provide considerable implications for retaining women in engineering and other STEM professions. Women in the engineering profession should assess their own skills and work situation. A personal vision should be developed making a conscious effort to understand one's own level of identity as an engineer and self-efficacy and outlook toward one's career. Since engagement has been linked to resources available within the organization as well as one's relationship with a manager (Schaufeli and Bakker, 2004; Saks, 2006), women engineers struggling within their work role may want to consider making a change. A new organization and/or a new manager may allow them to find meaning and purpose or a more challenging opportunity.

Interventions may be effective in developing individual skills related to persistence in the profession. For example, numerous studies have proven that self-efficacy is developed and can be improved by one or a combination of four mechanisms: performance accomplishments, vicarious experience, verbal persuasion and psychological states (Bandura, 1982). At the undergraduate level we recommend that significant efforts be undertaken within engineering schools to inform and prepare women for a career in engineering beyond the basic degree. Educators should provide opportunities at orientation sessions to provide information on the various aspects of an engineering career. Throughout the four-year process a focused and thorough plan for career success should be developed for each woman student. Educators should provide training to women as well as men in undergraduate engineering programs that address the systemic issues associated with second-generation gender biases (Ely, Ibarra and Kolb, 2011) that are thought to exist in today's organizations. Educators should provide opportunities that inform women entering an engineering career of the dynamics of the profession related to the male-dominated culture including reviewing the results of this study and those of other researchers. Professional skill development should be included within the undergraduate engineering curriculum. Educators should provide forums or seminars where women who currently work in an engineering role return to campus and discuss the engineering profession with the students. This would aid in developing the professional role confidence discussed by Cech et al. (2011). Establishing ongoing mentoring programs with women in successful engineering careers can aid students in developing their own vision of work within an engineering career.

To reduce the influence of the cultural aspects of engineering and other STEM occupations, women entering these professions should be paired with managers who are personally engaged as a manager and have the ability to establish work systems that promote women's engagement as an engineer. Managers should initiate conversations with employees specifically focused on aspects of job engagement as some work systems may discourage and inhibit engagement. Managers of women engineers are encouraged to consider challenging assignments for women engineers. It is recommended that these assignments provide novelty and continuous learning.

This study supports the work of other researchers who suggest organizational changes necessary to retain women in engineering as well as other STEM professions (Bilimoria et al., 2008; Fouad and Singh, 2011; Hewlett et al., 2008; National Research Council, 2007). Organizations should recognize the compelling business case associated with increasing gender diversity within all levels of the organizations including the number of women in leadership (Catalyst, 2004; Ernst & Young, 2009; McKinsey & Company, 2010).

Ely, Ibarra and Kolb (2011) recommend developing programs designed specifically for women in leadership as there are so-called second generation gender biases in today's workplace that are powerful and invisible barriers to women's success. Cultural beliefs and workplace structures, practices and patterns exist that can impede women's progress by favoring men and impeding women's ability to develop an engineering identity. Organizations are urged to provide development opportunities for women engineers that are specifically designed to address retention. As proposed by Ely et al. (2011) these programs would allow women to become aware of and informed about gender biases within their workplaces. Additionally the intent of the programs would be to allow for women to develop an identity as an engineer within their professional domain. Professional development has been found to be an important aspect of retaining women in the engineering profession (Fouad and Singh, 2011). Organizations should recognize the importance of work engagement in retaining women engineers and as such should provide ongoing opportunities for challenge, novelty, and learning.

Future Research

Our findings suggest many opportunities for future research. The small sample size, while yielding quite unambiguous results, nevertheless implies that future research should involve more women engineers and engineers in non-corporate roles and with comparisons to male engineers. It is also recommended that similar studies compare women engineers to women in other more gender balanced professions such as accounting. Future research is suggested to explore the relationship between the ideal self and engagement and how both of these concepts relate to career decisions. Theoretically there appears to be some overlap in how the concepts of the ideal self and engagement motivate decisions especially related to career. And while each concept is shown here as distinctly influencing persistence there may be some relationship where the ideal self drives engagement or that engagement is the mechanism where the ideal self influences persistence. Each of these relationships should be explored through future research studies.

CONCLUSION

Despite difficulties within their role as an engineer, women persist in their careers as they find meaning, are continuously challenged, and have positive interactions with others resulting in feelings of fulfilment, value and worth. We theorize that because these women have developed an identity as an engineer and have higher levels of self-efficacy and a positive outlook, their ideal self motivates them to continue to persist within their engineering careers. Consistent with Boyatzis' theory of the ideal self and Kahn's theory of engagement this study shows that women with sustained engineering careers exude hope, have a clear image of how their career fits their future state, and view engineering as part of their core identity. They fully engage with their work, finding meaning and purpose, making the most of challenge, novelty, and continuous learning opportunities, and obtaining a sense of personal fulfillment, worth and value.

NOTE

1. The research methods used in the study are described in greater detail in Buse, Bilimoria and Perelli (2013).

REFERENCES

Bagilhole, B. (2002), 'Challenging equal opportunities: Changing and adapting male hegemony in academia', *British Journal of Sociology of Education*, **23**(1), 19–33.

Bandura, A. (1982), 'Self-efficacy mechanism in human agency', *American Psychologist*, **37**(2), 122–47.

Betz, M. and L. O'Connell (1992), 'The role of inside and same-sex influencers in the choice of non traditional occupations', *Sociological Inquiry*, **62**(1), 98–106.

Betz, N.E. and G. Hackett (1981), 'The relationship of career-related self-efficacy expectations to perceived career options in college women and men', *Journal of Counseling Psychology*, **28**(5), 399–410.

Betz, N.E. and R.S. Schifano (2000), 'Evaluation of an intervention to increase realistic self-efficacy and interests in college women', *Journal of Vocational Behavior*, **56**, 35–52.

Bilimoria, D.S.J., S. Joy and X. Liang (2008), 'Breaking barriers and creating inclusiveness: Lessons of organizational transformation to advance women faculty in academic science and engineering', *Human Resource Management*, **47**(3), 423–41.

Blum, L. (2001), 'Transforming the culture of computing at Carnegie Mellon', *Computing Reseach News*, 2–9.

Boyatzis, R.E. (2008), 'Leadership development from a complexity perspective', *Consulting Psychology Journal: Practice and Research*, **60**(4), 298–313.

Boyatzis, R.E. and K. Akrivou (2006), 'The ideal self as the driver of intentional change', *Journal of Mangement Development*, **25**(7), 624–42.

Bureau of Labor Statistics, U.S. Department of Labor (2011), *Women in the Labor Force: A Databook.* Retrieved from US Bureau of Labor Statistics: http://www.bls.gov/cps/wlf-databook-2011.pdf.

Bureau of Labor Statistics, U.S. Department of Labor (2012), *Occupational Outlook Handbook 2012–2013 Edition.* Retrieved from Architecture and Engineering Outlook: http://www.bls.gov/ooh/architecture-and-engineering/home.htm.

Buse, K., D. Bilimoria and S. Perelli (2013), 'Why they stay: Women persisting in the engineering profession', *Career Development International*, **18**(2).

Catalyst (2004), *The Bottom Line: Connecting Corporate Performance and Gender Diversity.* Retrieved September 2011 from Catalyst: http://www.catalyst.org/file/44/thepercent20bottompercent20linepercent20connectingpercent20corporatepercent20performancepercent20andpercent20genderpercent20diversity.pdf.

Cech, E., B. Rubineau, S. Silbey and C. Seron (2011), 'Professional role confidence and gendered persistence in engineering', *American Sociological Review*, **76**(5), 641–66.

Chiu, L.H., S.Y. Chiu, J.H. Chiu and D.M. Chiu (2002), 'Engineering and technology education for women in the new century', *IEEE Engineering Science and Education Journal*, 145–52.

Corbin, J. and A. Strauss (eds) (2008), *Basics of Qualitative Research: Techniques and Procedures for Developing Grounded Theory*, California: Sage.

Ely, R.J., H. Ibarra and D.H. Kolb (2011), 'Taking gender into account: Theory and design for women's leadership development', *Academy of Management Learning & Education*, **10**(3), 474–93.

Ernst & Young (2009), *Groundbreakers Using the Strength of Women to Rebuild the World Economy.* Retrieved September 2011 from Ernst & Young: http://www.ey.com/Publication/vwLUAssets/Groundbreakers_Using_the_strength_of_women_to_rebuild_the_world_economy/$FILE/Groundbreakers.pdf.

Fouad, N.A. and R. Singh (2011), *Stemming the Tide: Why Women Leave Engineerings.* Retrieved from Women in Engineering: http://www.studyofwork.com/wp-content/uploads/2011/03/NSF_Women-Executive-Summary-0314.pdf.

Frehill, L. (2008), 'The Society of Women Engineers National Survey about Engineering', *SWE Magazine*, **54**(3), 10–13.

Gill, J., R. Sharp, J. Mills and S. Franzway (2008), 'I still wanna be an engineer! Women, education and the engineering profession', *European Journal of Engineering Education*, **33**(4), 391–402.

Gladwell, M. (2000), *The Tipping Point*, New York: Back Bay Books/Little, Brown and Company.

Glaser, B. and A. Strauss (1967), *The Discovery of Grounded Theory: Strategies for Qualitative Research*, New York: Aldine.

Glass, C. and K. Minnotte (2010), 'Recruiting and hiring women in STEM fields', *Journal of Diversity in Higher Education*, **3**(4), 218–29.

Hartman, H. and M. Hartman (2009), 'Do gender differences in undergraduate engineering orientations persist when major is controlled', *International Journal of Gender, Science and Technology*, **1**(1), 61–82.

Heilman, M.E., A.S. Wallen, D. Fuchs and M.M Tamkins (2004), 'Penalties for success: Reactions to women who succeed at male gender tasks', *Journal of Applied Psychology*, **89**(3), 416–27.

Hewlett, S.A., C.B. Luce, L.J. Servon, L. Sherbin, P. Shiller, E. Sosnovich and K. Sumberg (2008), *The Athena Factor: Reversing the Brain Drain in Science, Engineering, and Technology*, Cambridge: Harvard Business School Publishing Corporation.

Higgins, E. (1987), 'Self-discrepancy: A theory relating self and affect', *Psychological Review*, **94**, 319–40.

Hill, C., C. Corbett and A. St. Rose (2010), *Why So Few? Women in Science, Technology, Engineering and Math.* Washington, DC: AAUW. Retrieved 2011 from American Association of University Women: http://www.aauw.org/learn/research/whysofew.cfm.

Jorgenson, J. (2002), 'Engineering selves: Negotiating gender and identity in technical work', *Management Communication Quarterly*, **15**(3), 350–80.

Kahn, W.A. (1990), 'Psychological conditions of personal engagement and disengagement at work', *Academy of Management Journal*, **33**(4), 692–724.

Margolis, J., A. Fisher and F. Miller (1999/2000), 'Caring about connections: Gender and computing', *IEEE Technology and Society Magaine*, 13–20.

Maxwell, J.A. (2005), *Qualitative Research Design*, Thousand Oaks, CA: Sage Publications.

McKinsey & Company (2010), *Women at the Top of Corporations.* Retrieved from McKinsey & Company: http://www.mckinsey.com/locations/swiss/news_publications/pdf/women_matter_2010_4.pdf.

Miller, G.E. (2004), 'Frontier masculinity in the oil industry: The experience of women engineers', *Gender, Work and Organization*, **11**(1), 47–73.

Moss-Racusin, C.A., J.F. Dovidio, V.L. Brescoll, M.J. Graham and J. Handelsman (2012), *Science Faculty's Subtle Gender Biases Favor Male Students.* doi:10.1073/pnas.1211286109.

National Research Council (2007), *Beyond Bias and Barriers: Fulfilling the Potential of Women in Academic Science and Engineering*, Washington, DC: National Academies Press.

National Science Foundation (2010), *Science and Engineering Indicators 2010*, Arlington, VA: National Center for Science and Engineering Statistics (NCSES). Retrieved from http://www.nsf.gov/statistics/seind10/start.htm.

National Science Foundation (2011), *Employed US Scientists and Engineers by Level and Field of Highest Degree, Sex and Employment Sector 2006.* Retrieved from Characteristics of Scientists and Engineers in the United States 2006: http://www.nsf.gov/statistics/nsf11318/pdf/nsf11318.pdf.

National Science Foundation (2012), *Advance: Increasing the Participation and Advancement of Women in Academic Science and Engineering Careers.* Retrieved March 2009, from ADVANCE: http://www.nsf.gov/funding/pgm_summ.jsp?pims_id=5383.

Powers, A., B. Bagilhole and A. Dainty (2009), 'How women engineers do and undo gender: Consequences for gender equity', *Gender, Work and Organization*, **16**(4), 411–28.

President's Council of Advisors on Science and Technology (2012), *Engage to Excel: Producing one million additional college graduates with degrees in science, technology, engineering, and mathematics.* Retrieved from PCAST Documents & Reports: http://www.whitehouse.gov/sites/default/files/microsites/ostp/pcast-engage-to-excel-final_2-25-12.pdf.

Rich, B.L., J.A. Lepine and E.R. Crawford (2010), 'Job engagement: Antecedents and effects on job performance', *Academy of Management Journal*, **53**(3), 617–35.

Rouse, G.C. (2000), 'Orchestrating impartiality: The impact of "blind" auditions on female musicians', *Americal Economic Review*, **90**, 715–41.

Saks, A.M. (2006), 'Antecedents and consequences of employee engagement', *Journal of Managerial Psychology*, **21**(7), 600–619.

Schaufeli, W.B. and A.B. Bakker (2004), 'Job demands, job resources, and their relationship with burnout and engagement: A multi-sample study', *Journal of Organizational Behavior*, **25**, 293–315.

Stout, J.G., N. Dasqupta, M. Hunsinger and M. McManus (2011), 'STEMing the tide: Using ingroup experts to inoculate women's self-concept in science, technology, engineering, and mathematics (STEM)', *Journal of Personality and Social Psychology*, **100**(2), 255–70.

Suddaby, R. (2006), 'What grounded theory is not', *Academy of Management Journal*, **49**(4), 633–42.

3. To stay or to leave: Factors that differentiate women currently working in engineering from those who left the profession

Romila Singh, Nadya A. Fouad, Mary Fitzpatrick, Catia Figueiredo and Wen Hsin Chang

INTRODUCTION

Engineering is one of the most sex-segregated professional occupations in the United States today. Twenty percent of engineering graduates are women, the successful result of over three decades of intense early education interventions that have cost millions of dollars. President Obama established the Committee on STEM Education to determine how much and where this money was spent. CoSTEM found that, just in 2011, $3.4 billion dollars were spent by various federal agencies on STEM education. A third (approximately $1.1 billion) was directed to women, people with disabilities, and racial/ethnic minority students. Thirteen million dollars focused exclusively on interventions to increase the number of girls and women in STEM careers (CoSTEM, 2011). It can be argued that these interventions have been successful, because the 20 percent graduation rate is roughly double the graduation rate from the 1970s. In 2013, the Committee on STEM Education issued a five-year strategic plan, again noting the critical need for science and technological innovation, not just for US preeminence, but for security reasons as well. The foreword of this plan notes that "The health and longevity of our Nation's citizenry, economy, and environmental resources depend in large part on the acceleration of scientific and technological innovations, such as those that improve health care, inspire new industries, protect the environment, and safeguard us from harm." For the first time, the strategic plan explicitly includes the recommendation for STEM education and the workplace to be more inclusive of women and racial/ethnic minorities.

However, while 20 percent of engineering graduates are women, only 11 percent of practicing engineers are women (NSF, 2011), a rate that has been relatively constant for over two decades. Thus, nearly half of women who graduate in engineering decide, somewhere along the way, to leave an engineering career. But only 10 percent of men leave an engineering career (Society of Women Engineers, 2007). It would appear that different mechanisms influence retention and attrition for men and women. To address the strategic plan goals laid out by CoSTEM (2013), it is critical for organizations to understand factors that influence the retention decisions of men and women, but it is clearly urgent to understand what explains the loss of half of the women from engineering. We argue that the loss of women engineers represents a critical loss to society in terms of technical expertise, a loss to organizations in terms of investments in training and human capital, and a potential loss to individuals as they have to prepare for another career. In this chapter, we discuss the findings of a large-scale study to examine reasons women left engineering. While we often focus on the women who leave engineering, it is also true that half stay as engineers. We will, thus, also look at key differences between women engineers who left technical workplaces and those who are currently working in engineering. Using dominant vocational and management theories, we expose the points of convergence and divergence in the experiences of these two groups of women engineers.

THEORETICAL BACKGROUND AND FRAMEWORK FOR THE STUDY

Women engineers' intentions to persist or leave engineering careers can be meaningfully explored using two dominant theoretical perspectives from two different fields of inquiry – social cognitive career management theory (SCCMT) and turnover theory.

Social cognitive theory (Bandura, 1997) has been recently applied in vocational psychology to help explain how individuals make career choices and how they determine their level of performance. Bandura hypothesizes that individuals' conception of their confidence to perform tasks (self-efficacy) mediates between what they know and how they act and that people's beliefs in their ability to accomplish things helps to determine the actions they will take. Bandura also notes that self-efficacy is domain-specific. Thus, confidence to do tasks in one domain, such as conducting experiments, is not necessarily related to confidence to do tasks in another domain, such as leading a department or college. Bandura (1997) also postulates that self-efficacy is distinct from outcome expectancies, or the expectations one has of the result of behavior.

More recently, Lent and Brown (2013) extended the model to explain a variety of career decisions people make over the span of their careers, which they call the Model of Career Self-Management. The model proposes that self-efficacy and outcome expectations together predict career management goals, actions, and outcomes. The model also predicts that the context may provide supports or barriers to accomplishing those outcomes. This study compares women who are currently working in engineering with those who are not on a variety of SCCT related elements such as self-efficacy and perceptions of contextual supports and barriers.

The prevailing view in turnover literature is that job and career attitudes, in the form of dissatisfaction with one's job and or career and a lack of commitment to the organization as well as the profession, are positively related to intentions to leave the organization and the profession (e.g., Mobley, 1977; Rhodes and Doering, 1983; Steers and Mowday, 1981). Turnover intentions refer to deliberate and conscious willfulness to leave the organization (Tett and Meyer, 1993). The two key attitudes implicated in turnover theories are satisfaction and commitment. In our study, we examine career satisfaction and occupational commitment as precursors to intentions to leave the engineering profession. Career satisfaction captures individuals' satisfaction with their rate of progress toward achieving their overall career goals (Greenhaus, Parasuraman, and Wormley, 1990). It is frequently used as a measure of an employee's intrinsic assessments of career success (Judge, Cable, Boudreau, and Bretz, 1995; Seibert, Kraimer, and Liden, 2001) and has been negatively linked to occupational withdrawal intentions (Greenhaus, Parasuraman, and Collins, 2001).

Career commitment is defined as one's motivation to work in one's chosen occupation (Carson and Bedeian, 1994). Career commitment refers to one's feelings of attachment, identification, and involvement in the occupation and has been found to be negatively related to intention to change one's occupation (Blau, 1985). In this study, we examine whether there are differences between the two groups of women engineers on career satisfaction, career commitment, and intentions to leave the engineering profession.

SAMPLE

Seventy-one universities were identified by the American Society of Engineering Education as top institutions that graduate women, Latino(a), African American, and Asian engineers (some universities appeared in more than one category). Deans were contacted and invited to ask their engineering alumnae to participate in the study; 30 universities agreed to do so. The universities are geographically very diverse, and include both public and private institutions.

Email addresses were either given to the research team or links to the survey were sent to alumni directly from the university. The link took participants to a website, which had a link to the online survey. Although we started with a focus on specific cohorts from engineering colleges, we received feedback not to limit our study in this manner, which led women engineers from some additional 200 universities to be represented in the study.

Profile of Participants

A total of 5,562 women who graduated with a bachelor's degree in engineering participated and completed the study. Of this, 554 (10 percent) women obtained a degree but never worked as an engineer; 1,365 (29 percent) women previously worked as an engineer but have left the field since (279 of these left less than five years ago); and 3,324 (60 percent) women are currently working in engineering. We report here on those women who are currently working in engineering (labeled as "persisters") and compare them with women who left engineering within the past five years (labeled as "non-persisters"). These were the two groups that received the entire survey instrument; the other two groups filled out shorter versions of the survey. We chose five years as a cut-off point for comparison so as to ensure that recollections were recent enough to be accurate. We used ANOVAs, t-tests, and discriminant analysis to uncover areas of difference between the two groups of women engineers on a variety of factors related to persistence and turnover. We first discuss measures employed in the study and then present a broad profile of these two groups.

MEASURES

Responses to almost all scales were given on a five-point Likert scale and were computed by averaging the items. Higher values represented more positive self-efficacy beliefs, outcome expectations, positive job attitudes, more supportive organizations, supervisors, and co-workers, higher developmental experiences, greater promotion opportunities, stronger turnover intentions, and greater job search behaviors. With the exception of one scale, reliability estimates for all measures exceeded .70.

Self-Efficacy and Outcomes Expectations

As noted earlier, we identified three domains of self-efficacy and outcome expectations based on a review of the literature and the results of a study by Fouad et al. (2011). The three domains for self-efficacy and commensurate outcomes expectations were: engineering tasks, navigating organizational politics, and managing multiple life-roles. Thus, three scales measured participants' domain specific self-efficacy, and three scales measured participants' domain specific outcome expectations. All six scales were pilot-tested for content validity and reliability on a separate group of working women engineers that did not participate in the survey.

Engineering tasks self-efficacy

Engineering tasks were identified in the O*Net set of tasks common across the major engineering occupations (DOL, 2008) which included researching, designing, answering technical questions, operating software to execute designs, communicating with colleagues, supervisors and customers, troubleshooting problems, and documenting procedures. Based on these characteristics, we developed a 21-item set of questions to assess engineering task self-efficacy. One item was dropped because of poor factor loading. A sample item included, "I am confident that with proper training, I can design a new product or project to meet specified requirements." Responses were given on a 5-point scale (1 = not at all confident; 5 = very confident.) The reliability estimate for the final version of the scale was .93.

Engineering tasks outcome expectations

We developed an 11-item scale to assess outcomes that might be expected of doing engineering tasks. Consistent with recommendations in constructing outcome expectations scales (e.g., Bandura, 2004; Lent and Brown, 2006; Fouad and Guillen, 2006), we included items about outcomes from the perspective of others (co-workers, managers), self-evaluation, and material goods, such as receiving raises for doing a good job. Examples of items included "If I perform my job tasks well, then I will earn the respect of my co-workers," "If I achieve in my job, I expect

I'll receive good raises," and "When I am successful at my work tasks, then my manager(s) will be impressed." Higher scores indicated higher levels of engineering tasks outcome expectations. The scale demonstrated good internal consistency with a Cronbach's alpha of .84 in this sample.

Organizational self-efficacy

Confidence in navigating the organizational environment was measured using a 17-item measure developed specifically for this study. Respondents were asked to rate (1 = not at all confident; 5 = very confident) how confident they feel navigating different aspects of their work culture (i.e. building relationships, networking, understanding and managing workplace politics). An example item includes, "I am confident that I can network with others at work." Items were averaged and higher scores indicated higher organizational self-efficacy beliefs. The scale demonstrated good internal consistency with a Cronbach's alpha of .91 in this sample.

Organizational outcome expectations

A 20-item measure was developed for this study to assess an individual's beliefs in the outcomes associated with one's successfully navigating the work organization. An example item includes, "If I am a good at my job, then I will be better able to achieve my future goals." The measure was reduced to eight items after conducting factor analysis. Cronbach's alpha for this scale was found to be .75.

Managing multiple life-roles self-efficacy

Confidence in managing multiple work and non-work roles was assessed using a seven-item measure developed for this study. Examples of items include "I am confident that I can find ways to meet the demands of my multiple work and non-work roles" and "I am confident that I can fulfill all my non-work responsibilities despite having a demanding job/career." The scale demonstrated good reliability of .95 in this sample.

Managing multiple role outcomes expectations

A nine-item measure developed for this study assessed individuals' beliefs in the outcomes associated with their ability to manage multiple life roles. Higher scores represented higher outcomes expectations related to managing multiple life roles. Example of items include "If I can manage my multiple life roles, then I will feel good about myself" and "I expect that being able to successfully combine my multiple life roles will be rewarding to me." The scale demonstrated adequate internal consistency with a Cronbach's alpha of .68.

Career Attitudes

Established scales were used to measure the two job attitudes: career satisfaction and occupational commitment.

Career satisfaction

Career satisfaction was measured with an established five-item scale by Greenhaus, Parasuraman and Wormley (1990) that assessed the extent to which individuals felt satisfied with the progress they made toward a variety of goals such as career goals, advancement goals, and income goals. Items include "I am satisfied with the progress I have made toward meeting my overall career goals." Higher values indicated higher levels of career satisfaction. Reliability for the scale in this study was .90.

Career commitment

A 12-item Career Commitment Measure by Carson and Bedian (1994) was slightly modified to use the specific occupation of this study (engineering) rather than the generic words "my line of work/career/field" as in the original scale. The scale consists of three subscales: Career Identity, Career Planning, and Career Resilience and all three sub-scales were used in the current study. Examples of items include "Engineering has a great deal of personal meaning to me," "Engineering is an important part of who I am," and "The costs associated with engineering sometimes seem too great" (reverse-scored). Higher scores indicated higher levels of commitment toward the engineering profession. Reliability for the scale was found to be .89.

Workplace Supports and Barriers

Supports and barriers in the workplace were measured using established scales. Organizational barriers were measured using established scales for social undermining (Duffy, Ganster, and Pagon, 2002) and workplace incivility (Miner-Rubino and Cortina, 2007). Workplace supports were assessed through perceived organizational support and perceived supervisor and co-workers' support, work–family culture, and work–life benefits availability and use. Workplace barriers and supports are described below.

Social undermining

Social undermining, which refers to intentional offenses aimed at destroying another's favorable reputation, their ability to accomplish their work, or their ability to build and maintain positive relationships was assessed by a 13-item scale developed by Duffy et al. (2002). Participants were asked to report on the frequency (Response format: 1 = Never; 6 = Every Day) with which their supervisors engaged in undermining behaviors directed toward them within the last one year. Items were preceded with the statement "In the past one year, how often has your supervisor intentionally …" and included behaviors such as "Talked bad about you behind your back?," "Belittled you or your ideas?," "Made you feel incompetent?," and "Spread rumors about you?" Higher scale values indicated greater display of undermining behaviors. Reliability for this scale was found to be .95.

Workplace incivility

Uncivil behaviors, defined as characteristically rude or discourteous behaviors displaying a lack of regard toward others, were measured by a six-item scale (Cortina, Magley, Williams and Langhout, 2001). Participants were asked to indicate how often (response format: 1 = Never; 3 = More than Once or Twice) in the past year they observed conduct directed toward female employees that was condescending, patronizing, or otherwise rude and disrespectful. Sample behaviors include "To what extent did you observe any supervisor, senior manager, or colleague speak in a condescending or patronizing manner to a female employee?" Reliability for the scale was .85 in the current study.

Perceived organizational support

A nine-item perceived organizational support measure by Eisenberger et al. (1986) was used to assess the degree to which individuals felt that their organization recognized their contributions and cared for their well-being (Example item: "This organization strongly considers my goals and values.") Cronbach's alpha for the scale in this current study was .94.

Perceived social support from supervisors and coworkers

An established instrument by Caplan, Cobb, French, Harrison and Pinneau (1975) was used to measure perceived social support from supervisors and co-workers. This measure included four items for supervisory support and four items for co-worker support and assessed general forms of social support at work (example item: "How much can each of these people be relied on when things get tough at work?"). Higher values indicated greater perceived social support from supervisors and co-workers. Reliability for perceived supervisory support was found to be .91 and .84 for co-worker support.

Developmental experiences

This four-item measure assessed the extent to which the organization offered professional development opportunities and support to its employees (Wayne, Shore and Liden, 1997). Example item includes, "In the positions that I have held at my company, I have often been assigned projects that have enabled me to develop and strengthen new skills." Scores indicate the extent to which employees believed their managers took an active interest in providing them with developmental opportunities. Higher scores indicate greater perception of developmental experiences. Reliability estimates for this scale were .82.

Opportunities for advancement

This nine-item measure assessed the extent to which the organization offered promotional opportunities (Smith, Kendall and Hulin, 1969). Respondents indicated "yes," "no," or "don't know" to statements that described the promotional opportunities at their workplace.

Work–life culture

We modified the original 20-item work–family culture scale developed by Thompson, Beauvais and Lyness (1999) to include a shortened 15-item measure that tapped the managerial support for work–family issues and organizational time demands that allowed employees to manage their work and family obligations. Respondents were asked to indicate the extent to which their organization's culture encouraged its employees to have a balance between their work and family lives. A sample item is "In this organization employees can easily balance their work and home lives." Items were assessed using a five-point scale that ranged from 1 (Strongly Disagree) to 5 (Strongly Agree). Reliability for this scale was .92.

Work–life benefit availability and use

A list of 12 family supportive benefits commonly offered by organizations was presented to the participants who were instructed to place a checkmark next to each benefit offered by their organization and another checkmark next to each benefit offered by the organization that they currently use or had used in the past. Benefits that were not available or not used by the participants were coded as 0 and those that were available or were used were coded as 1. Two sets of overall scores were computed by summing the number of benefits checked within the two categories, one for total benefits availability and the other for total benefits used. Higher scores indicated a greater number of benefits that were available and used.

Turnover Intentions

An established scale was used to assess intentions to leave the profession.

Professional turnover intentions

A four-item instrument by Hom, Griffeth and Sellaro (1984) was modified to assess the extent to which participants were considering leaving their current occupation (i.e., engineering). Illustrative items include "I often think about quitting engineering." Responses given on a five-point scale (1 = Strongly Disagree to 5 = Strongly Agree) were averaged with higher scores indicating greater intentions to leave the profession. The reliability of the scale was .91.

DEMOGRAPHIC AND BACKGROUND PROFILE OF PERSISTERS AND NON-PERSISTERS

The top majors for this group were chemical, mechanical, civil, and electrical engineering. Forty-three percent received additional degrees; most had a Master's or MBA, and 2 percent had earned a PhD. The graduates represented over three decades of engineering education: 9 percent graduated prior to 1984, 10 percent between 1984 and 1989, 7 percent between 1990 and 1994, 11 percent between 1995 and 1999, 14 percent between 2000 and 2004 and 12 percent after 2005. Most women self-identified as Caucasian (84 percent), with 3 percent identifying themselves as Latina, 2 percent as African-American, 3 percent as multi-racial, and 8 percent as Asian or Asian-American.

Similar to women currently working in engineering, the majority of those who had left engineering less than five years ago also self-identified themselves as Caucasian (79 percent) followed by Asian-Americans (8 percent), 3 percent each representing African-American, Latina, and multi-racial groups, and 2 percent reported belonging to the "Other" category.

With regard to their marital status, 70 percent reported being married or in a committed relationship, while 23 percent reported never having married. Only a quarter reported being parents. Current women engineers in our sample were no less likely to be married as their counterparts who left engineering less than five years ago, but less likely to be parents.

Current engineers reported working an average of 43.5 hours a week, organization tenure of an average of eight years, and a median income of between $76,000 and $100,000 a year. Among this group of respondents, two-thirds reported that the gender composition of their work group was either mostly men or all men. About half (51 percent) reported working as individual contributors with no direct reports, while 30 percent worked as project managers, and 16 percent were in executive positions. The top industries represented included consulting (16 percent), aerospace (10 percent), electronics (6 percent), education (6 percent), construction (5 percent), computer engineering (4 percent) and utilities (4 percent).

There were no significant differences between women who are currently working in engineering and those who left engineering less than five years ago in terms of the hours worked (39 hours/week), length of tenure with their company (ten years), average range of salary reported (between $51,000 and $75,000), and both groups were likewise most likely to have graduated with chemical, mechanical, civil and electrical engineering degrees.

Unlike women who are currently working in engineering, women who left engineering were more likely to be in management and executive positions (53.8 percent) and project management roles (21.9 percent). The least common positions occupied by these engineers were non-management roles (24.4 percent). Unlike women who are currently in engineering, the majority of women who left less than five years ago were in an executive role. Finally, for those in management positions, the majority indicated that they had one to four direct reports and were most likely to work in groups that were predominantly male; however, a larger number who left engineering (26 percent) reported working in gender balanced groups.

In sum, current and former engineers do not differ in terms of race, marital or parental status, engineering major, salary level, or number of direct reports.

DIFFERENCES BETWEEN PERSISTERS AND NON-PERSISTERS

Self-Efficacy Beliefs among Persisters and Non-Persisters

Comparing the two groups of women engineers on the three sets of self-efficacy beliefs and outcome expectations, our results revealed no significant differences among any of these personal factors. In other words, compared to women who are currently working in engineering, women who are no longer working in engineering did not have significantly different levels of confidence in their abilities to perform engineering tasks, navigate the political environment at work, or juggle multiple life roles. Further, they did not have any differing levels of expectations from engaging in any of these activities and behaviors.

Contextual or organizational supports

Lent and Brown (2013) noted that a variety of contextual supports and barriers can play an instrumental role in affecting attitudes, behaviors, and career choices. We examined several work-related contextual supports. At a very broad level, workplace support is reflected in the extent to which a company values the contributions of its employees and shows care and concern toward the employees' well-being. We also examined the supportiveness of a company by looking at the provision of training and development opportunities and clear and tangible avenues for advancement that were made available to employees. Our premise, based on past research, was that employees who benefitted from such tangible forms of organizational support will be less likely to think about leaving their organizations (Wayne et al., 1997). Finally, workplace support can also be gauged at a more immediate and micro level by understanding the interpersonal nature of relationships with one's supervisors and co-workers. To this end, we examined social support provided to women engineers by their supervisor and co-workers. It's been shown that employees who work with supportive supervisors and co-workers are less likely to harbor intentions to quit.

Our examination of workplace supports and barriers resulted in three findings. First, current engineers perceived more training and development opportunities than women who left engineering. Current engineers also perceived greater opportunities for advancement. Second, current engineers reported fewer work–life benefits available to them, but were significantly more likely to have used those benefits. Third, current engineers reported greater support from both co-workers and supervisors, and greater organizational support for work–life balance. There were no significant differences between the two groups on any other workplace supports.

Contextual or organizational barriers

According to the SCCMT framework, barriers exemplify any contextual influences that detract and hinder from goal pursuit, choice action, and fulfillment. We examined two broad categories of barriers in this study, both of which were anchored in the work environment. The first set of factors tapped into the perceptions of incivility in the workplace that was captured by the extent to which supervisors, senior managers, and co-workers treated women in a condescending, patronizing, or discourteous manner (Miner-Rubino and Cortina, 2007). The second set of factors believed to affect behaviors and choice actions focused on more role-level barriers such as the extent to which women engineers experienced role ambiguity, role conflict, or role overload.

We found a few differences in barriers between current engineers and those women who left engineering. One difference was that former engineers had reported greater instances of working in an environment that belittled and treated women in a condescending, patronizing manner. Former engineers were also more likely to report being systematically undermined by their supervisors.

In sum, current engineers reported greater perception of supports, especially opportunities for training and advancement, and fewer barriers compared to women who left engineering. Former engineers were more likely to report incivility and undermining behaviors in the workplace.

Predictors of Turnover: Satisfaction, Commitment, Withdrawal Cognitions

Some of the strongest and most proximal correlates of turnover intentions are job attitudes such as satisfaction and commitment. In this study, we asked women engineers to report their levels of career satisfaction and career commitment as well as their intentions to withdraw from the profession. As might be expected, current engineers reported significantly higher levels of satisfaction with the engineering profession than former engineers. Current engineers were also less likely to indicate intentions of leaving the profession. We also found strong negative correlations between commitment and satisfaction factors with intentions to leave the engineering profession. In other words, if engineers felt satisfied with their careers and committed to the engineering profession, they were less likely to express intentions to leave the engineering profession.

DISCUSSION

One of the trends in the literature on women in engineering has centered around the notion that women who either quit engineering or are not successful in engineering careers do so because of their lack of self-confidence in their technical abilities. Our finding is contrary to this anecdotal evidence as well as a few other small-sample studies that point to women's lack of self-confidence as a primary driver for their lack of persistence in engineering. For example, Buse, Bilimoria, and Perelli (2013) interviewed 31 women engineers, ten of whom had left the field. Also based on the social cognitive career management theory, the authors coded comments related to general self-efficacy, and concluded that the current engineers had higher levels of self-efficacy. Perhaps because we directly assessed specific domains of self-efficacy, our results differed from Buse et al. (2013). Specifically, we did not find any significant differences among persisters and non-persisters in terms of women's confidence in their ability to perform engineering tasks, navigate the political environment at work, as well as their confidence in their ability to manage multiple roles. It may be that we did not directly assess self-efficacy domains that may differentiate persisters and non-persisters. For example, Cech, Rubineau, Silbey and Seron (2011) demonstrated that professional role self-confidence differentiated women who stayed in a STEM major and those who left the major more than expertise confidence. The latter might be considered similar to our assessment of engineering task self-efficacy while the former might be similar to the domain of organizational self-efficacy. However, the organizational self-efficacy scale was designed to assess confidence in navigating organizational politics, rather than confidence in the "ability to fulfill the expected roles, competencies and identity features of a successful member of their profession" (Cech et. al., 2011, p. 642). As we noted earlier, persisters and non-persisters differed in their perception that the organization offered support in the form of training and development and advancement. Although Cech et al. (2011) studied engineering students, future research is encouraged to examine the role of professional role self-efficacy in differentiating between those engineers who remain in the profession versus those who leave.

Another common notion that is commonly offered to explain why women engineers leave engineering has to do with women's desire to stay home with the children. What is not captured in this narrative, but revealed in our data, is that women engineers who decide to quit engineering do so as a last resort, after exploring and exhausting all options for flexible work within their organizations. As evidenced in our study, women currently working in engineering reported making use of the few work–life benefits that were offered to them compared to their counterparts who quit engineering. What was more compelling is that former engineers reported working in organizations characterized by cultures that were not supportive of their needs to balance work and family obligations. In other words, lack of workplace flexibility and non-supportive work–life cultures operate to force women engineers to quit technical workplaces when faced with equally compelling sets of work and parenting responsibilities, rather than women's lack of willingness to persist in engineering when they become mothers.

Our research clearly points out that women engineers' self-confidence does not appear to be related to their departure from engineering. Moreover, they work hard and long hours, and are committed to the engineering profession. What does set the current and former engineers apart is the workplace climate that they encounter: whether it is supportive or chilly. Overall, our findings revealed that women currently working in engineering, as compared to those who left engineering, experienced a supportive workplace that provided them with opportunities for training, development, and advancement within their organizations. Moreover, current engineers worked with empathic and understanding supervisors and co-workers, especially supervisors who were supportive of their need to balance work and non-work roles.

Another element of a supportive work environment that emerged as a differentiator between women working in engineering and those who were not was the presence of a supportive work–life culture. Although current women engineers reported fewer work-life benefits available to them as compared to their counterparts who had left engineering, they were significantly more likely to have used those benefits. This finding, combined with the result that current women engineers reported their supervisors as more likely to be sensitive to work–life balance concerns, suggests that current engineers' supportive work environments manifests in a variety of tangible and intangible forms ranging from concrete opportunities for training, development, and advancement and provision of work–life benefits, to less tangible supports that signals that they value their women engineers.

We also detected a complementary trend, albeit in the form of workplace barriers: women who were currently working as engineers experienced far fewer barriers at work in the form of incivility and undermining behaviors as compared to those who left less than five years ago. Following the suggestions of Duffy et al. (2002) and Miner-Rubino and Cortina (2007), we believe that undermining and incivility behaviors are indicative of a toxic work environment that can have the potential of driving people out the door. Taken in conjunction, the results with regard to the experience of workplace barriers and supports point toward workplace climate as being the biggest differentiator that sets apart women who are currently working in engineering from those that have left the technical field.

Our final set of results reveal that women engineers who are currently working in engineering had higher levels of career satisfaction and commitment toward the engineering profession than those who left less than five years ago. Moreover, both career satisfaction and engineering commitment were negatively related to professional withdrawal intentions. This finding is in line with the themes discussed so far and further underscores the point that workplaces that support the careers of women engineers are more likely to reap benefits in terms of satisfied employees who are committed to the profession.

In conclusion, there have been several surveys designed to capture the workplace experiences of women engineers (e.g., SWE, 2007) and while these offer some useful insights, few, if any, provide much evidence on what differentiates women engineers who leave engineering workplaces from those who continue to persist in these careers. Our theoretically anchored study was designed to shed some light into this area and hopefully, our results offer a few answers and insights into which personal (e.g., self-efficacy beliefs) and organizational factors (e.g., workplace climate in the form of supports and barriers) act as key differentiators in the career choices made by women who are still working in engineering and those who have already left.

REFERENCES

Bandura, A. (1997), *Self-Efficacy: The Exercise of Control*, New York: W.H. Freeman.

Bandura, A. (2004), 'Cultivate self-efficacy for personal and organizational effectiveness', in E.A. Locke (ed.), *Handbook of Principles of Organizational Behavior*, Malden, MA: Blackwell, pp. 120–36.

Blau, G.J. (1985), 'The measurement and prediction of career commitment', *Journal of Occupational Psychology*, **58**(4), 277–88. doi:10.1111/j.2044-8325.1985.tb00201.x.

Buse, K., D. Bilimoria and S. Perelli (2013), 'Why they stay: Women persisting in US engineering careers', *The Career Development International*, **18**(2), 139–54. doi:10.1108/CDI-11-2012-0108.

Caplan, R.D., S. Cobb, J.R.P. French, R.V. Harrison and S.R. Pinneau (1975), *Job Demands and Worker Health* (NIOSH Publication Number 75-160), Washington, DC: U.S. Government Printing Office.

Carson, K.D. and A.G. Bedeian (1994), 'Career commitment: Construction of a measure and examination of its psychometric properties', *Journal of Vocational Behavior*, **44**(3), 237–62. doi:10.1006/jvbe.1994.1017.

Cech, E., B. Rubineau, S. Silbey and C. Seron (2011), 'Professional role confidence and gendered persistence in engineering', *American Sociological Review*, **76**, 641–66.

Cortina, L.M., V.J. Magley, J.H. Williams and R.D. Langhout (2001), 'Incivility in the workplace: Incidence and impact', *Journal of Occupational Health Psychology*, **6**, 64–80.

CoSTEM (2011), *Council on Science Technology Engineering and Math.* Retrieved from http://www.whitehouse.gov/sites/default/files/microsites/ostp/pcast-stemed-report.pdf.

Department of Labor (2008), O*Net: Engineering Occupations. Retrieved from http://www.bls.gov/ooh/Architecture-and-Engineering/.

Duffy, M.K., D.C. Ganster and M. Pagon (2002), 'Social undermining in the workplace', *Academy of Management Journal*, **45**, 331–51.

Fouad, N.A. and A. Guillen (2006), 'Outcome expectations: Looking to the past and potential future', *Journal of Career Assessment*, **14**, 130–42.

Fouad, N.A., M.E. Fitzpatrick and J.P. Liu (2011), 'Persistence of women in engineering: A qualitative study', *Journal of Women in Math, Science and Engineering*, **17**, 69–96.

Greenhaus, J.H., S. Parasuraman and K.M. Collins (2001), 'Career involvement and family involvement as moderators of relationships between work–family conflict and withdrawal from a profession', *Journal of Occupational Health Psychology*, **6**(2), 91–100. doi:10.1037/1076-8998.6.2.91.

Greenhaus, J.H., S. Parasuraman and W.M. Wormley (1990), 'Effects of race on organizational experiences, job performance evaluations, and career outcomes', *Academy of Management Journal*, **33**(1), 64–86. doi:10.2307/256352.

Hom, P.W., R.W. Griffeth and C.L. Sellaro (1984), 'The validity of Mobley's (1977) model of employee turnover', *Organizational Behavior and Human Performance*, **34**, 141–74.

Judge, T.A., D.M. Cable, J.W. Boudreau and R.D. Bretz (1995), 'An empirical investigation of the predictors of executive career success', *Personnel Psychology*, **48**(3), 485–519. doi:10.1111/j.1744-6570.1995.tb01767.x.

Lent, R.W. and S.D. Brown (2006), 'On conceptualizing and assessing social cognitive constructs in career research: A measurement guide', *Journal of Career Assessment*, **14**(1), 12–35. doi:10.1177/1069072705281364.

Lent, R.W. and S.D. Brown (2013), 'Social cognitive model of career self-management: Toward a unifying view of adaptive career behavior across the life span', *Journal of Counseling Psychology*, **60**(4), 557–68. doi:10.1037/a0033446.

Miner-Rubino, K. and L.M. Cortina (2007), 'Beyond targets: Consequences of vicarious exposure to misogyny at work', *Journal of Applied Psychology*, **92**, 1254–69.

Mobley, W.H. (1977), 'Intermediate linkages in the relationship between job satisfaction and employee turnover', *Journal of Applied Psychology*, **62**, 237–40.

National Science Foundation, Division of Science Resources Statistics (2011), *Women, Minorities, and Persons with Disabilities in Science and Engineering: 2011*. Special Report NSF 11-309. Arlington, VA. Available at http://www.nsf.gov/statistics/wmpd/.

Rhodes, S.R. and M. Doering (1983), 'An integrated model of career change', *The Academy of Management Review*, **8**(4), 631–9. doi:10.2307/258264.

Seibert, S.E., M.L. Kraimer and R.C. Liden (2001), 'A social capital theory of career success', *Academy of Management Journal*, **44**(2), 219–37. doi:10.2307/3069452.

Smith, P C., L. Kendall and C.L. Hulin (1969), *The Measurement of Satisfaction in Work and Retirement*, Chicago, IL: Rand McNally.

Society of Women Engineers (SWE) (October 18, 2007), *Where Are All the Women Going?* Press release. Available at http://www.swe.org/stellent/idcplg?IdcService=SS_GET_PAGE&ssDocName=swe_007553&ssSourceNodeId=110.

Steers, R.M. and R.T. Mowday (1981), 'Employee turnover and post-decision accommodation process', in L. Cummings and B. Staw (eds), *Research in Organization Behavior* (Vol. 3), Greenwich, CT: JAI Press, pp. 235–81.

Tett, R.P. and J.P. Meyer (1993), 'Job satisfaction, organizational commitment, turnover intention, and turnover: Path analyses based on meta-analytic findings', *Personnel Psychology*, **46**, 259–91.

Thompson, C.A., L.L. Beauvais and K.S. Lyness (1999), 'When work–family benefits are not enough: The influence of work–family culture on benefit utilization, organizational attachment, and work–family conflict', *Journal of Vocational Behavior*, **54**, 392–415.

Wayne, S.J., L.M. Shore and R.C. Liden (1997), 'Perceived organizational support and leader-member exchange: A social exchange perspective', *Academy of Management Journal*, **40**, 82–112.

4. Deciding to stay or go: Understanding the career intentions of women in the Australian mining industry

Margaret Nowak, Melissa Marinelli, Linley Lord and Dede Bonner

INTRODUCTION

Women seeking to develop careers paths in science and technology, engineering and mathematics fields (STEM occupations), areas characterised by an almost entirely male workforce, have been a focus of attention in research and discussions relating to gender equality in the workplace. While there have been increases in women's representation in STEM careers, a challenge for management has been their retention. An important objective in seeking increased retention rates is to build a critical mass of women who can become role models for women who follow (Stout et al., 2011).

In Australia there has been a focus on the attraction and retention of women in non-traditional occupations in the resources sector (Cabrera, 2006; Chamber of Minerals and Energy, 2008; Guillaume and Pochic, 2009; Barrera et al., 2010). Human resource (HR) practitioners have traditionally had remuneration and promotion, employee awards, and staff development in their armoury to reinforce commitment and reduce turnover. These focus on the external drivers and career success indicators and assume homogeneity amongst employees in career values and career motivation.

Literature on women's workforce experiences has been critical of the assumption that women can be encompassed by male centric models of motivation towards career success and advancement and workplace behaviour (Eagly and Karau, 2002; O'Neil et al., 2004; O'Neil and Bilimoria, 2005; O'Neil et al., 2008; Rudman and Phelan, 2008). An alternative approach to attraction and retention is to understand career values and drivers of individual employees and seek policies and career trajectories that take these into account.

The term 'career success' can signify disparate measures of achievement ranging from salary increases to measures of psychological well-being. Considerable discussion has focused on how career success should be defined, with distinction being made between objective and subjective career success (Judges et al., 1995; Feldman and Ng, 2007; Herrbach and Mignonac, 2012; Smith et al., 2012). For Judges et al. (1995) objective success refers to tangible indicators such as pay, promotions and positions whereas subjective success refers more to achievements such as work satisfaction resulting in staff retention and higher job performance. Other researchers building on Schein and Van Maanen's work have distinguished internal success (individual sense of achievement, work challenge, work–life balance) from external success that is publicly demonstrable, such as promotion (for example Sturgess, 1999).

Many organisations base employee rewards and career development systems on the assumption that all employees are equally motivated by the prospect of a promotion and other external manifestations of career support such as recognition programmes and employee development programmes (Pemberton and Herriot, 1994). A significant gap exists in our understanding of individuals' internal career motivators. This is especially true for women in the workforce (Perry, 1993; Pelos, 2000; Quesenberry, 2007).

In this chapter we focus on the career motivation of women in the mining industry in Australia arising from recent research on their careers and career drivers. The project explored the concept of career anchors (Schein, 1974) to understand career drivers for women working in mining companies. Schein (1974, 1975, 1978) suggested that life experiences give an increasingly accurate and stable 'career-self-concept', which identifies as a 'career anchor' and which informs how and why individuals make career decisions. Schein describes a 'career anchor' as 'a motivational/attitudinal/value syndrome that guides and constrains the person's career' (Schein, 1974, p. 4). A career anchor is a 'descriptive and predicative tool' that is 'inside the person, functioning as a set of driving and constraining forces on career decisions and choices' (Schein, 1978, p. 127). We posit that there will be a relationship between the individual's career self-concept and how they define career success.

Schein (1974, 1990) identified eight career anchors as follows: technical/functional competence, managerial competence, autonomy, security/stability, entrepreneurial creativity, service/dedication to a cause, challenge and lifestyle. Three components contribute to career anchors, the first two deriving from experience in the work setting and the third from reaction to norms and values in the social and work situations. These are self-perceived and relate to talent and abilities; motives and needs; and concepts, attitudes and values.

The theory argues that when individuals achieve congruence between their work environment and their career anchor they are more likely to have positive career outcomes (Feldman and Bolino, 1996) including work effectiveness, job satisfaction and job stability (Schein, 1990).

One of the advantages of Schein's career anchor theory is that it looks at the dynamic of the development of stable career identity, taking the discussion beyond career choice. Its value, in consideration of organisational reward systems, is that it is able to direct the discussion towards the variety of career paths within an occupation and of career tracks within an organisation (Feldman and Bolino, 1996). It suggests that the individual's career path/career track choices stabilise in predictable ways related to their interests, abilities and values. This predictability can be of value to organisations as they design career development and rewards systems. Organisations that effectively personalise reward and career development opportunities to align with the individual's dominant career anchors should experience benefits in the form of improved work effectiveness, job satisfaction and lower employee turnover.

Feldman and Bolino (1996) argue that individuals may have more than one career anchor as a consequence of multiple career and life goals or high personal ambivalence, and the existence of more than one anchor will influence career outcomes. Multiple anchors may be complementary or mutually inconsistent. They argue for three basic dimensions of career anchors, talent-based, need-based and value-based. The concept of individuals potentially having more than one anchor is used by Herrbach and Mignonac (2012) in their discussion of the question of the meaning of 'career success' and Tremblay et al. (2007) find a link between subjective success and some career anchors.

A number of career anchor studies have specifically investigated women's careers (Konrad et al., 2000; Pelos, 2000; Quesenberry, 2007; Herrbach and Mignonac, 2012). However, they have not generally yielded clear patterns of career anchor difference. For example, Konrad et al. (2000) found women were more likely to be aligned with lifestyle and challenge career anchors compared to men who showed a preference for the security/stability anchor. Pelos (2000) found that one of the most common reasons women entered entrepreneurship was to achieve a satisfying balance of family and work demands, but found no significant gender-based differences in comparison to all-male populations. Herrbach and Mignonac (2012) found that career anchors moderate the relationship between gender discrimination and career success.

This study extends the research on women and career anchors by exploring the career attitudes and motivations of women currently working in the mining industry in Australia.

THE STUDY AND ITS METHODS

Data Collection

Industry contacts were used to identify women working in mining organisations or within the broader mining industry in professional roles, with a technical or scientific background (for example: engineering, geology, metallurgy) and a letter of invitation was sent to appropriate candidates. Twelve women were selected for this exploratory study. They were employed in a number of organisations, but predominantly by one major mining company, and worked across several organisational functions including business improvement, mine planning and development, mine operations, environment and asset management. They had a range of experience from new graduate to senior executive and a variety of tenure in the industry.

The data were collected in two ways. Firstly, participants completed a career orientations questionnaire to assess perceptions about career needs, motivations and values. The first part of the questionnaire comprised demographic questions covering age, family status, qualifications, work experience, and mode of employment. The second part, previously used by one of the researchers (Marshall and Bonner 2003), contained 40 items adapted from Schein's original questionnaire (Schein, 1974). Completing this section of the questionnaire involved assigning a score from 1 (Never True for Me) to 6 (Always True for Me) for each item. Participants were asked to review their responses and select three items that were the most true for them. These items were weighted and the points for each item transcribed into a table that served to group items pertinent to each career anchor.

Upon returning the completed questionnaires, semi-structured interviews were undertaken at a location convenient to the participants (four of 12 women) or by telephone (eight of 12 women). Interviews lasted from 30 minutes to 90 minutes and were electronically recorded, transcribed and analysed. Interviews focused on career histories; of particular interest were their self-perceived career highlights and low-lights, and specific instances of changes in roles and employers. Further questions probed career motivations, typical workplace frustrations and advice that they would give to other women wanting to work in their organisation. In many cases the interview became a conversation, generating rich data and a strong rapport between the interviewer and participants (Kvale, 1996; DeVault, 1999; Holstein and Gubrium, 1999).

Data Analysis

Patterns of career anchors were identified across the group of 12 participants including primary preferences, clusters of career anchors, and career anchors that were not preferred. The dominant career anchors for each participant were also identified. The interview transcripts were coded using a conventional content analysis approach (Hsieh and Shannon, 2005) to identify statements related to career orientation, decision and motivation. In particular, the reasons for entry into employment in the mining industry, and explanations of a change of role or organisation within the industry were captured. The software program NVivo was used to assist with data management.

Through this analysis, we gained an understanding of women's career motivations in the mining industry. In the following section, we present key insights from the data analysis focusing on the dominant career anchors in both the career anchor questionnaire and interviews. We also examine the reasons why these women have chosen to remain in or change roles or organisations during their careers to date. We illustrate sections of the discussion with selected quotes from the interviews.

INSIGHTS FROM WOMEN IN THE MINING INDUSTRY

Questionnaire Analysis

Prior to the semi-structured interviews, each woman completed a career orientations questionnaire (Marshall and Bonner, 2003). The scores for each participant are presented in Figure 4.1. The two highest career anchor scores for each participant are highlighted in Table 4.1.

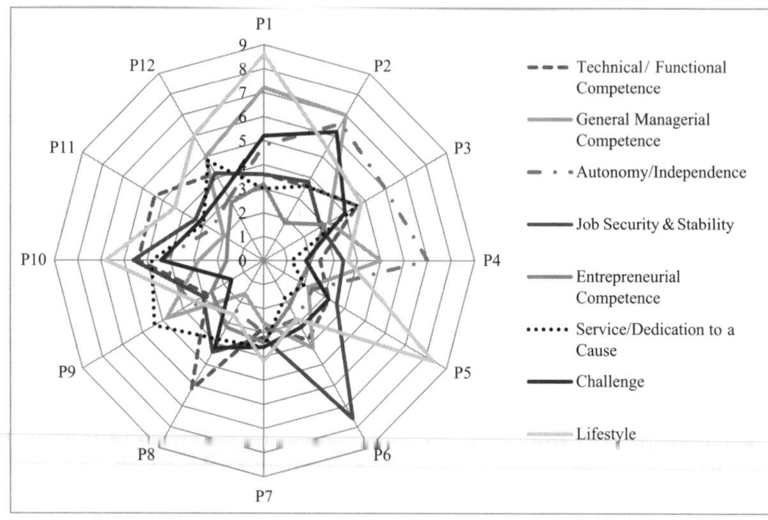

Figure 4.1 Career anchor questionnaire scores

Table 4.1 Career anchor questionnaire scores by participant

Career Anchor Dimension (Feldman & Bolino, 1996)	**Schein's Career Anchors**	**P1**	**P2**	**P3**	**P4**	**P5**	**P6**	**P7**	**P8**	**P9**	**P10**	**P11**	**P12**
Talent based	Technical/ Functional competence	3.6	3.6	4.6	2.4	3.2	3.8	2.8	**6.2**	2.8	5.4	**5.4**	4.2
	General managerial competence	**7.2**	**7**	3.2	**5**	2.2	**4.2**	2.6	1.6	**4.8**	2.8	2	**5**
	Entre-preneurial competence	3.2	1.8	3	2	1.8	2.2	3.4	3.2	2.6	1.6	1.8	2.8
Needs based	Autonomy/ Independence	4.8	**6.6**	**6**	**7**	2.4	2.8	3	2.4	3.6	4.4	2.6	3
	Job security & Stability	3.6	3.8	2.8	3.4	**3.6**	**7.6**	3.2	**4.4**	3	**5.6**	3.4	4.2
	Lifestyle	**8.6**	5.4	**4.8**	3.6	**8.4**	2.8	**4.2**	2.6	3.4	**6.8**	**4.4**	**6**
Values based	Service/ Dedication to a Cause	3.0	3.6	4.6	1.2	2	1.8	**3.6**	3.8	**5.4**	4.8	3	4.8
	Challenge	5.2	6.2	4	1.8	3.2	3.2	**3.6**	4.2	1.6	4.4	3.2	3.4

The respondents' questionnaire results demonstrated multi-item peaks, conforming to Feldman and Bolino's (1996) position that multiple career and life goals impact on the individual's career anchors. In three-quarters of our sample (nine cases) a strong peak is apparent around items that Feldman and Bolino (1996) defined as talent situated anchors of technical/functional competence (TF) or managerial competence (GM). Another peak occurs around items defined as the needs situated anchors of autonomy (AU), job security and stability (SE) and lifestyle (LF). The remaining three respondents (three cases) focused largely on needs situated anchors with lifestyle coupled with autonomy and job security. The respondents did not focus strongly on values based career anchors such as dedication to a cause and challenge in the job. The results show the career anchors of respondents were largely complementary rather than mutually inconsistent. Complementarity of career anchors would be of advantage to an employer seeking to manage an incentive system designed to encourage employees' commitment to the organisation.

Interview Data

The cumulative career history obtained through the semi-structured interviews, reveals that career motivation and drive is strongly associated with Lifestyle (12 of 12 women), Challenge (eight of 12 women) and Security/Stability (seven of 12 women) career anchors. The career anchors of Entrepreneurial (zero of 12 women) and Service/Dedication to a cause (one of 12 women) appear to be least influential.

There are points of both congruence and difference between the analysis of the career anchors questionnaire and the semi-structured interviews. Key similarities include the dominance of the lifestyle career anchor in both the questionnaire and the interview data, the absence of entrepreneurial bent, and the presence of multiple career anchors or orientations for each participant. A notable difference is that the need for challenge is more prevalent and prominent in the interview data.

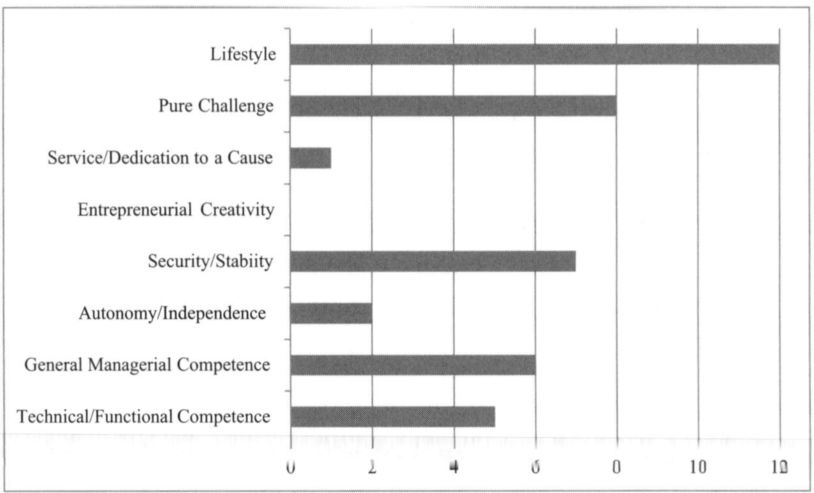

Figure 4.2 Career anchors indicated by interview data

Lifestyle

Lifestyle emerged as the dominant career anchor in both the interviews and questionnaire. In the interview data, lifestyle encompasses the concept of 'work–life' balance or integrating work and non-work activities but extends beyond this. The influence of children and other family members on career decisions is discussed, as is the desire to experience satisfaction in both work and out of work pursuits.

> Just making sure what I want out of life is still available where they're offering / because I don't live to work, I work and I do things outside of work (P10).

However, lifestyle is also strongly linked to work location and mode of work. In the mining industry, work may be situated in small towns, in larger rural posts, on remote sites necessitating rotational or fly-in/fly-out (FIFO) work, or in city areas. Work location impacts a sense of community through social networks and friendships, the availability of facilities such as housing and schools, and psycho-social factors such as anonymity and independence, which can be elusive in small mining towns and mine sites. With lifestyle as a career anchor, the women in our study make career choices to maximise or improve their desired lifestyle and to accommodate life changes.

In Schein's questionnaire, lifestyle questions are general in nature. They query the desire to pursue and combine personal, family and work concerns, or the desire to seek work opportunities that do not interfere with personal and family concerns. The interview data reveals a more nuanced view of this desire to accommodate aspects of life. Lifestyle is important to women at varied stages of career and with differing family statuses, not only women with family commitments. Lifestyle is a strong career driver that exists in tandem with rather than instead of, ambition and satisfaction derived from work. When an improvement in lifestyle is desired, or an adjustment to work role is made to accommodate new caring responsibilities, it is not to the detriment of the level of challenge provided by the work role.

Challenge

While not appearing as a 'top' career anchor in the questionnaire data, interview conversations with the participants were peppered with the need for continued stimulation and challenge. Challenge as a career driver is revealed through a desire for learning and growth, a need for constant variety and a tendency to boredom. Avoiding boredom was a definite driver for career decisions.

> I think for me, it is all about that variety of change, and how you change the role that you are in, so you have something stable but being able to change aspects of your role to keep you interested (P4).

Examining Schein's definition of the Challenge career anchor and elements of the questionnaire relating to it provide some explanation for the discrepancies between the interview data and questionnaire responses. According to Schein's definition an individual with a career anchor of pure challenge would not give up the 'opportunity to work on solutions to seemingly unsolvable problems, to winning out over tough opponents, or to overcoming difficult obstacles' and 'novelty, variety and difficulty become ends in themselves' (Schein, 2006, p. 12). In Schein's questionnaire, the questions pertaining to challenge do not directly query the need for variety, stimulation and the desire to learn. It is these additional aspects of challenge that appear to be most important to the women in our study and guide their career decisions.

Multiple career anchors

The interview data reveals that most of the women had more than one career driver. Differences in the career anchors indicated by the questionnaire and the interview data may be owing to the time period that each data collection method covers. By design, the questionnaire captures the influences at the time of implementation. These motivations are a sum of previous decisions and experience and reflect the current career orientation. In contrast, the interview data covers career history and reveals career anchors that were relevant in the past and the future. This supports previous work on the changing nature of career anchors as careers progress – both as experience is accumulated and as priorities shift (Tremblay et al., 1998; Chang et al., 2012; Herrbach and Mignonac, 2012; Rodrigues et al., 2013). Rodrigues et al. (2013) have suggested that there can be three potential drivers of changing career orientations, ageing, changing non-work roles such as caring, and pursuit of long-term career drivers. Time-sensitive analysis could be an avenue for future research.

The dominance of various career anchors have not been assessed in the interview data as the coding only assessed whether they were present in the women's career histories or not. Further analysis of individual job movements could assess this.

Shall I Stay or Shall I Go?

Examining the reason why the women in our study have chosen to change work roles in their careers allows us to delve more deeply into their career motivations and attitudes. The reasons given for changing roles are captured by five key themes. These are:

- career building
- intrinsic aspects
- extrinsic aspects
- people and work environment
- structural factors.

These are discussed in further detail below.

Career building

A desire to move up the ladder was one reason given by several women for changing roles. The women are ambitious and want to progress in their careers. They are actively looking for and applying for promotions. As expressed by a mining engineer with eight years of work experience:

> I was more than ready to step up into a senior level, so I waited until I found what looked like a good opportunity (P1).

If they do not receive it in their current company they will not hesitate to find a more senior role elsewhere:

> The previous job … , actually I was in my role for three and a half years and I did the interview to apply for the role coming next, and I didn't get it, but I didn't get a 'No'. I got a 'yeah, maybe within sometime', and I just got fed up with it. At the same time, this one was a better offer so I accepted it (P3).

With an eye on their future prospects, several of the group changed roles to take advantage of greater opportunities including further skill development both within and across industry sectors.

> My thought is 'I've got a foot in the door now, I can make my career whatever I want it to be. If I want to go and work on a mine site I can, if I want to go to managerial I can'. There's much more opportunity (P11).

> I got the opportunity for promotion in Perth, honing my technical skills, so getting into mine planning and feasibility studies (P9).

> I wanted to get more experience than just oil and gas. Mining was a logical step, a boom industry (P12).

This is consistent with Tremblay et al. (1998) and Chang et al. (2012) who found that desire for change was not necessarily linked to dissatisfaction, but can be associated with a desire for greater satisfaction through career progress.

Intrinsic Aspects

Intrinsic aspects relate to the need for stimulation and challenge in a work role. Many women sought variety and change in their work.

> I achieved all that I wanted to achieve at that operation and for myself, and it marked up five years with [Group B] and I needed a change (P8).

The women in our study moved roles frequently, on average every 12 months, and some also moved companies a number of times. This may be a feature of the mining industry and its project based work structure. It can also be seen as an indication of the need for stimulation through new challenge and learning and an aversion to boredom.

> The role has changed probably every six month which is really good; I love that. (P5)

> I wanted to learn. I wanted to keep learning (P8).

> I was bored brainless. I just didn't have anywhere near enough work to do, so I recently switched again (P1).

Others expressed the feeling of being at a dead end or not seeing a future pathway from their roles in their organisations.

> They didn't give the job to anyone and I was like ' this is all political games and I don't understand what is going on here'. That was the moment I was like 'Phh. Where do I go from here?' (P3)

In contrast, a sense of satisfaction and achievement was a reason for remaining in a role or with a particular company. This arose from making a contribution to the business, influencing a project, improving processes or seeing a job completed.

> So I just felt that I could make a difference in the office, help build up the business, and I guess, in some ways, make a name for myself, either within the company, or within our clients as well (P11).

Extrinsic Aspects

Further reasons for changing roles relate to extrinsic motivations including lifestyle, reward and security. Of these aspects, the most dominant influences relate to work location and lifestyle. As previously discussed, lifestyle emerged as a dominant career anchor. Family, including children and other family members, influenced job role changes. For the five of 12 women in our sample with children, the arrival of family was important to career decisions. For some, it meant a decision to change roles or to negotiate part-time or job share roles in order to accommodate their changing responsibilities.

> Just two women saying 'Well, let's apply for this on a job share basis' and trying to demonstrate through the application process that we were greater than the sum of our parts (P9).

Regardless of family status, wanting an improved lifestyle drove changes in work location or mode of work. This was manifested as desire to move to larger metropolitan cities after spending several years working in mining towns, or to move to a residential role after working in FIFO work mode.

> I started my career as fly-in/fly-out but then I wanted to go residential just to build a network of friends (P9).
>
> My good friends had all left, I had a bad ex and it was a small town (P1).

Receiving recognition was another reason for remaining in a role or with an organisation:

> I enjoy it, I don't hate going to work every day and you feel like you're getting recognised for what you're doing (P4).

Recognition was more frequently cited as a reason for remaining in a job than financial compensation. This may be owing to high remuneration in the mining industry in Australia, a result of the recent resources boom (Australian Bureau of Statistics, 2013). The influence of money on retention was mentioned by a few women, but this was particularly in relation to remaining in an uncomfortable workplace or a dull job during times of lesser economic prosperity.

A desire for job stability or security was another reason for remaining in a role or for choosing one opportunity or company over another. Again, during less prosperous times, having a secure job or taking a less desirable role outweighed the desire for variety, challenge and change. Job stability also featured in the dialogues of some women with long-term partners or children. Dolan et al. (2011) found that there was a strong relationship, for women in engineering, between their perceptions of career success and their aspiration for balance between work and life and for job security.

People and work environment

The factors influencing staying in a role or moving on were similar. A notable difference was the emphasis on working environment and working with others as reasons to stay in a job or with a company. A good work environment was described as collaborative, interactive and open, one in which people are looked after. Having fun at work was mentioned by more than one woman. A diverse and international workplace was also seen as beneficial. Demeaning, competitive or condescending behaviour was not favoured.

Positive relationships built in the workplace provided a sense of belonging and connection and were a reason to remain.

> I think most of the highlights come … when I have good relationships with the people around me (P3).

> The team is really friendly and they look after us really well and I am happy (P5).

The opportunity to manage people and to use leadership skills were also commonly cited influences on remaining in a role. While also providing significant challenge, a sense of achievement was gained from developing people and imparting knowledge to them, and from achieving results through others.

> I'm actually starting to get to use some leadership skills in conjunction with developing an actual cohesive team (P1).

Company values and integrity were viewed as important to retention. Some women preferred the more personal feel of a smaller company, and others preferred the clout and resources of a larger company. Regardless of size, the way business was conducted was noted and unethical behaviour was a prompt to seek work elsewhere.

> It starts from [Company A's] values and beliefs and it extends all the way down to [Mine A's] values and beliefs. They're so visible every day and that's what I love about my company (P8).

Structural factors

A final influence on the decision to change roles are external or structural factors and include organisational needs, company restructure and market factors such as economic downturn or boom and commodity prices. Women with extended tenure in the mining industry had experienced fluctuations in the mining economy and associated restructures, redundancies and reduced work hours.

> When [Site A] shut, I moved over to the iron ore operations in [Town C] (P4).

> I was even working contract work during the GFC [ed: global financial crisis] because people will say they only want you for a couple of hours, because that's all they can afford (P9),

Their choice to remain in the mining industry through these economic cycles is testament to the satisfaction gained from their work within the industry.

DISCUSSION

This study explored the career motivations and attitudes of women in the Australian mining industry using the concept of career anchors (Schein, 1974). Data have revealed the dominant career anchors and our analysis reveals the following key contributions.

Career Anchors

First was the multiplicity of career anchors that drove career decisions that were surfaced. Previous studies using the career anchor framework have similar findings and challenge the concept of uni-dimensional career anchor dominance. A large proportion of engineers involved in Martineau et al.'s (2005) study presented undifferentiated career anchor profiles, that is: they indicated that career decisions were influenced by multiple career anchors. The authors link this to a preference for hybrid and managerial careers. Rodrigues et al. (2013) prefer the term 'career orientation' rather than career anchor to capture influences on the contemporary career, with participants in their study commonly displaying more than one dominant or primary and secondary career orientation. The authors found that consideration of multiple career orientations provided 'rich insights for understanding people's career choices and patterns' (p. 149).

Second, the career anchors questionnaire revealed the dominance of certain anchors. The women in our study are inclined towards either general managerial competence or technical/functional competence, with the general managerial competence appearing more frequently as a dominant anchor (top two scores). This contrasts with previous findings using the career anchor concept to explore careers of scientifically based professionals. Rodrigues et al. (2013) found that pharmacists 'seek to enact functional managerial roles and show little interest in crossing occupational boundaries'. For IT professionals, a desire for technical competence appeared more frequently that managerial competence in career histories (Chang et al., 2012). In contrast, several of the women in our study were interested in broad roles within the mining industry that involved 'doing it all'.

The questionnaire responses also revealed needs-based career anchors (Autonomy/Independence, Job Security & Stability, and Lifestyle) to be most prevalent, with a particular dominance of the Lifestyle career anchor. The career decisions of pharmacists (Rodrigues et al., 2013) and global managers (Suutari and Taka, 2004) were also driven by lifestyle, but not to the extent of our mining women. The dominance of the Lifestyle career anchor is linked to a preference by engineers for project-based career paths (Martineau et al., 2005).

Career conversations with the women confirm that lifestyle is an important driver for career decisions, but provide a more nuanced view of this career orientation. Lifestyle extends beyond the concept of work–life balance to include the impacts of job location. Variety in job location is perhaps a unique feature of the mining industry. The collective sense from the interview data is that the variety and choice of locations and work modes (residential, FIFO, drive-in/drive-out) available through working in the mining industry are a positive drawcard for the women we interviewed. The opportunity to move between different modes of work and a variety of locations enables continuity of a desired lifestyle that enabled several women to enjoy careers in the industry spanning in excess of 20 years. The story told by our women differs from the reported impediments to women's employment in the mining industry (Mayes and Pini, 2008) and the work–life conflict reported by Canadian mining women (Women in Mining Canada, 2010).

In contrast to the responses to the questionnaire, a desire for challenge and stimulation emerged in the interviews as an important career anchor. Sufficient challenge and variety will retain these women, while a lack of opportunity to fulfil their need for challenge will lead them to seek employment elsewhere. This need for challenge aligns with recent work on women in the resources industry. Qualitative research undertaken with 31 senior women in the resources sector in Western Australia (Teo et al., 2013) suggested that, for the women interviewed, internal or intrinsic drivers were more important in defining career success in contrast to visible external drivers such as promotion. The internal drivers they identified included being challenged at work, having a sense of personal achievement, doing social good, sense of self-efficacy and work–life balance.

Chang et al. (2012) identified a career anchor of Learning Motivation that may better align to the aspects of 'challenge' that we have identified. Learning motivation is defined by Delong (1982) as the 'desire to achieve a specific goal related to self-growth, or satisfy one's quest for knowledge' (from Chang et al., 2012, p. 317). Rodrigues et al. (2013) see challenge as a desire for novelty and innovation, and as seeking change and variety at work. These studies also noted a difference between Schein's definition of Pure Challenge and the nature of challenge revealed by participants.

While demonstrating some similarities, the dominant career anchors of our mining women differ from those of previous studies drawing on different professions, industries and nations. The question of the variability of career anchors across occupations, professions and culture has been raised previously (see for example Rodrigues et al., 2013). The findings of our preliminary study lend support to this hypothesis.

Deciding to Stay or Go

Third, in addition to exploring career anchors, the career conversations enabled us to more deeply understand reasons for choosing to remain in or leave a work role. Factors beyond Schein's eight career anchors emerged. Most women cited a combination of factors as influencing career decisions over their career histories and these vary with career stage and economic climate.

The motivations to stay within the mining industry identified by our study provide an alternative view to previous work on barriers to women's retention within the industry. Commonly cited are structural issues such as the lack of flexible work arrangements, gender-biased work practices and processes, a work environment that is not conducive to family, and requirements for travel and work in remote locations. Workplace culture, characterised by a masculine ethos, a prevalence of harassment and discrimination and a culture of overwork, is also a frequently cited problem. These factors are seen to act in combination to inhibit the participation and retention of women in the mining industry (Mayes and Pini, 2008; Brouggy, 2010; Women in Mining Canada, 2010).

An assumption in current literature is that retention of women is best addressed by focusing on the issues related to job departures. Our findings suggest that a set of factors separate from the issues encountered in the workplace influence career motivation and act as pull factors for this group of women within the mining industry. In a similar vein, recent work focusing on engineering women has identified the influence of self-efficacy, belonging, and the challenge provided by the occupation as reasons why women stay (Ayre et al., 2013; Buse et al., 2013; Singh et al., 2013). Research on women in leadership careers within the resource sector reveals professional development, networking and receiving and providing mentoring as central to career success and sustainability (Teo et al., 2013). These influences extend beyond the barriers and problems oft cited in literature on women's workplace experiences. Herzberg (1968) posits that different factors influence job satisfaction and motivation, and job dissatisfaction, and that the two states act independently of each other and cannot be treated as opposites. This resonates with our findings on push and pull factors relating to retention of women who are enjoying successful careers and provides the opportunity to build on current thinking about the retention of professional women in the mining industry. The women in our study negotiate barriers and pursue mining careers throughout their various life stages. The variety of opportunities available within the mining industry is a great attraction for these women.

The women's stories indicate that good work culture and work environments do exist within the industry. Further, the opportunity to lead others and to assist in their development provides a sense of satisfaction, achievement and fulfilment. This is mirrored in work by Teo et al. (2013) who determined 'mentoring others' and 'people development' to be aspects of career success and sustainability for women in the Australian resources industry.

Methodological Considerations

The combination of data collection tools – the career anchor questionnaire coupled with career conversations (our semi-structured interviews) – revealed rich data about women's career decisions. We suggest that the coupling of the two techniques is a more sophisticated way of identifying what retains women in the mining industry. The career anchor questionnaire provided a quick and relatively low resource use mechanism to capture women's career motivators and provide feedback to participants. This revealed important information about the plurality of career anchors and trends of dominant career anchors within the group. Conducting career conversations with each woman allowed us to understand their individual career stories, and to delve more deeply into their motivations by querying specific career episodes. This gave us insight into their career motivations over time.

The data that emerged from these conversations both complemented and contradicted the questionnaire outcomes. Variances lead us to return to the wording and definitions underpinning the questionnaire. We found that Schein's definitions of certain anchors differed from the women's collective meaning – for example: Challenge and Lifestyle. Differences can also be linked to the nature of the tools: information collected by the questionnaire reflects the current career orientation, while interview data reveals career anchors and other motivations across the career history.

Implications

Our findings are useful for organisations with an interest in the retention of women working in scientific and technically based professions within the mining industry. Insights from Schein's theory into the underlying career drivers of employees can be used to develop or expand current employee retention and career management programmes. Congruence between an individual's career anchors and organisation provided opportunities to satisfy those career anchors will positively impact job satisfaction and retention and limit job turnover intent (Chang et al., 2012). Improving retention of women in technical and science based professions in the mining industry may result from providing opportunities for challenge, variety and continuous learning through frequent role rotation, chances to gain broader experience, and occasions to lead and mentor others. Organisations need to recognise the importance of lifestyle as a career driver that acts in tandem with, rather than exclusive to, ambition and achievement. It is also essential to extend the understanding of 'lifestyle' beyond the popular work–life balance and family-friendly paradigms that tend to focus on women with children. Our findings indicate that 'lifestyle' also encompasses relational aspects such as being part of a community and having established friendship groups. The tight-knit communities that typify remote, rural and site based mining experience provide opportunities to satisfy these social needs. Women's experience as a highly visible minority in such communities can also be an impetus to move on to new opportunities. These social needs should be considered when guiding career development.

CONCLUSION

In this chapter, we presented key insights from an exploratory study into career drivers and motivations of professional women working in the Australian mining industry. We suggest that using Schein's career anchor theory, via the combination of career anchor questionnaire and career interview, provides a means for gaining rich understanding of how women with STEM careers in the mining industry have constructed their careers. We have an understanding of the career values that are critical to their decisions about career within their organisations and the industry as a whole.

Clear patterns of career motivation have emerged, despite the exploratory nature of this research, signalling that an extension of this study to a larger sample is warranted. This would enable the refinement of an interview schedule that could be used as part of targeted career development programmes. It would also allow further exploration of matters such as the influence of time and time of life on career anchors and their components. The relevance of industry context should also be considered. The differences in career anchors across professions that are reported in the literature indicate that individuals may self-select a particular industry and the associated structure, career paths and culture to align with their career values, and that this will be reflected in their career anchor patterns. We believe that these understandings can assist organisations to improve the retention of professional women in the mining industry.

REFERENCES

Australian Bureau of Statistics (2013), 'The Employee Earnings and Hours, Australia, May 2012', Canberra.

Ayre, M., et al. (2013), '"Yes, I do belong": The women who stay in engineering', *Engineering Studies*, **5**(3), 216–32.

Barrera, S., J. Gardner and B. Horstman (2010), 'Women's experiences in the Western Australian mining industry: A snapshot in 2010', 3rd National Our Work Our Lives Working Women's Centre Conference, Darwin, Australia.

Brouggy, L. (2010), 'Gender, retention and human resource management: A study into the retention of women in the Australian mining industry', Discipline of Work and Organisational Studies, Thesis for Bachelor of Economics and Social Sciences (Honours), University of Sydney, Australia.

Buse, K., D. Bilimoria and S. Perelli (2013), 'Why they stay: Women persisting in US engineering careers', *Career Development International*, **18**(2), 139–54.

Cabrera, E. (2006), 'Opting out and opting in: Understanding the complexities of women's career transitions', *Career Development International*, **12**(3), 218–37.

Chamber of Minerals and Energy (2008), *Attraction and Retention of Women in the Western Australian Resources Sector*, Perth: Chamber of Minerals and Energy.

Chang, C.L.H., J.J. Jiang, G. Klein and H.G. Chen (2012), 'Career anchors and disturbances in job turnover decisions: A case study of IT professionals in Taiwan', *Information & Management*, **49**(6), 309–19.

Delong, T.J. (1982), 'Rexamining the career anchor model', *Personnel*, **59**(3), 50–61.

DeVault, M.L. (1999), 'Talking and listening from women's standpoint: Feminist strategies for interviewing and analysis', in A. Bryman and R.G. Burgess (eds), *Qualitative Research*, London: SAGE, **IV**, 86–111.

Dolan, S.L., A. Bejarano and S. Tzafrir (2011), 'Exploring the moderating effect of gender in the relationship between individuals' aspirations and career success among engineers in Peru', *The International Journal of Human Resoure Management*, **22**(15), 3146–67.

Eagly, A.H. and S.J. Karau (2002), 'Role congruity theory of prejudice toward leaders', *Psychological Review*, **109**(3), 573–98.

Feldman, D.C. and M.C. Bolino (1996), 'Careers within careers: Reconceptualizing the nature of career anchors and their consequences', *Human Resource Management Review*, **6**(2), 89.

Feldman, D.C. and T.W.H. Ng (2007), 'Careers: Mobility, embeddedness, and success', *Journal of Management*, **33**, 350–77.

Guillaume, C. and S. Pochic (2009), 'What would you sacrifice? Access to top management and the work-life balance', *Gender, Work & Organization*, **16**(1), 14–36.

Herrbach, O. and K. Mignonac (2012), 'Perceived gender discrimination and women's subjective career success: The moderating role of career anchors', *Relations Industrielles*, **67**(1), 25–50.

Herzberg, F. (1968), *Work and the Nature of Man*, London: Staples Press.

Holstein, J.A. and J.F. Gubrium (1999), 'Active interviewing', in A. Bryman and R.G. Burgess (eds), *Methods of Qualitative Research*, London: SAGE, **II**, 105–21.

Hsieh, H.F. and S.E. Shannon (2005), 'Three approaches to qualitative content analysis', *Qualitative Health Research*, **15**(9), 1277–88.

Judges, T., D.M. Cable, J.W. Boudreau and R.D. Bretz Jr (1995), 'An empirical investigation of the predictors of executive career success', *Personnel Psychology*, **48**(3), 485–519.

Konrad, A., J.E. Ritchie Jr, P. Lieb and E. Corrigall (2000), 'Sex differences and similarities in job attribute preferences: A meta-analysis', *Psychological Bulletin*, **126**(4), 593–641.

Kvale, S. (1996), *Interviews: An Introduction to Qualitative Research Interviewing*, Thousand Oaks, CA: SAGE.

Marshall, V. and D. Bonner (2003), 'Career anchors and the effects of downsizing: Implications for generations and cultures at work: A preliminary investigation', *Journal of European Industrial Training*, **27**(6), 281–91.

Martineau, Y., T. Wils and M. Tremblay (2005), 'Multiple career anchors of Quebec engineers: Impacts on career path and success', *Relations Industrielles/Industrial Relations*, **60**(3).

Mayes, R. and B. Pini (2008), 'Women and mining in contemporary Australia: An exploratory study', *The Annual Conference of the Australian Sociological Association*, Melbourne, Australia.

O'Neil, D.A. and D. Bilimoria (2005), 'Women's career development phases: Idealism, endurance, and reinvention', *Career Development International*, **10**(3), 168–89.

O'Neil, D.A., D. Bilimoria and A. Saatcioglu (2004), 'Women's career types: Attributions of satisfaction with career success', *Career Development International*, **9**(5), 475–500.

O'Neil, D., M. Hopkins and D. Bilimoria (2008), 'Womens careers at the start of the 21st century: Patterns and paradoxes', *Journal of Business Ethics*, **80**(4), 727–43.

Pelos, S. (2000), *Career Orientations of Female Entrepreneurs: A Study Using Schein's Career Anchor Theory*, San Fransisco, CA: University of San Fransisco.

Pemberton, C. and P. Herriot (1994), 'Cutting through the career jungle', *Professional Manager*, **January**, 18–19.

Perry, E. (1993), *Women in the Middle Years: Assessing Internal Careers and Linkages to Work and Family*, Tulsa, OK: University of Tulsa Press.

Quesenberry, J. (2007), *Career Values and Motivations: A Study of Women in the Information Technology Workforce*, Pennsylvania: Penn State University Press.

Rodrigues, R., D. Guest and A. Budjanovcanin (2013), 'From anchors to orientations: Towards a contemporary theory of career preferences', *Journal of Vocational Behavior*, http://dx.doi.org/10.1016/j.jvb.2013.04.002.

Rudman, L.A. and J.E. Phelan (2008), 'Backlash effects for disconfirming gender stereotypes in organizations', *Research in Organizational Behavior*, **28**, 61–79.

Schein, E.H. (1974), *Career Anchors and Career Paths: A Panel Study of Management School Graduates*, Sloan School of Management, Cambridge, MA: MIT.

Schein, E.H. (1975), 'How career anchors hold executives to their career paths', *Personnel*, **52**, 11–24.

Schein, E.H. (1978), *Career Anchors: Matching Indiviudal and Organizational Needs,* Reading, MA: Addison-Wesley.

Schein, E.H. (1990), *Career Anchors: Discovering Your Real Values*, San Diego, CA: Pfeiffer & Company.

Schein, E.H. (2006), *Career Anchors: Self Assessment*, San Francisco, CA: Pfeiffer.

Singh, R., N.A. Fouad, M.E. Fitzpatrick, J.P. Liu, K.J. Cappaert and C. Figuereido (2013), 'Stemming the tide: Predicting women engineers' intentions to leave', *Journal of Vocational Behaviour*, **83**(3), 281–94.

Smith, P., P. Caputi and N. Crittenden (2012), 'How are women's glass ceiling beliefs related to career success?', *Career Development International*, **17**(5), 458–74.

Stout, J.G., N. Dasgupta, M. Husinger and M.A. McManus (2011), 'STEMing the tide: Using ingroup experts to inoculate women's self-concept in science, technology, engineering, and mathematics (STEM)', *Journal of Personality and Social Psychology*, **100**(2), 255–70.

Sturgess, J. (1999), 'What it means to suceed: Personal conceptions of career success held by male and female managers at different ages', *British Journal of Management*, **10**, 239–52.

Suutari, V. and M. Taka (2004), 'Career anchors of managers with global careers', *Journal of Management Development*, **23**(9), 833–47.

Teo, T., L. Lord and M. Nowak (2013), 'Sustaining successful leadership careers: Top management women in the resources sector of Western Australia', *Fourth Asia-Pacific Business Research Conference,* Singapore.

Tremblay, M., M. Gianecchini and T. Wils (2007), 'Determinants of subjective and objective success among Canadian and French engineers', *XVII Congres Annuel de L'Association Francophone*, Reims, France.

Tremblay, M., T. Wils and C. Proulx (1998), *Determinants of Desired Career Paths among Canadian Engineers*, Cirano Serie Scientifique, Montreal, Canada.

Van Maanen, J.E. and E.H. Schein (1977), 'Toward a theory of organizational socialization', Working paper, Sloan School of Management, 960–77.

Women in Mining Canada (2010), *Ramp Up: A Study on the Status of Women in Canada's Mining and Exploration Sector*, accessed from http://0101.nccdn.net/1_5/1f2/13b/0cb/RAMP-UP-Report.pdf.

5. Family issues for women engineers

Mary Ayre, Julie Mills and Judith Gill

In many English-speaking economies less than 15 per cent of professional engineers are women (NSF, 2012; Kirkup et al., 2010; Kaspura, 2013), and furthermore women are more likely to leave the profession than men (Frehill, 2009; Hunt, 2010; Kirkup et al., 2010; Kaspura, 2013). It has been suggested that difficulties of combining motherhood and the attendant childcare responsibilities with an engineering career contribute to women's attrition from the profession after about ten years (Blackwell and Glover, 2008; Fouad and Singh, 2011; Plett et al., 2011; for example).

This chapter considers the issues that affect work–family decisions of women engineers in Australia and some other Western countries. After examining the evidence that these issues are at least partly responsible for women leaving the profession, we explore ways that women who have stayed in the profession have resolved these issues, focusing particularly on the Australian context. Their solutions may suggest strategies to other women engineers faced with conflict in their work–life integration, and also strategies for implementation and support by managers and employing organisations who wish to improve the retention of women in the engineering profession.

THE AUSTRALIAN STUDIES

In Australia, the progress of women in the engineering profession has been tracked over 13 years by Engineers Australia (EA), the national engineers' professional body, through a series of three surveys of its members. Known informally as CREW1, 2 and 3, after the title of the first survey, The Careers Review of Engineering Women, these studies have been invaluable in identifying and calibrating the different positions of men and women in the Australian profession in many different fields, including work–family integration (Roberts and Ayre, 2002; Mills et al., 2008; Kaspura, 2013), the focus of this chapter.

The present study investigates the career experiences of all the women who graduated from a single engineering program (civil engineering) at a single Australian technical university (ATU) between 1974 (the year the first woman graduated) and 2008. It is a two-part study: an online survey followed by semi-structured interviews with 16 volunteers. All 16 were interviewed and their interviews fully transcribed and analysed using a thematic approach. The results pertaining to work–family integration are compared here with profiles drawn from the CREW studies.

Of ATU's 76 female civil engineering graduates to 2008, we were able to contact 65 using the university's alumni database and personal contacts within the cohort. Fifty-six completed the survey – that is, 86.2 per cent of those contacted and 73.7 per cent of the whole cohort. By comparison, the numbers participating in the (national, multi-disciplinary) CREW studies were 767 in CREW1, 1817 in CREW2, and 932 in CREW3. The ATU response rate was higher than any of the national CREW surveys: 86.2 per cent compared with 42.2 per cent, 36.9 per cent and 19.9 per cent of those contacted for CREW1, 2 and 3, respectively.

The ATU survey questions were based closely on the CREW studies, with only slight modifications needed to accommodate the different circumstances of the ATU population. In all the studies it was found that the distributions of age, and year of graduation, were remarkably similar. The single-discipline, single-institution nature of the ATU study, however, eliminated several of the extraneous variables present in the CREW studies, thus improving the validity of any relationships identified between the variables.

The ATU study had an additional important advantage over the CREW studies. The use of the ATU's alumni database to contact the graduates ensured that the invitation to participate reached those who had left the profession as well as those who had stayed. In the case of the CREW studies, invitations to participate went only to current members of EA. Thus the CREW invitations would have reached very few women who had left engineering since it is unlikely that those who have left the profession maintain their membership of EA. Hence the CREW studies could not be used to provide valid retention rates, and we therefore give an overview of international data on retention of women engineers before comparing ATU's retention data.

RETENTION OF WOMEN ENGINEERS: INTERNATIONAL DATA

A clear indication that an engineering career is more problematic for women than men is that women are more likely to leave the profession. In the UK in 2008, 35 per cent of female graduates in science and engineering were still working in those fields, and 56 per cent of their male counterparts (Kirkup et al., 2010). A study of US engineers in 2009 found that after 18 to 20 years, about 50 per cent of male, but only about one-third of female qualified engineers were still working in engineering (Frehill, 2009). A different US study the following year found more optimistically that only 12.9 per cent of women trained as engineers were doing unrelated work, but this still exceeded the comparable proportion of men (9.8 per cent) (Hunt, 2010). According to Australian 2011 census data, 51.2 per cent of Australian women holding engineering qualifications were employed in engineering at the time compared with 63.6 per cent of men (Kaspura, 2013).

ATU Retention

In the ATU study, 53 of the 56 respondents (94.6 per cent) were still working in engineering, which appears remarkably high compared with the rates given above. Of the three who were not currently working in engineering, one was taking a career break, one was looking for another engineering position and one did not provide a reason. Although 20 of the 76 ATU graduates were uncontactable or did not respond, we know from other respondents that a number of these were still working in engineering, or taking a short career break intending to return to the profession. Thus, even if we assume that all of the 'missing' graduates had left the profession, the ATU retention rate, at 70 per cent, would exceed the others cited above, except Hunt's. With retention rates exceeding both Australian and other national rates, the ATU data suggested that this study could offer new information about what keeps women in the profession. In this chapter we focus on the ATU findings relating to family responsibilities and their impact on the careers of our respondents. Other findings from the ATU study are reported elsewhere (Ayre et al., 2011).

INTEGRATING WORK AND FAMILY

In the early twenty-first century, even in the developed world where there is legal equality between the sexes, the mother nearly always retains the primary responsibility for childcare. This applies in two-parent families in which both parents are in paid work, as well as when the mother is not employed outside the home (Bagilhole et al., 2007; Hewlett et al., 2008; Watts, 2009). Working mothers have to find ways to integrate caring responsibilities with work commitments. The heavily masculinised culture of the engineering workplace has been shown to make this particularly difficult for women engineers. A frequently noted feature of this culture is the strong underlying assumption that childcare responsibilities are the mother's domain, and hence will inevitably affect her commitment to her work.

Planning for Parenthood

There is evidence that family issues start to influence the careers of women engineers while they are still students. Female engineering students are reported as being aware of the possibility, perhaps likelihood, of having their commitment questioned by employers when family responsibilities start to affect their availability outside the normal working day (Womeng, 2006; Hughes, 2011; Fender et al., 2011).

Once in employment, women engineers are even more aware of the possible effects on their careers of having children, and many factor these in when planning for parenthood (Preston, 2004; Womeng, 2006; APESMA, 2010). In Australia for example:

> 50 per cent of respondents said that their career had affected their planning for parenthood. Of those that answered it had, 37.4 per cent responded it affected whether to have any children, 73.7 per cent the timing of children, 43.8 per cent the number of children and 7.5 per cent other (APESMA, 2010, p. 7).

Several of the ATU interviewees mentioned timing their families or needing to change their job when they had children. Anne, for example (all names changed for anonymity), who after 12 years as a construction engineer is now a partner in a small consulting company, commented:

> Construction is an industry that you need to put your family on hold … which is why I'm 36 and have a three-month-old baby. I got married at 32. I did everything late because I spent my twenties working [in construction]. A lot

> of construction companies don't pay maternity leave. You're very lucky if you even get a holiday.

It has been shown that women engineers have fewer children than women in other professions (Blackwell and Glover, 2008; APESMA, 2007, 2010; Fouad and Singh, 2011). This is a clear indicator that there are particular difficulties in this profession for women trying to integrate family responsibilities with their career.

Reduced Fertility

A recent longitudinal study of UK professionals found that over the period 1971–1991 only 40 per cent of women in science, engineering and technology had children, compared with 80 per cent of women in health-related occupations (Blackwell and Glover, 2008). In the US the proportion of women holding bachelor's degrees in any subject who have had children is about 75 per cent (Livingston and Cohn, 2010), while a survey of US female engineers found that 40 per cent had children living at home with them (Fouad and Singh, 2011). Although these two data sets are not directly comparable since the Livingston and Cohn data refer to a lifetime and Fouad and Singh's data were provided by a survey (thus a 'snapshot'), they suggest that, as in Britain, US female engineers are less likely to have children than women in other professions. In Australia a similar picture emerges. Recent surveys by APESMA (The Association of Professional Engineers, Scientists and Managers Australia – the trade union of this group) have found that about 45 per cent of their female members have children (APESMA 2007, 2010), but only 33 per cent of the female engineers, and this is the lowest figure amongst all the science and technology professions that APESMA represents (APESMA, 2007).

An even smaller proportion, only 22 per cent, of the female engineers who responded to the CREW1 and CREW2 surveys were responsible for children (Mills et al., 2008), and although the corresponding figure in CREW3 has risen to 30 per cent (Kaspura, 2013), it still trails the 45 per cent figure for all Australian female scientists (APESMA 2010). However, it is interesting that the ATU group, which had the same age profile as the CREW studies, were more likely to have responsibility for children than their CREW3 counterparts (40 per cent compared with 30 per cent), and also for elderly parents (10.9 per cent and 6.6 per cent respectively).

These low proportions of those with childcare responsibilities are only partially accounted for by the young age profiles of the CREW respondents: 50 per cent of female respondents to CREW1 and CREW2 were aged 20–29, and 43 per cent of CREW3's (Roberts and Ayre, 2002; Mills et al., 2008; Kaspura, 2013). CREW3 findings also echo evidence from the UK and the US that female engineers are delaying having their first child (Blackwell and Glover, 2008; Hewlett et al., 2008). For example, Kaspura (2013) reports that only 5.5 per cent of the CREW3 20–29 age group were responsible for children.

Parents' responsibility for children includes decisions about how they are to be cared for during the working day. Working parents need to arrange childcare of some kind, and this can be difficult if childcare providers' hours do not match the parents' working hours, and particularly so where there is an expectation that working hours should frequently extend beyond normal business hours.

Long Hours

Engineering has a reputation for a long hours culture, and anyone unwilling to conform with this expectation struggles to maintain respect and professional credibility (Bagilhole et al., 2007; Hewlett et al., 2008; Sappleton and Takruri-Rizk, 2008; Watts, 2009; APESMA, 2010). In an ATU interview, Frances, aged 32, a senior engineer as yet without children, mentioned the long hours expectation and its negative implications for engineering mothers, including possibly herself in the future:

> The profession doesn't offer a lot of scope for women if they want to look at having a family. Engineering can be very full on and it can be very demanding. The hours are not set – they're very grey. I mean although we do have set hours for our work, you've got to come in [outside these] if needed. … One day I might have children. I'll have to think about what happens there.

Using the Australian Bureau of Statistics practice of categorising 35 or more hours per week as being full-time work, data from the CREW3 and ATU surveys confirm that substantial numbers of both female and male engineers regularly work longer hours than that. A total of 42 per cent of female respondents to CREW3 and 58.4 per cent of the men worked more than 40 hours per week. Many of these worked 49 hours or more: 10.3 per cent of female and 18.9 per cent of male CREW3 respondents. Interestingly, the ATU survey respondents were even more likely to work 40 hours or more (53 per cent), and about 11 per cent worked more than 50 hours, despite generally being more likely to use their employers' family-friendly policies than the CREW3 group, as is shown below.

Family-Friendly Employment Provision

In addition to being unwilling to work longer hours than the usual working day, many working mothers value flexibility in the timing of their agreed hours. Flexible hours (or 'flexitime') are one way to help manage the restricted opening hours and burgeoning costs of childcare. Other desirable options for both male and female parents, but particularly females, are part-time employment, paid maternity leave, carer's leave, leave without pay, job sharing and work-based childcare. These provisions, often known as 'family-friendly policies', are all available in varying degrees across the developed world in engineering employment as in other fields. Utilisation of these policies, however, by both female and male engineers, is often far less than might be expected (Womeng, 2006; APESMA, 2010; Fouad and Singh, 2011), as discussed below.

The CREW2 and 3 studies found that the availability of family-friendly policies in engineering employment in Australia had increased markedly since 1999, and by 2012 all of the policies listed above, with the exception of job-sharing, were available to 78 per cent or more of women engineers (Kaspura, 2013). Availability of part-time employment for female respondents, for example, increased from 49 per cent to 78 per cent over the period and paid maternity leave from 45 per cent to 86 per cent (Mills et al., 2008; Kaspura, 2013).

Comparison of the ATU study with the CREW studies finds that although ATU availability of family-friendly employment provisions approximately matched CREW availability, take-up in all categories was proportionally higher for the ATU group than for the CREW groups. Figure 5.1 below illustrates these data for flexible work hours, part-time employment, and paid maternity leave.

The higher proportion of ATU women than CREW3 women having responsibility for children (40 per cent and 30 per cent as already mentioned) was almost certainly one reason for greater take-up of family-friendly provisions in the ATU group. This likelihood is strengthened by the finding that the ATU mothers were twice as likely to have responsibility for two or more children than the CREW3 mothers: 32.4 per cent and 16.6 per cent (Kaspura, 2013) respectively. However, as discussed below, women engineers often experience reduced status and other penalties when making use of family-friendly provisions and this is a deterrent to take-up. Such 'penalties' are less likely to occur in the public than in the private sector, and as shown later in the chapter, the ATU group were nearly twice as likely to work in the public sector than the CREW3 respondents. It will be argued that choosing to work in the public sector is a key factor in the ATU group's persistence in the profession.

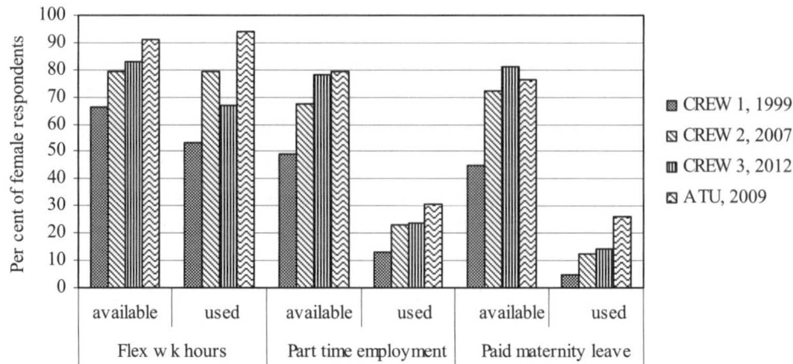

Figure 5.1 Availability (% of female respondents) and use (% of those who have availability) of family-friendly policies, CREW and ATU surveys of Australian female engineers

It is also noticeable in Figure 5.1 that whereas take-up of flexible work hours approximates to availability, take-up of part-time employment and paid maternity leave are considerably less than their availability. Part-time work, now formally available to nearly 80 per cent of Australian female engineers, is used by 31 per cent of those who have availability (Kaspura, 2013). This figure almost exactly matches the proportion of those who have responsibility for the care of children, and thus strongly suggests that this facility is principally used for childcare reasons. Another indicator is that women engineers' take-up of part-time work occurs almost exclusively in the key childcare age groups of 30s, 40s and 50s, peaking at 49.5 per cent in the 40s age group (Kaspura, 2013). In other studies it has been found that the arrival of a second child accentuates work–family conflict for women engineers, triggering a demand for part-time employment eight times greater than from mothers of one child (Sappleton and Takruri-Rizk, 2008).

Penalties for Using Family-Friendly Policies

It is noted, however, across the developed world, that women engineers find it difficult to return to a part-time position after maternity leave at the same level of seniority as they held previously, and consequently either have to revert to technical roles, or decide not to return at all (Womeng, 2006; Bagilhole et al., 2007; Blackwell and Glover, 2008; Frehill, 2009, Marinelli, 2011).

Female respondents to CREW1 and CREW2 also reported being penalised for changing to part-time work or using other family-friendly provisions by not being offered key roles, challenging work and promotions. As remarked by a female CREW2 respondent:

> Management do not reward people working part time regardless of the contribution they make to the organisation. While things are improving, I have had to fight tooth and nail to gain promotions because I am 'only part time' (Mills et al., 2008, p. 19).

Although reasons for low take-up of family-friendly policies were not explored in CREW3, grievances of this nature are echoed in other recent Australian studies such as the APESMA reports (2007, 2010) and in the follow-up interviews to the ATU survey.

Nancy, a senior manager aged 42 with two young children, who returned to her workplace on a part-time basis after maternity leave, described her treatment on return:

> I felt it did count against me, going out of the workforce. I really felt like I took a backward step when I went off to have the kids … There was a change of management. I think that the managers that came in had quite a paternalistic attitude and they still do, like 'we know what's best for you'. They demoted me when I came back part-time from maternity leave. Strictly speaking they're not supposed to do that but I wasn't demoted in terms of salary … I was demoted in terms of position. It was all done as part of a restructure, so I couldn't really complain as there were [apparently] other reasons for it.

An undermining annoyance that may also be felt as a penalty is the attitude of full-time colleagues who seriously or jokingly complain that a consequence of a colleague reducing her hours is that they have more work to do. Taunts of this nature can come from women without children as well as from men (Faulkner, 2009a; Frehill, 2009). Rosie, aged 43, another senior manager with two young children in the ATU group, reported:

> The fact is that you get treated differently, you get criticized and marginalized because you have that flexibility compared to other people, men in particular, who don't have that flexibility, who have chosen not to have that flexibility … just smart comments about leaving early to pick up children and being a part-timer … If a young female was looking at the results of [the ATU survey] she might think well I can have a family and I can work from home and I can have this flexibility, but it comes at a cost.

The sting in 'smart' comments about regularly leaving 'early' when working part-time is aggravated by the long hours expectation in this industry, mentioned above.

Reluctance to use employers' family-friendly policies is not confined to Australia. The same penalising consequences of using these provisions are reported from the UK (Bagilhole et al., 2007); Europe in general (Womeng, 2006); and in the US (Fouad and Singh, 2011). Other penalties too have been identified, arising from entrenched perceptions that women's potential or actual parenting role automatically reduces their commitment to their job. For example, employers have been known to prefer male employees over females in the allocation of training and funding resources (Preston, 2004). Watts (2009) noted that, on announcement of their pregnancies, some of her civil engineering interviewees started being marginalised and denied decision-making roles, and that this process was even more evident after taking maternity leave. Describing the typical engineering workplace as portraying an 'anti-family culture' (Bagilhole et al., 2007, p. 41) seems appropriate in most, if not all, Western countries.

As outlined below, the cultural climate also affects women engineers' professional identity, leading to stalled careers and attrition from the profession.

Identity Issues

Another perspective in the debate about the impact of family responsibilities on women's progression and retention in the engineering profession is the influence of identity: that is how individuals define themselves as a result of their background, experiences, values, hopes and ambitions. Identities influence behaviour when deciding how to act or react in particular circumstances. In different contexts, different facets of an individual's identity may dominate, for example parental identity at home, and professional identity when at work (Capobianco, 2006; Gill et al., 2008; Plett et al., 2011).

Briefly, the characteristics of an engineering professional identity have been defined as being a problem solver, team player and lifelong learner, and taking great pride in the work (Anderson et al., 2010). Typically, owing to usually being markedly outnumbered, a female engineer's professional identity is also influenced by how she sees herself as differently positioned in the profession from men. This perspective is strongly mediated by her interpretation of the attitudes and judgements of others about women engineers, such as her managers, colleagues, and the general public (Faulkner, 2009b; Powell et al., 2009; Meyers et al., 2012).

To be successful in the profession, it has been shown that as well as having the necessary engineering skills and expertise, and taking pride in the work (the attributes of a strong professional identity), engineers must also enjoy respect and recognition from their colleagues: that is, belong in the profession. Since men as the dominant group set the culture in engineering and hence what is valued and respected, it is often difficult for women to achieve belonging status, and even more difficult if a woman is also a mother (Tonso, 2006; Gill et al., 2008; Faulkner, 2009b).

Even with strong professional identity women engineers often need to adopt various strategies to fit in and belong in the profession. One of the most usual is to try to minimise differences from men: being 'invisible as women' (Faulkner, 2009b) or 'becoming a bloke' (Mills et al., 2006). Several of the ATU interviewees mentioned how they had had to 'prove' themselves as engineers, more than their male colleagues had to. Nancy described this process:

> Because you're a woman, they [men] don't think you speak with the same authority and they'll sort of treat you that way: sort of 'oh what would you know?' And you have to prove yourself, you know, you have to be tougher for that reason. ... They're very quick to point the finger. Yeah. I think a man in the same job gets given a lot more latitude.

However, once women become pregnant, or as parents claim family-friendly provisions, it is no longer possible to pass as one of the boys. In marked contrast to male engineers, Faulkner notes, "[women] frequently report that their visibility as mothers reduces further their visibility as engineers where men with children continue to be taken seriously as engineers and are not defined by being parents" (Faulkner, 2009b, p. 178). As well as sharing Nancy's experience of having her authority doubted because of her sex, ATU interviewee Brenda, a senior manager in the public sector, was further challenged on her credibility as an engineer when she was pregnant:

> I came across men who reported to me but had difficulty accepting decisions I had made. I was being tested frequently on my knowledge and also at times was inappropriately spoken to. When I later became pregnant, some of the older men questioned whether I should be allowed to work on construction sites.

A woman finding herself "newly aware of being seriously isolated in hostile macho cultures" (Hewlett et al., 2008, p. 54) has to adopt new coping strategies to continue to feel she belongs. Weakened feelings of belonging can lead to jostling of identities, in some cases resulting in another component of an individual's identity becoming more dominant, causing "many women [to] revisit their priorities and recalibrate their lives" (Hewlett et al., 2008, p. 55), with the possible result that they leave their profession altogether (Plett et al., 2011).

Evidence that Work–Family Issues May Contribute to Women's Attrition

It has been shown earlier that women engineers in the US, the UK and Australia leave the profession at a faster rate than their male counterparts. The discussion above suggests that at least part of this female attrition is caused by a combination of the practical difficulties of combining childcare with an engineering career, and the culture of the engineering workplace, which tends to sideline and marginalise women engineers with parenting responsibilities.

Many international researchers confirm that increased family responsibilities are a contributory factor to female attrition from the profession (Frehill, 2009, 2012; Fouad and Singh, 2011; Hunt, 2011). In Australia, census data from 2006 and 2011 show that women engineers' participation in the labour force starts to fall with the first child and continues to drop steadily with each additional child, and faster than in other professions with comparable qualification requirements (Kaspura, 2013) as shown in Figure 5.2 below.

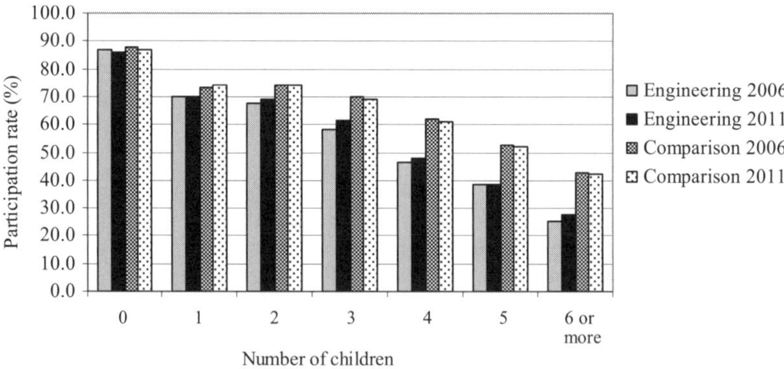

Figure 5.2 Labour force participation of Australian female engineers with 0–6 children compared with females in other professions

The difficulty of obtaining satisfying part-time work has often been cited as one of the reasons for women in their thirties leaving the profession (Greenfield, 2002; Mills et al., 2006; Blackwell and Glover, 2008; Fouad and Singh, 2011). Brenda stressed the importance of this provision:

> It's important that engineering jobs provide flexibility so as to retain female engineers as I've known women [engineers] who've changed their occupation when they had a family due to lack of flexibility by their employer. Fortunately having worked for state governments I have had great support and have taken maternity leave to have my three children and have moved between full- and part-time work.

From her perspective as a manager in a small consulting company, Frances was very aware of the possible consequence of losing good women engineers unless part-time work was available. Discussing the availability of part-time work in her company, she blamed the masculine engineering culture for the resistance to making this provision:

> Because [engineering] has always been male dominated it hasn't had that flexibility – it hasn't had to – and I guess they [many women] give up once they have children ... I think the industry is having to change because of the shortage of good engineers. So you either have nobody or you have somebody that's less efficient or you have somebody that works half the time that's twice as efficient. I think it's just slowly starting to shift.

Other research has demonstrated that managers who understand and support their employees' work-family commitments benefit by a reduced likelihood of their women engineers leaving (Frehill, 2009; Fouad and Singh, 2011).

STRATEGIES FOR SUCCESS

Following a decade of research on why women are more likely to leave the profession than men, there has recently been considerable interest in the women who stay (Cech et al., 2011; Fouad and Singh, 2011; Hughes, 2011; Plett et al., 2011; Buse et al., 2013). We focus here on how women engineers who have children have confronted, negotiated or avoided the career hazards described above that accompany motherhood in this profession. The ATU study's data are particularly relevant here because of its subjects' high rates of responsibility for children, and staying in the profession.

Public or Private Sector

A striking statistic from the ATU survey was that 43.6 per cent of respondents worked in the public sector, compared with 24.5 per cent of the female respondents to CREW3 (Kaspura, 2013), despite public sector engineers' salaries being in general lower than those in the private sector (Kaspura, 2012). In Australia, the 'public sector' includes both government departments and public sector corporations (the latter being a former government enterprise, now partially privatised. Australian public sector corporations include utilities, transport authorities and universities).

The Australian public sector is credited with generous employment conditions compared with many private sector companies, especially the smaller ones (KPMG, 2009). Since the Australian government is also very supportive of working mothers, its employment conditions include good family-friendly policies (KPMG, 2009). The data obtained from the ATU survey shown in Figure 5.3 below appear to support the view that there is indeed more availability of family-friendly provisions in the public than in the private sector.

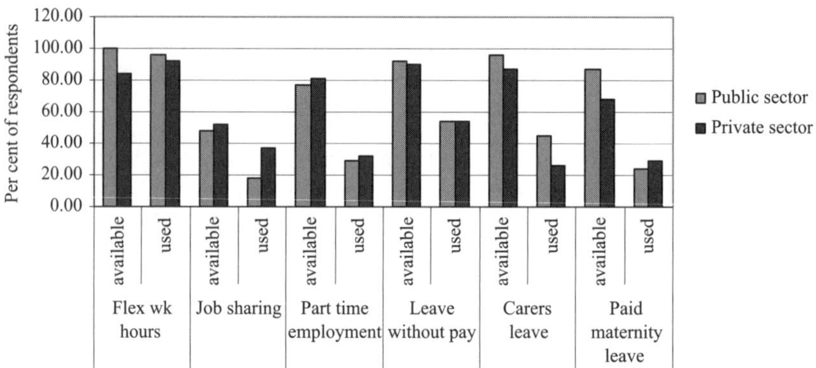

Figure 5.3 Availability of family-friendly policies (% of respondents) and use (% of those with availability): ATU survey respondents employed in public and private sectors

Although the data do not show that all these facilities are actually used more in the public than private sector, consideration of the popularity of the public sector with the ATU group suggests that the greater availability of the family-friendly policies may be one of the attractions to working in the public sector by women engineers who plan to have a family.

Even more striking than the proportion working in the public sector was that 32.1 per cent of the ATU respondents worked in the transport sector, compared with 4.4 per cent of the female respondents to CREW3, and 3.9 per cent of the males. Part of the explanation is that transport authorities are some of the only public sector engineering organizations remaining after decades of privatisation. There may also be other reasons such as there being more likelihood of nine-to-five work in transport than in the construction or mining sectors, and possibly a perception that transport work contributes to the social good, a feature that it is often claimed women seek in engineering work (Buse, 2009; Plett et al., 2011; for example).

The more generous provision of family-friendly policies is also found in the larger private sector companies. Kaspura (2013) finds that availability of family-friendly policies is related to the size of an employing organisation (public or private), and that, with the exception of flexible work hours and part-time work, the availability of the other four provisions listed in Figure 5.3 increases with the organisation size. Further, he finds that women engineers are less likely than men to be employed in organisations with fewer than 50 employees (10.9 per cent women, 17.2 per cent men), and more likely than men to be employed in organisations with more than 500 employees (68.2 per cent and 62.3 per cent respectively). The same preference for large organisations is found amongst the ATU respondents, where the corresponding figures were 14.6 per cent working in organisations with fewer than 50 employees, and 60 per cent in organisations with more than 500.

When comparing usage in the public and private sectors, no clear picture emerges from either the ATU or the CREW3 data relating use of family-friendly policies to size of employing organisation. This possibly confirms the evidence that a congenial supportive workplace is necessary to encourage use of these facilities. Whatever the policies of an employing organisation, their implementation depends on the attitudes of the local manager who may or may not be positive and supportive towards women employees with parental responsibilities (Frehill, 2009).

The flexibility in employment conditions available in the public sector for all employees and a culture that is more accepting of use of these provisions than is usual in the private sector was mentioned by all of the ATU public sector interviewees. They stated this as being a strong reason they had chosen to work for the government. Those who had not yet had any children, as well as those with established families lauded the security, flexibility, and the regular hours available in the public sector. Helen, an ATU interviewee with two young children, summarised this as follows:

> I think the main reason I chose a government position is the stability that goes with that. Particularly knowing it was going to be at that time of my life when I was going to be having a family. I guess it's the work life balance, the family friendly environment and being able to take maternity leave and being able to go back on a part time basis – the security of it. And also being able to transfer from one position to another within the Department – being able to do a temporary contract knowing that you've got a permanent position to go back to and that sort of thing. The other thing about being with [my government department] is with their flexitime arrangements and so forth; there doesn't seem to be as much pressure to do really long hours. They seem to be a bit more used to the fact that people have families and they can't necessarily do long hours.

Even when these provisions exist, however, for the ATU respondents as for others in the profession as noted earlier, returning to their previous position after maternity leave especially if changing to part-time, was not necessarily automatic. Several said they had to renegotiate their status, responsibilities and conditions, but were clearly confident that they were negotiating from a position of strength (a combination of their rights, and the department's need for their known skills) and this factor had enabled their success.

Many Ways to Share Childcare

Six of the 16 ATU volunteer interviewees were working part-time, five of them because of family responsibilities. All five had two or three children, aged between six months and 13 years. Four of the five worked in the public sector, as had the fifth until she was very recently headhunted by a large multi-national company, and was 'able to take with her', as she put it, the same flexible working conditions she had enjoyed in her government position. The sixth interviewee working part-time was young, in her twenties, and as yet childless. She had negotiated an 80 per cent contract for quality of life reasons, ascribing her employer's willingness to allow this to their seeing 'it as a good thing to have a happy employee who's productive'.

None of the women working part-time for family reasons relied principally on family members to provide childcare, and some of them had devised rather unusual solutions based on equitable sharing of responsibility with their partners. Nancy, whose two children were aged two and a half and five, is an example:

> We both work four days a week and we have a different day off each. That was something that we sort of negotiated before we had kids. I said to him … if we're going have kids we do it, and we share it evenly. And so that's what

> we did and it's worked really well for us. We're both enjoying working four days. We enjoy that day we have off. And the rest of the time they're in family day care.
>
> [*Authors' note: Family day care is an Australian system of childcare where a small number of children are looked after in the home of an approved carer. It resembles a family situation rather than a day care centre, but the carer is not a family member*].

Jennie, a project manager, and her husband each work a 60 per cent contract (three days a week), leaving only one day when both are working and other childcare arrangements have to be made. Despite the even greater reduction in their salaries, like the first couple they are very satisfied with this arrangement while their children are young. They plan to return to full-time work when the children are older, and, as public sector employees are confident that this will be possible.

Anne, the partner in a small consulting company, had two children, aged three, and three months. At certain times, such as when her company is preparing a tender against a deadline, she cannot leave the office whatever emergency arises with the children. The solution she and her husband had devised to allow for these unpredictabilities may appear to some to be even more radical than both parents dropping to fractional salaries described above:

> I have to have a way so that if my children are sick, I can't not come to work. We decided that we need my husband to be at home, so we'll sacrifice my husband's salary now, so that I can focus on the business. He's resigned from his job and is in charge of the two little ones for the time being, so it's a bit of a learning curve for both of us.

The enterprise, confidence, and notably recognition by both parents of joint responsibility for day-to-day childcare, of all these couples in resolving childcare quandaries offer one explanation for the success of these women engineers in their careers. The other is that they have chosen employers with enlightened family-friendly policies.

SUMMARY AND CONCLUSION

The principal family issues which affect the careers of women engineers are the timing and size of family, the long hours culture, the availability and acceptability of using family-friendly employment provisions, and the impact on professional identity of a male-dominated traditional attitude towards childcare responsibilities. These factors directly and indirectly influence a woman's career in many ways ranging from being undervalued and marginalised to feeling she no longer belongs in the profession, causing her to leave and take her talents elsewhere to find professional fulfilment.

The masculine culture that fosters negative attitudes towards colleagues with maternal responsibilities can also affect a woman's own view of her fit in the profession, and hence whether she wishes to continue in it. Individually or cumulatively, sexist attitudes have been identified as powerful influences in the known attrition of women from the profession especially during their thirties and forties, a time when male engineers, including those who are parents, are gaining promotion and consolidating their careers.

A study of female graduates of a single engineering discipline at a single Australian university found a good retention rate compared with data from other English-speaking countries. This study also found that these women were more likely to be caring for children and elders, and more likely to use their employers' family-friendly provisions than other Australian women engineers. They were also more likely to work in the public sector, with a marked concentration in the transport sector.

In interviews with volunteers from this group, those who were parents made it very plain that they had chosen their employer with a view to the availability of flexible work hours, part-time work, paid maternity leave and other family-friendly policies. In nearly every case the selected employer was in the public sector, known to have family-friendly working conditions. These women were demonstrating 'self-confiden[ce] in their abilities to navigate their organization's political landscape and juggle multiple life-roles' (Fouad and Singh, 2011, p. 37), an important factor in staying in the profession.

Some of this group had also devised some unusually equitable patterns of shared childcare with their partners, well in advance of the current cultural pattern in Australia of the male partner working full-time and the female part-time (Broomhill and Sharp, 2007). Although admittedly these options are not available to everybody since they rely on the presence of a supportive domestic partner, they are cited because they emerged from the study being reported as possible ways of resolving some work–life integration issues.

Interviewees working in the private sector who had not yet had children were clearly aware that it may be difficult to continue their career with their present employer when they did start a family, and were quite prepared to move to a more family-friendly employer if necessary when the time came. Notable was their confidence that such a move with no interruption to career was a realisable option. Buse et al. (2013,

p. 144) also noted how persistent women engineers "demonstrated initiative and seized control … in managing conflict with superiors … and effecting formal job changes."

The implications for employers are plain. A workplace culture that does not recognise that family responsibilities are a concern shared by both parents, not just the mother, militates against a woman engineer being able to combine her work and family responsibilities without loss of seniority and prospects. Her employer is in danger of losing a skilled and valuable professional who may look for better conditions elsewhere in the industry or leave engineering altogether. Another danger is that this culture will discourage women from staying with a company, as well as discouraging prospective female employees.

Cultural attitudes are difficult to shift. It has been shown that it is not enough simply to codify policies and procedures: there must also be firm leadership in implementing them at all levels (Frehill, 2009; Fouad and Singh, 2011; Buse et al., 2013). These authors recommend specific training of supervisors in work–life concerns, and 'flexibility goals' (Frehill, 2009, p. 39) to be set and rewarded. It is also important to be alert to unforeseen career penalties for using family-friendly policies, such as reduced status on return from maternity leave. Another recommendation is for a readiness to re-examine a manager's view, for example in a performance review, that a woman using family-friendly policies is less committed to her work than employees without children (Fouad and Singh, 2011).

Based on the evidence from our ATU study, we endorse all these recommendations to improve retention of women engineers. We also suggest that they may be applicable in other professions where there is marked attrition of women, with, or about to assume, parental responsibilities.

REFERENCES

Anderson, K.J.B., S.S. Courter, T. McGlamery, T.M. Nathans-Kelly and C.G. Nicometo (2010), 'Understanding engineering work and identity: A cross-case analysis of engineers within six firms', *Engineering Studies*, **2**(3), 153–74.

APESMA (Association of Professional Engineers Scientists and Managers Australia) (2007), *Women in the Professions: Survey Report*. Melbourne, Australia: APESMA.

APESMA (2010), *Women in the Professions: The State of Play 2009–10*. Melbourne, Australia: APESMA.

Ayre, M., J.E. Mills and J. Gill (2011), *Not All Women Leave: Reflections on a Cohort of 'Stayers' in Civil Engineering*. Paper presented at the 2011 ASEE Annual Conference, 26–29 June, Vancouver, Canada, on CD-ROM.

Bagilhole, B., A. Powell, S. Barnard and A. Dainty (2007), *Researching Cultures in Science, Engineering and Technology: An Analysis of Current and Past Literature*, UK Resource Centre for Women in Science, Engineering and Technology.

Blackwell, L. and J. Glover (2008), 'Women's scientific employment and family formation: A longitudinal perspective', *Gender, Work & Organization*, **15**(6), 579–99.

Broomhill, R. and R. Sharp (2007), 'The problem of social production under neoliberalism: Reconfiguring the male-breadwinner model in Australia', in M. Griffin Cohen and J. Brodie (eds), *Remapping Gender in the New Global Order*, New York: Routledge, pp. 85–108.

Buse, K. (2009), *Why They Stay: The Ideal Selves of Persistent Women Engineers*. Doctor of Management Qualitative Research Paper, Case Western Reserve University, Cleveland, OH.

Buse, K., D. Bilimoria and S. Perelli (2013), 'Why they stay: Women persisting in US engineering careers', *Career Development International*, **18**(2), 139–54.

Capobianco, B. (2006), 'Undergraduate women engineering their professional identities', *Journal of Women and Minorities in Science and Engineering*, **12**(2–3), 95–118.

Cech, E., B. Rubineau, S. Silbey and C. Seron (2011), 'Professional role confidence and gendered persistence in engineering', *American Sociological Review*, **76**(5), 641–66.

Faulkner, W. (2009a), 'Doing gender in engineering workplace cultures. I: Observations from the field', *Engineering Studies*, **1**(1), 3–18.

Faulkner, W. (2009b), 'Doing gender in engineering workplace cultures. II: Gender in/authenticity and the in/visibility paradox', *Engineering Studies*, **1**(3), 169–89.

Fender, J., V. Davidson, J. Vassileva, N. Ghazzali and E. Croft (2011), *Perceptions and Experiences of the Workplace among Canadian Computer Science and Engineering Students: A Gender Analysis*. Paper presented at the 15th International Conference of Women Engineers and Scientists (ICWES 15), Adelaide, Australia, 19–22 July.

Fouad, N.A. and R. Singh (2011), *Stemming the Tide: Why Women Leave Engineering*. Milwaukee, WI: University of Wisconsin.

Frehill, L. (2009), *SWE Retention Study and Work/Life Balance*. Society of Women Engineers, 34–40.

Frehill, L. (2012), 'Gender and career outcomes of US engineers', *International Journal of Gender, Science and Technology*, **4**(2), 148–66.

Gill, J., R. Sharp, J.E. Mills and S. Franzway (2008), 'I still wanna be an engineer! Women, education and the engineering profession', *European Journal of Engineering Education*, **33**(4), 391–402.

Greenfield, S., J. Peters, N. Lane, T. Rees and G. Samuels (2002), *SET Fair: A Report on Women in Science, Engineering and Technology*. London: Department of Trade and Industry.

Hewlett, S.A., C.B. Luce, L.J. Servon, L. Sherbin, P. Shiller, E. Sosnovich and K. Sumberg (2008), *The Athena Factor: Reversing the Brain Drain in Science, Engineering and Technology*. HBR (Harvard Business Review) Report. Harvard: Center for Work-Life Policy.

Hughes, R. (2011), 'Are the predictors of women's persistence in STEM painting the full picture? A series of comparative case studies', *International Journal of Gender, Science and Technology*, **3**(3), 547–70.

Hunt, J. (2010), *Why Do Women Leave Science and Engineering?* Montreal: McGill University.

Kaspura, A. (2012), *The Engineering Profession: A Statistical Overview*. Canberra, Australia: Engineers Australia.

Kaspura, A. (2013), *The Engineers Australia Survey of the Working Environment and Engineering Careers, 2012*. Canberra, Australia: Engineers Australia.

Kirkup, G., A. Zalevski, T. Maruyama and I. Batool (2010), *Women and Men in Science, Engineering and Technology: The UK Statistics Guide 2010*. Bradford, UK: The UKRC.

KPMG (2009), *Understanding the Economic Implications of the Gender Pay Gap in Australia*. Sydney, Australia: Diversity Council Australia.

Livingston, G. and D.V. Cohn (2010), *Childlessness Up Among All Women: Down Among Women with Advanced Degrees*. Washington, DC: Pew Research Center.

Marinelli, M. (2011), *Making the Move or Keeping the Connection? Engineering Women as Managers: An Australian Study*. Proceedings of the 15th International Conference of Women Engineers and Scientists (ICWES). 19–22 July, Adelaide, Australia, on USB.

Meyers, K.L., M.W. Ohland, A.L. Pawley, S.E. Silliman and K.A. Smith (2012), 'Factors relating to engineering identity', *Global Journal of Engineering Education*, **14**(1), 119–31.

Mills, J., W. Bastalich, S. Franzway, J. Gill and R. Sharp (2006), 'Engineering in Australia: An uncomfortable experience for women', *Journal of Women and Minorities in Science and Engineering*, **12**(2–3), 135–54.

Mills, J., V. Mehrtens, E. Smith and V. Adams (2008), *CREW Revisited in 2007: The Year of Women in Engineering: An Update on Women's Progress in the Australian Engineering Workforce*. Canberra, Australia: Engineers Australia.

NSF (National Science Foundation) (2012), *Women, Minorities and Persons with Disabilities in Science and Engineering*. Arlington: National Science Foundation.

Plett, M., C. Hawkinson, J.J. VanAntwerp, D. Wilson and C. Bruxvoort (2011), *Engineering Identity and the Workplace Persistence of Women with Engineering Degrees*. Paper presented at the 2011 ASEE Annual Conference, 26–29 June, Vancouver, Canada.

Powell, A., B. Bagilhole and A. Dainty (2009), 'How women engineers do and undo gender: Consequences for gender equality', *Gender, Work & Organization*, **16**(4), 411–28.

Preston, A.E. (2004), 'Plugging the leaks in the scientific workforce', *Issues in Science and Technology*, **20**(4), 69–74.

Roberts, P. and M. Ayre (2002), *Counting the Losses… The Careers Review of Engineering Women: An Investigation of Women's Retention in the Australian*

Engineering Workforce. Canberra: National Women in Engineering Committee, Engineers Australia.

Sappleton, N. and H. Takruri-Rizk (2008), 'The gender subtext of science, engineering, and technology (SET) organizations: A review and critique', *Women's Studies*, **37**(3), 284–316.

Tonso, K. (2006), 'Student engineers and engineer identity: Campus engineer identities as figured world', *Cultural Studies of Science Education*, **1**(2), 273–307.

Watts, J.H. (2009), 'Allowed into a man's world: Meanings of work–life balance: Perspectives of women civil engineers as "minority" workers in construction', *Gender, Work & Organization*, **16**(1), 37–57.

Womeng Consortium (2006), *Creating Cultures of Success for Women Engineers*. Brussels: European Commission.

6. Onwards and upwards: Insights from women managers and leaders in engineering

Melissa Marinelli and Linley Lord

In Australia, women's participation rates in the engineering profession are comparable to that of the United States and Europe (Engineering UK, 2013) with only 10 percent of degree qualified engineers working in engineering and related professions being women (Kaspura, 2010). The low participation rates are attributed to small numbers of women enrolling into engineering courses and a high attrition rate post-graduation (Mills et al., 2008). This is despite government and industry body initiatives and the implementation of programs by organizations to attract, engage and retain women into the engineering profession. The low participation rates can be seen to contribute to the lack of engineering women in senior roles.

Knowing many successful women in the profession in Australia prompted the authors to ask: "What do we know about engineering women in senior roles?" Observations suggested that despite low participation rates, women in the engineering profession do make it to senior roles, including those considered to be management and leadership roles, and achieve success. A review of the existing research into engineering women revealed that little is known about these women. Previous studies, in Australia and other developed economies, have centered on the attraction, education and retention of women into the profession and the associated barriers, challenges and issues (for example: Miller, 2004; Gill et al., 2008; Hewlett et al., 2008; Watts, 2009).

Moving beyond the engineering profession, research on women in management and leadership, and that specific to making the transition to manager and leader, is focused on factors facilitating and impeding advancement (for example: Marongiu and Ekehammar, 1999; Tharenou, 2001; Goodman et al., 2003), the assessment of organizational policies and practices (Nesbit and Seeger, 2007) and career paths and leadership styles (Cabrera, 2007; Eagly and Carli, 2007). There is limited research on the advancement of women in engineering to senior positions and of engineering women becoming managers and leaders.

These gaps in the collective knowledge about engineering women prompted a research project investigating the experiences of engineering women who had advanced to senior roles, specifically that of manager and leader, within technical organizations. The project aimed to understand this transition to managerial and leadership roles, to uncover the factors impacting career advancement and to reveal how management and leadership is conceptualized, from the perspective of engineering women who occupy these roles. Through its focus on successful transitions and embedded in a philosophy of "what can we learn from the experiences of these women?", the research findings inform a more inclusive view of management and leadership in engineering and guide policy and practice aimed at improving retention and increasing women's representation in senior roles in engineering.

This chapter draws from this research project. We review the existing literature on women engineers and women's advancement to manager/leader roles. The methods of the study and the findings are presented. The findings are twofold. First, we find that our women engineers perceive their manager/leader roles to be multifaceted and varied, encompassing organizing, technical and relational aspects. They associate these roles with the clear purpose of delivering a capability, which they achieve by employing a highly relational approach with a focus on responsibility for and relations with others in the organization.

Second, our data suggests that the foundations for transition to senior roles are built on the combination of three factors: individual attributes, expertise and skill, and interpersonal aspects such as credibility, visibility and validation. From this foundation, the decision to make the move to a managerial or leadership role is impacted by the organization and is frequently facilitated by others, rather than being self-initiated. The chapter concludes with a discussion of these key findings in relation to existing knowledge.

WOMEN IN THE ENGINEERING PROFESSION

The minority status of women in the engineering profession in Australia is well documented. In 2011, 10.9 percent of formally qualified engineers in the labor force were female, an increase from 9.8 percent in 2006 (Kaspura, 2010, 2012). Engineering has the lowest proportion of female enrolments in any field of education in Australia, hovering between 15.5

percent and 16 percent for the period of 2001 to 2008 (Lewis et al., 2007). A recent summary of women's participation trends in engineering education and workforce in Australia is presented by Marinelli and Calais (2011). Key observations include significant gender differences in the uptake of full- and part-time engineering employment, an evident gender pay gap, and gender segregation of the engineering labor force across industries and roles.

The Association of Professional Engineers, Scientists and Managers Australia (APESMA) survey, revealed that the attrition rate of women engineers is almost 40 percent greater than men engineers of equivalent experience (APESMA 2007) and peaking at seven and ten years post-graduation (Mills et al., 2008). Similar patterns have been observed in the United States where women are twice as likely as men to leave engineering and science careers and also have higher exit rates than women in other professions (Hewlett et al., 2008).

Research on women in engineering in Australia has examined girls' participation and success in school level engineering enabling subjects, their knowledge of engineering study pathways and understanding of the engineering occupation (Gill et al., 2005; Gill et al., 2008). Mills et al (2006) explore women's educational and workplace experiences, revealing that while women obtain a sense of satisfaction from engineering work, they have an awareness of their minority position, experience feelings of unpreparedness for the engineering work environment and require the development of coping skills to get by.

The cultures of engineering and the engineer and the implications of these for women engineers and gender balance in engineering are further explored by Bastalich et al. (2007). The "Career Review of Engineering Women" study commissioned by Engineers Australia (Roberts and Ayre, 2002; Mills et al., 2008) shows while smaller proportions of male and female engineers reported their workplaces in a negative light, demeaning and inappropriate behavior is prevalent with over one in four women engineers indicating that they had experienced sexual harassment, discrimination and bullying in the workplace. Australian researchers have also sought to create new understandings of engineering workplace culture. To do so, they have drawn on the concept of "sexual politics" to explain the reason for the "engineering's resistance to gender diversity and equity" (Franzway et al., 2009, p. 93).

An emerging body of research from Australia and the United States explores the persistence and advancement of women in the engineering profession (Ayre et al., 2011; Fouad et al., 2011; Buse et al., 2013). Moving away from the barriers and issues standpoint, these studies offer an alternative and complementary perspective. A further area of interest is the advancement of women in the engineering profession and the experiences of women engineers in senior roles. This remains a relatively under-researched area.

WOMEN'S ADVANCEMENT TO MANAGERIAL AND LEADERSHIP ROLES

Management and leadership are distinct fields of scholarship. Mintzberg (2009) questioned: "We can separate leading and managing conceptually. But can we separate them in practice?" (p. 8). Buchen (2005) describes the hybrid role of manager–leader and questions the comparison and opposition of the roles in the context of role competencies. In this chapter, the focus is on the transition from technical engineering roles to broader senior roles and as such the terms of manager and leader are used interchangeably and in combination. Both are considered positions of influence for women.

Various metaphors have been used to describe the limited advancement of women in to positions of influence. The concrete wall and the glass ceiling are associated with impenetrable barriers suggesting the progress is rarely made beyond a certain point (Eagly and Carli, 2007). Eagly and Carli (2007), in recognition that more women were reaching senior roles, coined the "labyrinth of leadership". The labyrinth describes a convoluted, challenging but achievable journey of advancement to senior organizational roles.

Research on women in management identifies a number of factors influencing the entry and progress into management. Managerial advancement models based on the interaction of these facilitating and impeding factors have been proposed (Tharenou et al., 1994; Marongiu and Ekehammar, 1999; Marongiu-Ivarsson and Ekehammar, 2000).

Internal factors such as instrumentality, adaptive coping strategies (Marongiu-Ivarsson and Ekehammar, 2000), self-promotion and entrepreneurism (Eagly and Carli, 2007) are positively linked to managerial aspiration and advancement. These traits are viewed as masculine and highlight the mismatch between the current leadership stereotypes and feminine traits. Emerging managerial strategies and leadership theories are centered on interpersonal qualities such as cooperation and collaboration that are commonly attributed to women (Kellerman and Rhode, 2007). Women may have a more transformational approach and a relational practice (Eagly and Johannesen-Schmidt, 2001; Fletcher, 2001). Awareness of the benefits of these behaviors is growing.

External, organizational factors with a positive influence on women's advancement include women's representation at all levels in the workplace, including managerial positions and opportunities for skill development (Malach-Pines and Kaspi-Baruch, 2008). Nesbit and Seeger (2007) found little improvement in managerial representation by women in Australian firms despite the use of a wide range of initiatives, including flexible work arrangements, mentoring and diversity training, designed to increase representation. External factors including workplace structures, social policies, and gender roles create differing work and domestic conditions for men and women (Kellerman and Rhode, 2007).

Gender bias in promotion processes and gender-linage of occupations have been observed in the workplace (Tharenou et al., 1994). Gender stereotypes affect the perception and acceptance of women as managers and leaders, as the attributes associated with leadership and management are typically masculine (Marongiu and Ekehammar, 1999; Eagly and Johannesen-Schmidt, 2001). When women's representation is at a token level (Kanter, 1977), the effect of gender stereotypes is particularly strong.

THE STUDY AND ITS METHODS

In late 2009, semi-structured in-depth interviews were conducted with 22 degree qualified women engineers who at the time of interview self-identified as working in a managerial or leadership capacity within technical organizations in Australia. That is, that they were in roles related to their engineering expertise and experience.

Using criterion sampling (Creswell, 2007), participants were recruited from the membership of Engineers Australia – the professional body for engineers in Australia – in four Australian states. This approach was complemented by the author's professional network and snowball sampling with additional participants referred by existing study participants. Women meeting the criteria listed below were interviewed:

- degree qualified engineers;
- female;
- currently working in Australia for a company employing over 100 people;
- currently working as a manager and leader in their organization;
- had worked in this capacity for a minimum of 12 months.

For the purpose of the study, a manager/leader is a person in an organizational role that includes one or more of the leadership, management or business responsibilities detailed in the Engineering Australia Engineering Executive (EngExec) competency guidelines (Engineers Australia, 2006). These include, for example, demonstrating strategic direction and entrepreneurship, managing change and improvement or developing supplier and customer relationships. Participants were restricted to those working for companies employing over 100 people and thus required to have a workplace program and comply with reporting requirements detailed under the then titled Equal Opportunity for Women in the Workplace Act 1999. Organizations of this size can be expected to have a range of managerial positions in line with the EngExec guidelines.

The women were employed in a range of industries and organizations, including the infrastructure, building and construction, resources, defense and transport industries. Types of organization included engineering and technical service companies, government organizations, owner companies and engineering consultancies. The types of managerial and leadership role that the women occupied were also varied. The group encompasses relatively new managers to experienced senior executives.

Interviews focused on the participant's experience in managerial roles. Of particular interest was the journey to their first management role and their definition of their transition from a technical role to that of a management/leadership role. The findings presented in this chapter stem from a phenomenological interpretation of data elicited in the interviews described above (Moustakas, 1994). From the individual experiences of the women that were interviewed, we explore the initial phases of their transition to managerial and leadership capacity. Excerpts from the participants' interview transcripts are included to illustrate the findings.

INSIGHTS FROM WOMEN MANAGERS AND LEADERS IN ENGINEERING

We begin by exploring the concept of a manager and leader in engineering from the perspective of these women: what is a manager in engineering and what do they do? Then, with an understanding of the roles that these women have chosen to pursue, we examine the elements that created a foundation for their transition and the factors that were important to and enabled them to make the move to a new managerial role.

A Manager and Leader in the Engineering Profession

When asked about the role which they associated with first becoming a manager and leader, the women named a range of positions. These included:

- associate
- team leader/specialty manager/discipline leader
- project manager
- engineering officer
- lead engineer
- design manager
- specialist
- construction manager
- business transformation manager.

The majority of the women were offered a position in their existing function or area of expertise. The most common transition was from project engineer to project manager or from discipline engineer to team leader, taking on responsibility for projects or programs, or for a team of engineers or other technical professionals.

What does a manager do?

The women clearly expressed the purpose of their managerial or leadership role. From their perspective, being a manager and leader meant delivering projects and capabilities – for example: the construction of infrastructure such as roads or hospitals, managing the operation and maintenance of existing assets, providing services of a technical nature through engineering consultancy, or implementing programs of change through an organization. As one participant noted:

> Ultimately, I'm here to deliver a capability (E11).

To achieve these purposes, the manager/leader in engineering performs a wide variety of tasks requiring a range of skills. Word used to describe their roles included multifaceted, varied and "a bit scattered". One participant, now occupying a senior role in the defense force, explained colorfully:

> It's just about every bloody thing under the sun (E13).

Several of the women expressed a need to and the challenge of balancing the many aspects of the role. The main tasks performed by the women in their initial managerial roles can be broadly grouped as (i) Relational: relating to managing other people and leading a team; (ii) Organizing: associated with resource allocation, budgets and schedules; and (iii) Technical: relating to undertaking technical work, or providing technical expertise to achieve required outcomes. Table 6.1 presents the key tasks performed by the women in their initial management roles:

Table 6.1 Key tasks of the initial management role

Relational	• Managing others • Training and developing others • Building and leading a cohesive team • Communication, collaboration and liaison • Managing change • Bringing in work • Providing authority
Organizing	• Managing resources • Managing projects or programs • Fixing and restructuring • Managing change
Technical	• Technical expert • Bringing in work • Doing the work

When describing their work as managers and leaders, the overriding focus was their responsibility for and relation to other people within the organization. For all women, becoming a manager and leader required managing others. Through their teams and as part of those teams, the delivery of services or projects was achieved. As one interviewee noted:

> Managing people is so underrated, but such a very important part (E14).

Caring language was commonly used to describe the manager–subordinate relationship. Managing others was described as "looking after a team" or "keeping staff happy". This focus on the well-being and development of staff was a mechanism for building and leading a cohesive team because:

> It was important that we knew where we were going and who was working on what job and who to go to with what and that they felt part of the team … yeah, it was about bringing everybody together (E22).

Other relational tasks included communication based activities such as advocacy, liaison and communication internally and with external and industry stakeholders, and business development. Building relationships was seen as a key activity:

> I really enjoy getting in and understanding what the client's needs are and then relaying them to the team. I enjoy the client liaison more than anything, actually being out there on the front line (E21).

Organising tasks such as scoping, bidding for and managing projects, resource allocation and financial management of projects were prominent in the descriptions of managerial work.

> We've got about 55 engineers who do [X] in Australia and so we also share work between the other offices. I guess I coordinate that as well (E16).

> Looking after an $80 million budget, how much do we put into [area 1], how much do you put into [area 2]? Trying to weigh up how you divvy up the dollars and what strategies you have in place for the asset that you've got (E18).

Despite having moved into roles that were labeled as manager, several of the women also performed technical work in addition to their managerial tasks. As one participant explained:

> I do have some technical roles as well – I have to run projects, interface with clients, set other peoples tasks, review and check the work (E1).

This was particularly prevalent in managerial and leadership roles within engineering consultancies in which team leaders and lead engineers performed technical reviews provided expert advice and "chipped in and did the work" when deadlines were pressing.

Foundations of Transition

Analysis of the experiences of women engineers revealed a range of elements that provided a foundation for their transition and influenced the initial move to a managerial role. These can be broadly grouped as: (i) individual attributes and motivations, (ii) expertise and skills, and (iii) interpersonal factors (Figure 6.1). While the interplay between these three elements can vary, it appears that it is their combination that lays the foundation.

Individual attributes and preferences

The women displayed personal qualities and personality characteristics of being hard working, ambitious, internally motivated, driven by acknowledgement and were tenacious. They expressed a desire for autonomy and authority, particularly with regards to decision making. As one explained:

> The power! I'm interested in power! (E2)

Remarkably, these individual attributes did not necessarily correspond to a desire to seek out a managerial role. While all women interviewed had self-identified as managers and leaders in their profession, two distinct *preferences* were identified – those that wanted to advance their careers by taking on managerial and leadership roles and those more reluctant to do so.

A larger proportion of the women interviewed wanted to advance their careers by taking on managerial and leadership roles. Those that sought out opportunities, described themselves as having an interest in broader roles and saw value in non-technical skills, even early in their careers:

> I think I was just curious and I didn't ever see myself as purely technical, no. I always thought that my skills were broader and I could bring more to the profession than just technical skill. And I was interested in more than that (E7).

Moving to management was driven by a sense of dissatisfaction, boredom and under-utilization resulting from remaining in a technical role. They anticipated that taking on a broader role would meet needs to use other skills.

> I just felt so underutilized, well only, using a very small part of my skill set as a design engineer (E21).

Another motivation for taking a broader role was the perceived beneficial impact on career. One team leader described the opportunity to advance as "a good opportunity to get experience, too good an opportunity to miss". Another woman working as a project manager, explained:

> It's a big project and it's better for my career and it's more of a responsibility (E20).

A smaller group of women had a stronger focus on technical expertise and specialism. They enjoyed this aspect of engineering work and directed the same qualities of ambition and internal motivation towards technical expertise rather than seeking out roles with broader and increasing responsibility. Advancing to a management role was an inevitable consequence of possessing high levels of technical knowledge.

> You can't, even in the technical side, avoid some managerial experience (E4).

Expertise and skills

Gaining experience and acquiring proficiency was key to becoming ready to transition to a managerial role. Skills were acquired through a variety of means both internal and external to the workplace:

- Within the workplace:
  - completing a graduate program;
  - following a structured path of progression;
  - moving companies to experience a different type of business – as a consultant, a client or a contractor;
  - focusing on one technical area and becoming an expert;
  - broadening experience in policy, planning or advocacy roles;
  - site or field work.
- Outside of the workplace:
  - self-study
  - parenting
  - volunteer work
  - university teaching/lecturing.

In terms of the expertise that formed the foundation for management, some women were broad in their definition. Concepts of being a good engineer and "doing a good job as an engineer" were raised, but not elaborated upon.

> I can't be a good manager and leader without being a good engineer. I cannot not be both (E11).

Technical knowledge

Technical competence was seen as an essential foundation for becoming a manager in engineering related industries, with a perceived need for a solid grounding and broad technical experience. A manager with 20 years of work experience in the mining industry explained:

> You have to understand what it is that you are managing if you want to be a manger, so you need a good technical grounding and a breadth of experience in the field I think (E3).

Good performance at the technical or tactical level was noted as the basis for promotion:

> If you have performed well at the tactical level, and you desire to be part of that next phase, you apply, you get assessed, you get nominated, off you go (E13).

Technical competence was also discussed in relation to the promotion of others to more senior roles. A participant from the oil and gas industry matched technical grounding with the external perception of competence:

> When we are promoting people it ([technical grounding] definitely helps them because this is an issue of competence. So it depends on the person, but engineers do tend to be technical people and they do size people up on their technical competence (E8).

Site experience

The women also spoke frequently of practical and field experiences as a foundational element. Many of the women had spent time, even a number of years working in the field – on construction and building sites, at sea, on deployments, or in operating plants.

> I work[ed] with the technicians and at the time they change from old technology to fiber optic, so that was a good experience (E20).

The importance of learning from the experienced supervisors and field workers was emphasized.

> I was a site engineer for a number of large projects. I went in there with "No, I am here to learn. You guys have been working virtually all your life, teach me what you need to." I learnt how to operate graders and loaders and backhoes and dump trucks and all those things that some of the guys thought were beneath them (E15).

Interpersonal aspects

Linked to the accumulation of knowledge and skill, ***interpersonal aspects*** are also key to being ready for transition. Important interpersonal themes are credibility, visibility and validation by others.

The women's experiences indicated that ***credibility*** with peers and with others in the organization is established through solid technical proficiency. One's technical background was important in establishing "street-cred":

> I think that you need to have been able to have some experience to give you … in some area on the ground … to give you a bit of street-cred when you are talking to the people who you are looking after (E5).

> If I don't make it through as a laborer how on earth am I going to stand on site [as a manager] one day? It did me the world of good (E17).

Linked to credibility and reputation, ***visibility***, or being known, noticed or seen by others within the organization was also crucial. Several women stressed the importance of being visible within the company, as others in the organization were often the instigators, facilitators and gate-keepers of advancement opportunities. This was particularly the case in large organizations.

> I think it's important to be quite visible in the company, I think you need to mix with the people who are high, get yourself known to an extent (E16).

A team leader working for a large engineering consultancy explained how her lack of visibility delayed her promotion to associate level and her first managerial role. In her case her superiors related "visibility" to marketing ability, a key skill for bringing new work into the consultancy.

> The thing that they said to me was, you know, I wasn't good at marketing. They felt I wasn't visible enough. And I guess part of that is sort of a woman's thing where we don't promote ourselves well enough (E10).

Finally, ***validation*** is associated with the accumulation of skills and experiences and the building of credibility. Establishing credibility, and having this validated through the respect of others, offers a measure of confidence that appears to be key in being ready to take the leap. Being recognized by the organization appears to be particularly important:

> I'm on the [company] future leaders program which means they have identified people that they think are going to evolve through to these positions, so that's an indication that I think I'm seen as having the potential to lead (E6).

Making the Move: Opportunities, Triggers and Catalysts

Having gained solid and varied experience, established credibility, visibility and obtained validation from others, the engineering women revealed a range of opportunities and factors that influenced their decision to move beyond the engineering role. Figure 6.1 illustrates these factors as stemming from the organization, from others within the organization, or from the women themselves.

The organization

The *organizational culture* has a strong influence on the move to the managerial role. For one woman, her early move into a management position was "the way things are done around here" and was driven by the expectation that degree qualified, rather than experienced people, occupied such positions.

> Yeah, it was very early. Company A were good like that. Company A were very much a sink or swim company … as a result they put you in these positions very quickly (E4).

For women working in large organizations with highly structured career management and promotion paths, the move to a managerial role was linked to promotion to a certain role. A team leader working in a large technical consulting firm explained the *organizational process*.

> I got made Associate, I then got the [Name] section. Basically, once you are promoted to Associate, you are then responsible normally for a group of people (E10).

An *organizational change* event sometimes created an opportunity to step beyond the technical. Events such as a company restructure, de-amalgamation or growth created vacancies or additional positions and acted as a catalyst for some women to step forward or speak up.

> A new CEO came in. He did a talent pool mapping to identify the talent within the organization, the people that they would want to promote or retain. One of the opportunities I had was to speak to the consultant that was doing this and voice aspirations and they got communicated back (E14).

> When the [organizational] split came up there were obviously a number of jobs that came available and I applied for one of the manager positions … (E2).

Facilitated by others

The opportunity to advance was frequently facilitated by other individuals within the organization. Many women were offered a position or asked to step up into a role in their existing function or area of expertise, for example: lead engineer in their engineering discipline, or manager of the function within which they were working. For some it appeared to be a fairly natural next step:

> The Manager decided to go overseas for a couple of years, just for the experience of it, and so I suppose at the end of the day both he and our National Manager recommended that I just take over his post (E16).

Another applied for a role corresponding to their existing position at a new company and were instead offered a higher managerial role by that company:

> I sent an email to the HR Manager out of the blue asking if I could come and work there. I just wanted to be able to practice what I had been doing, just as I had always done as a specialist but when they interviewed me they thought that I could set up a team. It was 'okay, well, why not?'. I had no idea what it meant (E19).

A common mode was that of the "temporary position" where a position was created by the illness of a manager, an overseas move or retirement. Several women were asked to fill the manager's position temporarily, while recruitment processes endeavored to permanently fill it.

> My boss was going on leave for a month and they needed somebody to take over the project whilst he was away, do all of the interfacing, so I took over that. I thoroughly enjoyed it (E21).

The temporary position provided a taste of the managerial role. Frequently, the women in these temporary roles decided to apply for the permanent position, feeling that they were "doing the job anyway".

> It got to where that position was going to be called and I thought 'I've been doing it for so long and it's working' and with any new job the first three to six months is where you do all your hard work. I thought 'I've done all the hard work, I may as well just apply for the position' so I did and I won that position (E18).

It's up to me

A striking observation was that it was not common for participants to seek out a role themselves. There was a sense of aspiring to more senior roles but it was rare for the women in the group to actively search for and apply for their initial management role. There were a few notable exceptions, in which women felt compelled to step up to take a role. One team leader explained how her manager's role became vacant and a meeting was called to discuss candidates for replacement:

> I asked to take on this role because I didn't like the alternatives. It wasn't really the role that was appealing, it was not wanting to work for some of the other people (E1).

Another team leader described how the team of 17 engineers that she was part of was without a leader, and that this was causing issues for the group, particularly for graduate level engineers who were in need of technical guidance and assistance. She explained:

> They kept saying 'Oh no, we don't have anyone to fill that position.' And in the end I said, 'Well, I'll do it if no one else is doing it' (E22).

The transition process to a managerial role is more influenced by organizational or structural factors. This is in contrast to the foundations laid for the transition described in the previous section, which are for the most part personal and internal.

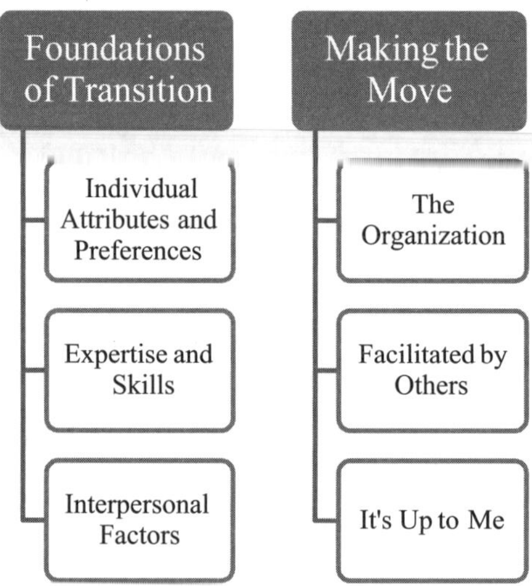

Figure 6.1 *Influences in the initial phases of transition from technical to managerial/leadership roles*

DISCUSSION

Work role transition and job mobility, encompassing a change in employment status and job context, are conceptualized by Nicholson (1984). Ng et al. (2007) propose that job mobility is influenced by a combination of structural, individual and decisional factors, indicating that changes in career are determined by multiple interplaying factors and that difference across industries and occupations can be expected. More recently Forrier et al. (2009) have developed a conceptual framework of career mobility. Like Ng et al., the career mobility framework aims to more fully cover the complex influences in careers by including agentic and structural influences, and the interplay between agency and structure.

The findings presented in this chapter expand our knowledge of a particular work role transition experienced by women in engineering careers. Our aim was to investigate the experiences of engineering women who had advanced to manager/leader roles within their organizations. Our focus was primarily on the transition into their first managerial/leadership role and the initial stages of that transition.

The Manager/Leader Role in Engineering

The roles occupied by the women interviewed for our study were described as having relational, organizing and technical aspects. All aspects are important but there was a particular emphasis on the relational aspects of the role, including responsibility for others, relationships with others and communication.

Relational practice in the context of women engineer's work behavior has been the focus of work by Joyce Fletcher. In an American study of female design engineers, Fletcher (2001) investigates the engineering workplace using a gendered lens. She reveals a way of working termed relational practice that is "rooted in a stereotypically feminine value system" (p. 4) which she explains is in direct contrast to the dominant definitions of success and competence in organizations. This dissonance results in relational work behaviors being devalued and ultimately disappeared. However, Fletcher identified that relational working is intentional and strategic, i.e. "the belief that this way of working was a more effective way of achieving goals and getting the job done" (p. 84).

Recent work by Mintzberg (2009) reflects relational aspects of the manager/leader role. In his model of managing, the manager exists in the centre of his/her business. Relational work is indicated through the acts of "leading", "linking", "communicating" and "controlling" their team, the rest of the organization and the outside world. In line with Fletcher's observations, action is achieved through other people as a result of this relational work. In contrast, Mintzberg does not describe the disappearing of such behaviors; instead they are presented as integral and essential aspects of the manager/leader role. This aligns with the relational theory of working developed by Blustein (2011), which conceptualizes work life existing amidst a relational matrix that impacts work-based experiences, behaviors and decisions.

This emphasis on relational aspects of the manager/leader role may be considered surprising in the context of the engineering profession where the image of "real work" is related to hands-on work, problem solving and technical talk (McIlwee and Robinson, 1992). Fletcher highlights that "supervisors were seen, not only by others but even in their own view of themselves, as no longer doing real work" (p. 90). In contrast, Trevelyan's (2007) ethnographic study of the practice of engineering in Australia revealed that a large proportion of work performed by engineers from the early stages of their career is coordinating work – a highly relational and an informal process.

Our findings support aspects of these previous works. The motivation to deliver capability through and from within their teams is reflected in the women's descriptions of their roles. The design of this study did not allow us to ascertain whether the women in our study "disappeared" their relational work during the performance of their manager/leader roles, but it is clear that their perception of their role is highly relational.

Given the prevailing narrative on "real" engineering work, the inclusion of technical aspects in the manager/leader role is not surprising. A continued connection to technical expertise may be a means of identification with the dominant professional culture and a means of continuing to fit in (Faulkner 2007). Trevelyan (2007) highlights the critical role of technical expertise in engineering coordination – it "convers informal authority" (p. 196) and facilitates the coordination of others (technical people) and their work.

Individual Attitudes and Preferences

Turning our focus to the transition into these roles, the influence of individual, interpersonal and structural elements, and the interplay between them is highlighted. This aligns, in part, with recent works in the field of job and career mobility (Ng et al., 2007; Forrier et al., 2009).

Individual attributes were important to the manager/leader transition. These included instrumental personality qualities such as ambition, internal motivation and being driven by acknowledgement. Previous research indicates that an instrumental personality profile is indicative of managerial advancement (Marongiu-Ivarsson and Ekehammar, 2000). Masculinity was found to have a strong influence on managerial advancement at initial and middle managerial transitions in the contexts of the Australian Public Service and Australian banking sector (Tharenou, 2001; Metz, 2004).

There was a strong focus on skill and knowledge building, supporting previous work on the impact of human capital on career advancement (O'Neil et al. (2013) present an updated review), career mobility (Forrier et al., 2009) and the positive influence of training and development on advancement to management (Tharenou, 2001), particularly in middle career and in moves to middle management.

Several participants described their managerial aspirations during our interviews, however not all possessed a desire to seek out a managerial role. Those who did harbor aspirations for the broader manager/leader role rarely voiced their managerial aspirations clearly or put themselves forward for such positions. Marongiu and Ekehammar (1999) note the need for women to emphasize their managerial aspirations more than men. Elsewhere, this is expressed as emphasizing achievements and interests to senior organizational members (Kumra and Vinnicombe, 2008) or self-promotion (Klenke, 2011). Sabattini and Dinolfo (2010) designate being "outspoken about career goals and desired assignments, and asking to be considered for promotion" (p. 6) as one of the unwritten rules of career development and advancement. In our study, general ambition and career aspiration were certainly displayed but there was a sense of letting good engineering work do the talking, rather than active self-promotion.

Interpersonal and Relational Aspects

While interpersonal aspects are incorporated into existing career mobility framework through elements such as social capital, values and norms, and ease of movement (Forrier et al., 2009), the dominance of the interpersonal and relational elements seen in our research is not reflected in the frameworks presented in recent works. We observed interpersonal and relational aspects operating in tandem with the more traditional managerial advancement predictors. Drawing on personality psychology terminology, we can describe women engineers as having an androgynous approach (Bem, 1974), employing both instrumental and relational qualities to facilitate their transition to the manager/leader role.

Aspects of interpersonal support and the impact of social capital on managerial advancement have been explored in previous studies. Evett's (1998) work on engineering women's careers in the United Kingdom identified a preferred strategy of "building a reputation" for managing gender within the organization. The mechanism for building the relationships that are intrinsic to reputation, credibility and visibility is technical expertise. Strong technical expertise – being a good engineer – establishes credibility with peers and others within the organization. This is the currency of the engineering profession conferring "informal authority in working relationships, which can result in a currency to trade for influence" (Trevelyan, 2007, p. 196).

O'Neil et al. (2013) note the recent growth in published research pertaining to the impact of social capital on women's career development. Tharenou (2001) examined the influence of mentor career support, career encouragement and male hierarchy on managerial advancement, revealing that neither career encouragement nor mentor career support predicted advancement to initial and lower management levels. The relative importance of the role of the sponsor, rather than the mentor, in the promotion process has been highlighted by Ibarra, Carter and Silva (2010). Typically, women lack sponsors, and this is given as a reason for women's lower promotion rates. In our study, women highlighted the role of influential others who opened doors, and offered or suggested more senior positions supporting this observation.

CONCLUSIONS

In this chapter, we examined the roles that engineering women occupy as they advance in their careers. The women's stories provide us with a clearer picture of what a manager/leader role entails for women in engineering. We also examined the influences on successful transition to the manager/leader role, specifically the foundations of transition and the opportunities, triggers and catalysts of the change in work role. This enabled us to identify some of the factors that affect career advancement for women in the engineering profession and the process of role transition in this context.

Relational practice appears to play an important role for women within the engineering context in making the transition to senior roles, specifically the manager/leader role. In fact, their ability to work in a relational manner and to leverage relationships established on the basis of technical excellence appears to be of key importance to the advancement of the women in our study.

Remaining connected to technical work also appears to be an important aspect of moving to a managerial/leadership role. The manager/leader role incorporates technical work and continued connection to real engineering work. Previous studies suggest that this is about establishing respect, generating influence and authority.

The significance of both individual and structural factors on the advancement of women engineers is observed. Individual attributes such as instrumentality, managerial aspiration and human capital, and the influence of the organization aligns, in part, with recent thinking in the field of job and career mobility. However, a key difference is the dominance of the interpersonal and relational elements seen in our research that is not reflected in current models.

REFERENCES

APESMA (2007), *Women in the Professions Survey Report 2007.*

Ayre, M., J.E. Mills and J. Gill (2011), 'Not All Women Leave! Reflections on a Cohort of "Stayers" in Civil Engineering', *American Society for Engineering Education 118th Annual Conference & Exposition*, Vancouver, Canada, American Society for Engineering Education.

Bastalich, W., S. Franway, J. Gill, J.E. Mills and R. Sharp (2007), 'Disrupting masculinities', *Australian Feminist Studies*, **22**(54), 385–400.

Bem, S.L. (1974), 'The measurement of psychological androgyny', *Journal of Consulting and Clinical Psychology*, **42**, 155–62.

Blustein, D.L. (2011), 'A relational theory of working', *Journal of Vocational Behavior*, **79**(1), 1–17.

Buchen, I.H. (2005), 'Training future manager-leaders', *Performance Improvement*, **44**(8), 20–22.

Buse, K., D. Bilimoria and S. Perelli (2013), 'Why they stay: Women persisting in US engineering careers', *Career Development International*, **18**(2), 139–54.

Cabrera, E.F. (2007), 'Opting out and opting in: Understanding the complexities of women's career transitions', *Career Development International*, **12**(3), 218–37.

Creswell, J. (2007), *Qualitative Inquiry and Research Design: Choosing among Five Approaches*, Thousand Oaks, CA: SAGE.

Eagly, A.H. and L.L. Carli (2007), 'Women and the labyrinth of leadership', *Harvard Business Review*, **85**(9), 63–71.

Eagly, A.H. and M.C. Johannesen-Schmidt (2001), 'The leadership styles of women and men', *Journal of Social Issues*, **57**(4), 781–97.

Engineering UK (2013), *The State of Engineering*, Engineering UK.

Engineers Australia (2006), 'Engineering Executive: Applicants Handbook', Centre for Engineering Leadership and Management, Canberra, Engineers Australia.

Evetts, J. (1998), 'Managing the technology but not the organisation: Women and career in engineering', *Women in Management Review*, **13**(8), 283–90.

Faulkner, W. (2007), 'Nuts and bolts and people: Gender-troubled engineering identities', *Social Studies of Science*, **37**(3), 331–56.

Fletcher, J.K. (2001), *Disappearing Acts: Gender, Power, and Relational Practice at Work*, Cambridge, MA: MIT Press.

Forrier, A., L. Sels and D. Stynen (2009), 'Career mobility at the intersection between agent and structure: A conceptual model', *Journal of Occupational and Organizational Psychology*, **82**, 739–59.

Fouad, N., M. Fitzpatrick and J.P. Liu (2011), 'Persistence of women in engineering careers: A qualitative study of current and former female engineers', *Journal of Women and Minorities in Science and Engineering*, **17**(1), 69–96.

Franzway, S., R. Sharp, J.E. Mills and J. Gill (2009), 'Engineering ignorance: The problem of gender equity in engineering', *Frontiers: A Journal of Women's Studies*, **30**(1), 89–106.

Gill, J., J.E. Mills, S. Franzway and R. Sharp (2005), 'I wanna be an engineer! A tale of high achieving women, professional power and the ongoing negotiation of workplace identity', *Redress*, **14**(2), 13–22.

Gill, J., R. Sharp, J.E. Mills and S. Franzway (2008), 'I still wanna be an engineer! Women, education and the engineering profession', *European Journal of Engineering Education*, **33**(4), 391–402.

Goodman, J., D.L. Firleds and T.C. Blum (2003), 'Cracks in the glass ceiling: In what kinds of organisations do women make it to the top?', *Group & Organisation Management*, **28**(4), 475–501.

Hewlett, S., C.B. Luce and L.J. Sevron (2008), 'Stopping the exodus of women in science', *Harvard Business Review*, **June**, 22–24.

Ibarra, H., N.M. Carter and C. Silva (2010), 'Why men still get more promotions than women', *Harvard Business Review*, **88**(9), 80–126.

Kanter, R. (1977), *Men and Women of the Corporation*, New York: Basic Books.

Kaspura, A. (2010), *The Engineering Profession A Statistical Overview*, 8th edn, Canberra, Australia.

Kaspura, A. (2012), *The Engineering Profession: A Statistical Overview*, 9th edn, Canberra, Australia.

Kellerman, B. and D. Rhode (2007), *Women and Leadership: The State of Play and Strategies for Change*, San Francisco, CA: Jossey-Bass.

Klenke, K. (2011), *Women in Leadership: Contextual Dynamics and Boundaries*, Bingley, UK: Emerald Group.

Kumra, S. and S. Vinnicombe (2008), 'A study of the promotion to partner process in a professional services firm: How women are disadvantaged', *British Journal of Management*, **19**, S65–S75.

Lewis, S., R. Harris and B. Cox (2007), *Engineering a Better Workplace: A Diversity Guide for the Engineeirng Profession*, Canberra, National Women in Engineering Committee, Engineers Australia and EA Books.

Malach-Pines, A. and O. Kaspi-Baruch (2008), 'The role of culture and gender in the choice of a career in management', *Career Development International*, **13**(4), 306–19.

Marinelli, M. and M. Calais (2011), *Painting the Picture: A Statistical Update on Women in Engineering in Australia*, ICWES 15: The 15th International Conference for Women Engineers and Scientists, Engineers Australia.

Marongiu-Ivarsson, S. and B. Ekehammar (2000), 'Women's entry into management: comparing women managers and non-managers', *Journal of Managerial Psychology*, **16**(4), 301–14.

Marongiu, S. and B. Ekehammar (1999), 'Internal and external influences on women's and men's entry into management', *Journal of Managerial Psychology*, **14**(5), 421–33.

McIlwee, J. and J. Robinson (1992), *Women in Engineering: Gender, Power and Workplace Culture*, Albany, State University of New York Press.

Metz, I. (2004), 'Do personality traits indirectly affect women's advancement?', *Journal of Managerial Psychology*, **19**(7), 695–707.

Miller, G.E. (2004), 'Frontier Masculinity in the Oil Industry: The Experience of Women Engineers', *Gender, Work & Organization* **11**(1), 47–73.

Mills, J., V. Mehrtens, E. Smith and V. Adams (2008), *CREW revisited in 2007 The Year of Women in Engineering – An update on women's progress in the Australian engineering workforce*, Barton, Engineers Australia.

Mills, J., W. Bastalich, S. Franzway, J. Gill and R. Sharp (2006), 'Engineering in Australia: an uncomfortable experience for women', *Journal of Women and Minorities in Science and Engineering,* **12**(2-3), 135–54.

Mintzberg, H. (2009), *Managing*, San Fransisco, Berrett-Koehler Publishers.

Moustakas, C. (1994), *Phenomenological Research Methods*, Thousand Oaks, SAGE.

Nesbit, P.L. and T. Seeger (2007), 'The Nature and Impact of Organisational Activities to Advance Women in Management in Australian Firms', *International Journal of Employment Studies*, 15(1), 1–23.

Ng, T.W.H., K. Sorensen, L.T. Eby and D.C. Feldman (2007), 'Determinants of job mobility: A theoretical integration and extension', *Journal of Occupational and Organizational Psychology*, **80**, 363–86.

Nicholson, N. (1984), 'A Theory of Work Role Transitions', *Administrative Science Quarterly*, **29**(2), 172–91.

O'Neil, D.A., M. Hopkins and D. Bilimoria (2013), 'Patterns and paradoxes in women's careers', in W. Patton (ed.), *Conceptualising Women's Working Lives: Moving the Boundaries of Discourse*, Rotterdam, The Netherlands: Sense Publishers, pp. 63–79.

Roberts, P. and M. Ayre (2002), *Counting the Losses: The Careers Review of Engineering Women: An Investigation of Women's Retention in the Australian Engineering Workforce*, National Women in Engineering Committee, Engineers Australia.

Sabattini, L. and S. Dinolfo (2010), *Unwritten Rules: Why Doing a Good Job Might Not Be Enough*, New York: Catalyst.

Tharenou, P. (2001), 'Going up? Do traits and informal social processes predict advancing in management?', *Academy of Management Journal*, **44**(5), 1005–17.

Tharenou, P., S. Latimer and D. Conroy (1994), 'How do you make it to the top? Examination of influences on women's and men's managerial advancement', *Academy of Management Journal*, **37**(4), 899–931.

Trevelyan, J. (2007), 'Technical coordination in engineering practice', *Journal of Engineering Education*, **96**(3), 191–204.

Watts, J.H. (2009), 'Allowed into a man's world: Meanings of work–life balance: Perspectives of women civil engineers as 'minority' workers in construction', *Gender, Work & Organization*, **16**(1), 37–57.

PART II

Organizational initiatives advancing women in STEM careers

7. Women as power resources: Putting theory into practice

Charlotte Holgersson, Pia Höök and Anna Wahl

The purpose of this chapter is to contribute to our knowledge of working for gender equality in STEM (science, technology, engineering and mathematics) organizations by describing the design and perspective of a specific women only change project involving women engineers in a manufacturing company and in a technical university. The results of the project will be analyzed and discussed in relation to implications for work for change.

Although most individuals in Sweden are positive towards gender equality on a rhetorical level, men and women face different conditions in the labor market. For example, the labor market is gender segregated with women and men mainly working in women and male dominated professions respectively. Men also dominate in higher positions in organizations and there continues to exist a wage gap between men and women (Hagberg et al., 1995; SOU, 1994, p. 3; SOU, 2003, p. 16; Statistics Sweden, 2012). Women engineers do not face the same conditions as men when pursuing a career in industry nor in academia. Among engineering students starting 2011, 28 percent were women, 72 percent were men (Statistics Sweden, 2011). The proportion of women PhDs in engineering, manufacturing and construction was 29 percent in 2006 and the proportion of women professors in engineering and technology was 8.3 percent in 2007. The proportion of women with an engineering background among researchers in industry was 25 percent in 2006 (Husu and Koskinen, 2010) and only six out of 146 engineers in executive teams among large listed technical companies (42 in total) are women (Ahlbom, 2010). Thus, women engineers, both in academia and industry, work in male dominated contexts on all organizational levels.

The purpose of the change project that will be presented and discussed in this chapter was to engage women engineers in a manufacturing company and in a technical university in working for gender equality within their own organization. The design of the change project drew on research in gender and organization. Feminist research has shown that the standard way of thinking and talking about organizations, both in practice and in research, is based on the dominance of men (Ferguson, 1984; Cockburn, 1991; Calàs and Smircich, 1991). Men in general and men in senior posts in particular are typically seen as self-evident representatives of organizations (Holgersson, 2013). Somewhat paradoxically the dominance of men in everyday practice results in a discursive invisibility of men *as men* (Collinson and Hearn, 1994). Women on the other hand tend to be constructed *as women*, i.e. as gendered. Furthermore, women are typically compared with the male norm and constructed as either same or different. Both the sameness and the difference constructions imply different forms of inadequacy on women's part (cf. Wahl, 1992, 1996).

This chapter focuses on attempts to challenge the construction of women as inadequate in organizations when designing and pursuing change projects. The first aim is to present the use of the theoretical concept of *women as power resources* (Wahl, 1998) when designing a change project and the second aim is to analyze the challenges involved in practicing the approach. The design of the project was influenced in several dimensions by gender theories and previous research about gender equality work. The theoretical influence resulted in specific criteria when identifying participants, the forming of the groups, theoretical input combined with reflective exercises and practices around interpretations. Practicing the approach resulted in a number of situations that highlighted organizations as male dominated and the complex prerequisites of gender equality work. These situations evolved around the naming of work for change, group composition, resources, accountability and definitions of change.

In the first section we discuss the methodological implications of women only groups in gender equality work. In the second section we present the theoretical influences in designing the project. Third we discuss the design of the project and relate it to feminist research. In the fourth section we discuss women as a power resource methodology in practice, followed by critical incidents of negotiations highlighting the women as power resources approach in process. Finally the impact of the project and results of design and processes are summarized in concluding comments.

WOMEN ONLY GROUPS IN GENDER EQUALITY WORK

Studies indicate that women are less content with the status quo and therefore more positive towards gender equality. That is not to say that all women support gender equality. Women's attitudes to gender equality can be related to women's awareness and strategies (cf. Sheppard, 1992; Wahl et al., 2005). Increased knowledge of gender relations leads to a comparatively greater will to bring about change (Höök, 2001). Moreover, gender equality work in organizations can affect what is allowed to be said in an organization (Rutherford, 2001). It can create an arena where women's "critical eye" might become a "critical voice" (Wahl, 1994), as well as influencing women's expectations on how to be treated and create lesser acceptance for discriminatory practices (Benschop and Dooreward, 1998).

It is common that gender equality initiatives target women, for instance management training for women or professional networks for women. Management training for women has only existed since the end of the 1960s. Vinnicombe and Colwill (1995) motivate women only trainings with the fact that women face different conditions than men: they seldom have the same support at home, they experience discrimination at work, and they often lack role models. Groups of women have a tendency of addressing topics that would not come up in all-male or mixed groups, such as: power and politics, sexuality, leader style, stress and career development. Usually these groups develop a supporting culture departing from common experience of exclusion (Vinnicombe and Colwill, 1995; Höök, 2001).

Early on, women-only training programs were supposed to compensate for women's deficiencies. They have consequently been criticized for making women's knowledge and experience invisible and for uncritically adapting women to a male norm (Marshall, 1984; Gatenby and Humphries, 1999; Ely and Meyerson, 2000). However, several studies show that women-only trainings serve other purposes as well. Several programs have a feminist consciousness raising purpose: making women aware of gendered power-relations and how they affect them in their roles as leader. Hammond (1986) argues that gender distribution should reflect the purpose of the program. If the main purpose is awareness raising, then women-only groups are preferable. Our own research has shown that there is a larger risk that mixed groups result in homosocial as well as heterosocial patterns of interaction reproducing existing gender arrangements (Höök, 2001; Wahl et al., 2008). The overall purpose of the training is typically reflected in the content, which then also influence how gender and power is constructed among participants. Studies show that a content that addresses gender and power opens up for critical reflection whereas a gender absent content has a tendency of silencing discussions on gender and power, although not as much in women-only groups as in mixed groups (Wahl, 1994; Höök, 2001; Snickare, 2012). De Vries (2010) argues that women-only programs can be designed in such a way that they challenge and change status quo if they are pursued within the frameworks provided by critical feminist theory on leadership, gender and the gendered organization. De Vries advocates a "bifocal approach" that combines a focus on women and their identity work as leaders and a focus on organizational change through the involvement of women and men as change agents. She concludes that even if the bifocal approach is not realized, a sole focus on developing women leaders has merit if it is based on awareness of the gendered nature of organization and leadership.

Nevertheless, studies show that even gender aware training programs for women only at least partly reproduce gender and other power arrangements (for example Gatenby and Humphries, 1999; Höök, 2001; de Vries, 2010). In Gatenby and Humphries' study, the women challenged gender power relations by collective feminist analysis, by practicing feminist leadership and by collective support. However, they also reproduced existing gender and power arrangements by constructing themselves and other women in a traditional manner particularly in relation to responsibilities for home and family (Gatenby and Humphries, 1999). Höök's (2001) analysis of a management-training program for women showed that the program resulted in women making sense of leadership and career from what Höök calls a center position, perceiving themselves as "owners" of the organization and legitimate interpreters of leadership. The center constructions of these women challenged pre-existing ideas on what constituted good leadership and a successful career and thereby constructing leadership and management career in a "new" way. Höök argues, however, that at some level reproduction is given, as the program is part of the very same system that it is trying to change. Still, after reviewing all studies within this area, one can conclude that possibilities for criticizing, challenging and changing existing gender and power arrangements are highest in programs with women only and with a content that explicitly address gender and power.

DESIGN OF THE PROJECT

The design of the project was founded on knowledge stemming from feminist research in general and feminist research on organization, women's collective action and gender equality work in particular.

A point of departure was a constructionist, process oriented view on gender (Acker, 1992; Wahl et al., 2001). According to this view, gender is constructed through human activities – what people do, say and think – that take place within material and discursive frameworks that both facilitate and delimit these activities (Acker, 1992). Thus gender relations are complex, dynamic and potentially unpredictable (Halford et al., 1997). Organizations can be seen as social arenas for organizing social relations such as gender (Hearn and Parkin, 2001) and an organization's gender relations are manifested through its gender structure and its symbolic order (Acker, 1992; Wahl, 1992; Gherardi, 1995; Wahl et al., 2001).

The project was partly inspired by early radical feminist writings on organization, emphasizing women's separatist organizing. For instance, Ferguson (1984) argues that opportunities for change stemmed from women's experience of subordination. Women's experiences from subordination could create an oppositional discourse, a discourse that could uncover and challenge the dominant discourse based on men's interest and privileges. Ferguson is, however, skeptical towards women's opportunities to change organizations from within. There is a risk that an oppositional discourse can become part of a dominant discourse. The solution lies in women's organizing outside existing organizations.

Ferguson's categorical conclusion can be questioned by arguing that an oppositional discourse *can* exist within male dominated organizations, for instance within the framework of gender equality work (Wahl et al., 2001). This, however, depends on the discursive and practical *content* of that work as well as the contextual power relations at play. If gender equality becomes part of the ideology that dominates in organizations, then it can be slotted into the existing gender arrangements instead of challenging it. This is why it is important that groups of women can be found in an organization that make sure that the work is not co-opted (Cockburn, 1991). Resonating with Ferguson, this could be seen as separatist organizing *within* existing organization and this can in turn be linked to Meyerson and Scully's discussion (1995) on tempered radicals, that is, women and men that seek to bring about fundamental change from within an organization.

Another source of inspiration, also addressing construction of gender and possibilities of change, was Eduards' writing on women's collective action (Eduards, 1997, 2002). According to Eduards, *women organizing as women* is pivotal for changing gender relations in societies. The collective actions of women challenge established notions on what women can and cannot do. By articulating demands women also convey an alternative image of themselves. They express both their right to make demands and the right for better conditions. They make themselves subjects, aware, active citizens, and in this way they broaden their political room for maneuver. Eduards does, however, not explicitly address organizational change.

Even though Eduards emphasizes women as a group, she also discusses the risk of doing so (Eduards, 1997). The risk lies in that highlighting women as a group or category can lead to this category being made permanent, even if analysis is made from a gender power perspective. She continues the discussion by asking whether the category women could be defined in such a way as to challenge the hierarchy, or whether all categorization – either political or theoretical – entails conservation of prevailing power relations. The crucial issue is if – and how – women can be constructed in a liberating way.

Promoting Women's Influence in Action

The empirical data originates from a research and development project designed and run by a group of feminist researchers in organization studies, in 2006–2007. Three Swedish organizations took part in the project: a manufacturing company, an energy company and a technical university. All three organizations were big and severely dominated by men at all levels and especially in top positions. The empirical material consists of the field notes taken throughout the process and the written reflections from the participating women. In this chapter, we have chosen to focus on the impact of the project within the manufacturing company and the technical university. The project involved three participating categories: project management, participants and reference group. Project management consisted of two researchers together with a consultant. Apart from managing the project the role of the two researchers were to lecture on feminist research and take active part in the discussions. The role of the consultant, trained in group dynamics, was to manage and interact in processes by creating reflective dialogue. Yet another researcher documented all meetings.

The reference group consisted of one or two senior executives, responsible for gender equality, from each participating organization. The reference group functioned like a board and was a way to secure commitment and support for the project on top level. The researchers met with the reference group twice a year, in addition to keeping them continuously informed via email. The reference group had an important role in selecting ten to 12 participants from their respective organization.

The criteria for selection of participants, defined by project management, were that the women were positive towards work for gender equality, felt comfortable with women-only groups and that they were interested in increasing their influence and commitment within the organization. The group of women was, however, to be mixed in terms of education, position and age. About half of the women were engineers, both managers and specialists within different operations.

The relation to participating organizations' top management was dealt with through the reference group and the conference (see overview in Table 7.1). The top management had approved of the project, and prerequisites for a continuous support were created through the set-up of the reference group with re-occurring meetings.

To achieve a suitable construction of women in the project, the idea of women as power resources was chosen (Wahl, 1992, 1996). Wahl's theoretical discussion departs from empirical studies on women managers, but it is argued here that her theoretical discussion is equally applicable to women in general. According to Wahl, women as a category can constitute a change potential when constructed as unutilized resources of power. That is to say, women can be a resource that *exercises power*, i.e. that can create and influence. An analysis of women as a power resource is in contrast to women as an unutilized or different resource, i.e. as an inadequate resource *to be used by those in power*. It is, however, impossible to predict the outcome of this exercise of power. This also includes a shift from an individual perspective on women and change, when regarded as a complement or inadequate, to a collective approach in that women exercise power in order to change organizations.

Höök (2001) applies the term *centre construction* to further develop the idea of women as power resource. Höök's analysis of a management training program show how this resulted in women participants constructing themselves as a power resource, while men taking part constructed them as a complementary or inadequate resource. Within the program, women constructed leadership and career from a center position, perceiving themselves as "owners" of the organization (cf. Cockburn, 1991) and challenging the discourse of women as inadequate as well as the same–difference divide.

Meetings and Themes

The project lasted for two years. During the first year the researchers met with the three participant groups individually at two different occasions. The first meeting was an opportunity to present the project, get to know each other and to convey basic knowledge on feminism as well as organization from a gender perspective. Between the meetings the participants were asked to do some assignments involving describing the gender segregations and cultural manifestations in their organizations, as well as reflect upon with realistic and utopic change initiatives. They were encouraged to make the assignments collectively, rather than on their own. The assignments were discussed at the following meeting. During the second meeting, the researchers lectured on knowledge on gender structures, discrimination and women's strategies, gendered careers and the gendered nature of competence as well as homo- and heterosocial processes. The consultant constantly "interrupted" the lectures by posing questions to lecturers and participants and created time to discuss and relate to participants' own experiences.

During the second year, a three-day workshop, a conference, two joint meetings (both of them lasted one evening plus one full day) and one full-day individual meeting with each participant group took place. The purpose with the three-day-long workshop was to create a network between the organizations, to convey further knowledge and to start planning and put together specific change initiatives. On the third day of the conference the change initiatives were presented to the reference group, in order for them to give their input and support.

After the three-day workshop, separate meetings with the participant groups followed. At these meetings the change initiatives were followed up, further knowledge on work for change was conveyed and support for the groups was discussed. Later but still during the second year, a conference with the title "Strategic Gender Equality Work: Knowledge, Dialogue and Impact" was arranged by the researchers in dialogue with the participating groups. The purpose was to create an opportunity report to the participating organizations about the project, and to exchange knowledge and experiences.

The participating women were encouraged to invite colleagues and managers from their own organization. The conference included lectures, presentations and panel discussions. Approximately 150 persons attended the conference, of which two-thirds came from one of the companies. Very few participants came from the technical university. After the conference, the researchers met with the participant groups to evaluate the conference and follow up on the change initiatives. On the last occasion, the researchers met with the groups and jointly summarized and evaluated the project.

Table 7.1 Overview of the different meetings in time, their basic theme and assignments

First separate meeting (June 2006)	Presentations of participants and project management and introduction of project Theme: Feminism in research, politics and ideology Assignment for next meeting: Study the organization from gender and power perspective
Second separate meeting (October 2006)	Theme: Gender in organization, discrimination, homosociality and heterosociality Assignment for next meeting: Formulate realistic and utopic change initiatives
Joint three-day workshop (January 2007)	Theme: Numbers, power and change Assignment at workshop: Formulate change initiative for their respective organization Assignment for next meeting: Start implementing change initiatives
Third separate meeting (April 2007)	Theme: Numbers, power and change (continuation) Assignment for next meeting: Follow up on change initiatives and invite colleagues to conference
One-day open conference and one-day joint follow-up meeting (September 2007)	Conference theme: "Strategic Gender Equality Work: Knowledge, Dialogue and Impact" Debrief and evaluation of conference and follow-up on change initiatives Assignment for next meeting: Follow up on change initiatives
Joint closing (December 2007)	Update and follow-up of participants' work situation and change initiatives

THE WOMEN AS A POWER RESOURCE METHODOLOGY IN PRACTICE

After this overview of the project, the main theoretical ideas that influenced the design of the project will be discussed. The theoretical ideas were manifested through the selection of participants, the pedagogy, the content, the expectations of the participants and the anticipated outcome. It inspired to design a project, which included groups of women only, more specifically women who already were gender aware and with some kind of formal power positions. Most of them had been involved in previous training for women, or been involved in other gender equality projects.

The participants were encouraged to network and to collaborate in terms of analyzing their organizations and designing collective change initiatives. In terms of pedagogy and content a feminist awareness raising process through the interplay between gender theory and sharing of own experiences was initiated. The content consisted of presentations of studies and films on different aspects of gender and power in organization. A reflective form of dialogue between researchers and participants, and between participants, was built into the design of the project. Lectures were always followed by reflective exercises in smaller groups and in exercises aiming at relating theory to own experience. The approach implied a constant shifting between knowledge dissemination and reflections. Participants were continuously encouraged to express what had been valuable or provoking during the session. They were also encouraged to continue the dialogue between meetings and to cooperate regarding change initiatives and assignments. Structures to continuously update absent participants were created by the project management and the process consultant.

Critique was seen as something good as it helped articulate room for improvement. The participants were seen as legitimate representatives for their respective organizations with a privilege of interpretation, i.e. power resources. Most importantly, a view on women in general and the participants in particular as power resources was fostered. The idea was to move beyond the patriarchal order of women being subordinate to and defined by the male norm when working for changes related to gender equality. The moving beyond the gender order included regarding women as accountable for interpretations of problems and as situated at the center of defining, initiating and evaluating changes. This meant encouraging the participants to interpret problems, to formulate possible solutions *and* to evaluate the results. These activities were continuously discussed with the participants. The challenge thus consisted in putting the concept of women as power resource into individual and collective practice in various and shifting ways. To live it and embody it in interaction with others, not just talking about it and analytically relate to it as a conceptual construct.

NEGOTIATIONS WHEN PRACTICING THE WOMEN AS POWER RESOURCES APPROACH

This section includes some examples of when the concept of women as a power resource was activated in the meetings and negotiated by the participating women and the researchers. In these situations, the subject position of the women was in focus, meaning that the incidents offered possibilities to discuss power in relation to formulating for example definitions, priorities and interpretations. They also pointed at power issues related to possibilities of obtaining resources and influencing organizational decisions. The situations often originated out of frustration or dissatisfaction in the groups. These were recognized as similar incidents when lack of organizational influence resulted in feelings of exploitation and fear. This was pointed out by the researchers as crucial experience and knowledge when working for change in organizations. The frustration was transformed into interesting reflections about power and feelings of powerlessness that helped the groups to move on in the project. The chosen examples include the issues of naming, separatist groups, available resources, accountability and definitions of change.

Naming

In all groups, there were women that expressed difficulties with the title "women as power resources". This inspired reflections regarding the approach and to the politics of naming in general. Women said that they did not feel comfortable with the title and thus were not able to stand up for it in other situations. The discussions that followed opened up exciting reflections related to the word "power" and "women", and expanded the understanding of the concept. The concept of power was provocative to many of the women, as it was interpreted as something being forced on to others. The concept of influence had a more positive connotation to some of them. In addition, some women found the concept to be potentially essentialist when defining "women". The researchers explained that the concept did not include definitions of women's resources in kind, but represented a way to think beyond sameness or difference to men. The researchers' response when negotiating the title of the project was that the three groups could use any name they wanted or preferred. The researchers declared, however, that they would continue to use the name they themselves preferred in the research community. At the end of the project, none of the participating groups had changed the title of their initiatives and even joked about their initial fear of using the concept of women as power resource.

Separatist Groups

Women raised the issue of men in two of the groups. They were frustrated by the absence of men in the project and this was negotiated with the research group. The women that were critical to the women only method pointed at the importance of involving men, and male managers in particular, in change processes related to gender equality. The research group responded by stating that the groups were welcome to include men in their change initiatives. Again, stressing the importance of women as power resource, in defining, designing and evaluating changes in the organizations. The women were then encouraged to think through on what terms they would involve men in their change initiatives, not to lose influence over the change processes.

Resources

Another example was the recurring discussions about how to set limits on time and energy used in the project. Some participants, especially in one of the groups, questioned why they should prepare assignments for the research group. This propelled a dialogue about the responsibility for resources and results in the project: Who is paying for our time? What is the meaning of all this, why do we engage in the project? These reactions could be interpreted as expression of the participants' fear of actually being exploited either by the researchers or by management. Many participants doubted their management's commitment to gender equality and were afraid of becoming alibis and doing a lot of work behind the scene without attaining the resources needed. They also doubted that they would receive credit for the results. This skepticism can be regarded as a result of the participants' previous experience of working with gender equality. The researchers' response to this was to consider this frustration as a specific competence and use it in this project. Participants were encouraged to set limits when it came to ambitions and workload. By asking how the project could be made worthwhile for the participants, they were supported in defining their own meaning in order to make the project a source of energy instead of being energy consuming. The researchers emphasized that this was a crucial issue since the feeling of being exploited by the project itself would be a sign that the approach had failed.

Accountability

During the first two meetings participants attempted to push the responsibility for extra group meetings onto the project management. The women criticized the project group for not arranging enough meetings. The researchers' response was to push back the initiative for group meetings to the participants by recalling the responsibilities of the researchers according to the project design. At the same time, the project leader announced that she would participate in extra meetings if desired. When it came to the planning of the conference, the participants suggested an alternative to the planned conference with internal invitations instead of invitations open to other organizations. This time the research group changed the entire concept according to the participants' suggestions, as the situation illustrated how the women wanted to make other priorities in line with how they evaluated the possibilities to make an impact on their own organizations. The fact that the research group changed the project plan in order to accommodate the wishes of the participants is an illustration of how the concept of women as power resources was implemented in the project.

Defining Change

The participants were preoccupied by what could be considered as organizational change: Does organizational change have to involve changing men? Was their personal development to be considered as organizational change? Could a change in their own knowledge, approach or working conditions be seen as organizational change? The women tended to downplay their own importance and put much emphasis on men in senior positions when defining organizational change. The researchers initiated a discussion about definitions of change, and what categories were considered subjects of evaluating change in organizations. Reflections on what was considered changes to the women in relation to what was considered accepted changes within the organization resulted in new and critical insights into power processes. Discussions about the women's right to define and evaluate change were repeated numerous times during the project, and were considered difficult to grasp.

THE IMPACT OF THE PROJECT

The impact of the project can be identified on an individual and an organizational level, and in both the short and the long term. The women participants most of all identified new knowledge and increased awareness as results of the project. New knowledge resulted in an increased sense of empowerment and in a willingness to act as change agents. The women participants identified the network they gained through the project as a source of support for future change efforts. A majority of women both at the manufacturing company and technical university advanced in their careers after the project was finalized. Almost half of the women at the manufacturing company had new positions within a year after the program was ended. They were very supportive towards each other in finding new positions. These new positions were not necessarily at a higher hierarchical level, but in contexts that were more appreciative of women. After a few years, all of the women had advanced to more senior levels within different units of the company, either directors or senior vice presidents. One woman moved on to become CEO of another company. At the university, a majority of the participants are today full professors. Four of these women occupy senior positions within the university hierarchy, either as directors or deans and one woman assumed the position of vice-chancellor of a university college.

On an organizational level, new change initiatives were carried out, both during and after the project. Among the change initiatives was the creation of networks. At the manufacturing company, a women's action network was created. The network meets regularly to monitor vacant senior manager positions, to identify women candidates who match these positions, and to encourage them to apply. The network at the manufacturing company argued for the need of balanced groups within the company. Another initiative at the manufacturing company was to convince senior management that the company needed a diversity director on a global level within the company and to offer the position to one of the researchers in the project management team. This intensified the diversity work at the manufacturing company. Diversity was made one of the strategic objectives for the years that followed the project. The new diversity director developed diversity key performance indicators addressing gender, nationality, age and business entity experience as well as inclusive work climate. Executive and employee networks as well as a network for male executives wanting to promote gender equality and increasing women on management positions have been set up. Moreover, a global community of more than 100 in-house trainers in diversity and inclusion has been created.

The women at the technical university did not manage to launch any major change initiatives during the project duration. They created a network that met once a month over lunch and where strategies for action were discussed. Some of the women also took the initiative to discuss the issue of gender equality in their own workplaces. Although the women from the technical university took much less action during the project, the women involved have later both launched extensive change initiatives and taken on senior positions and used these positions to put gender equality on the agenda and support other gender equality efforts within the organization.

CONCLUDING DISCUSSION

The approach of women as a power resource corresponds to the bifocal approach in women only programs introduced by de Vries (2010). Combining awareness raising and change initiatives, drawing on knowledge about both gender and organization, is a successful strategy in order to achieve organizational change. It resembles what Ely and Meyerson (2000) call a fourth frame approach in which the work culture is the target for assessment and revision and ultimately also change.

The project was inspired by a view of change as incremental, building on "small wins" rather than revolutionizing changes (Meyerson and Scully, 1995). But, as de Vries (2010) also notes, this approach is fundamentally flawed because of the difficulties any change initiatives inevitably will encounter. The project was, nevertheless, designed to allow a certain degree of freedom and openness to identify change where it took place. Change was realized where expected, but also in places where it would not have been expected to take place. As power works in so many different ways and on so many different levels (Halford and Leonard, 2001), so change processes are often complex and unpredictable.

The strategic choice of participants also contributed to the success of the project. The women had already reached positions with some authority within their respective organizations and were identified, by their superiors, as promising. Moreover, they were interested in contributing to change. Today, they are all still in STEM organizations, they have all ascended the organizational ladder and they continue to actively promote gender equality. Several have continued to work for change among men but they have also created new women-only-groups and joined existing women's' networks in order to continue to work for change. These women have all chosen to continue to work for change together with other women. They draw on both their individual position and the collective efforts of women to continue to work for change. The women are in a minority position (cf. Kanter, 1977) but drawing on their gender awareness and working collectively, they counteract the structural effects of such a position. This could be what Dahlerup (1988) identifies as "critical acts", that is, the actions of someone in minority who mobilizes resources to improve the situation for themselves and the whole minority group.

Finally, some concluding comments and reflections on differences between the two groups of women when practicing the approach of women as power resources will be shared. Obviously there were different reactions owing to the organizational context. The uncertain working conditions and scarce resources in academia made commitment to working for change complicated and contradictory. On one hand, these conditions enabled the articulation of criticism; on the other hand, they were not conducive to collective action. The women were more skeptical towards gender equality work, based on previous experience. The participants in the technical university were more afraid of being used as tokens, and they questioned the accountability of top management regarding gender equality issues. The conditions in the manufacturing company were different, more conducive to collective action, at least from a short-term perspective, but at the same time more difficult to voice criticism. There seemed to be both a greater sense of belonging to the organization and a greater demand for loyalty towards management in the companies compared to the technical university. Owing to the differences in conditions of working for change, it is essential to keep in mind that this affects when change will come about.

LESSONS LEARNED IN IMPLEMENTING THE PROJECT

We would like to conclude by sharing some lessons learned in this project, which can hopefully serve as inspiration to others:

1. Using gender theory proved to be significant to move beyond resistance.
2. Using a critical and reflective power perspective in all phases in practice helped in forming initiatives.

3. Turning frustration and anger into advantages was creative in working for change.
4. Manifesting the idea of the project in all stages – selection, pedagogy, content and expectations – achieved a sense of completeness.
5. Using the differences between two organizations was inspiring for participants, but was challenging to project leaders.
6. Following the process by being open to change during the project was both challenging and fruitful.

Using gender theory and research on gender equality work has proved to be significant when developing and designing work for change to move beyond resistance previously experienced. Results show how the implementation of the concept of women as power resources involves continuous communication, enactment and negotiation. Showing in what way a critical and reflective power perspective can be focused in all phases of the project in practice is the most important contribution, in particular the way in which women's experiences of frustration, anger, fear and other expressions of lack of power in organizations can be turned into central advantages and specific forms of competence in work for change in organizations.

The concept of women as power resources was manifested in designing the project through all stages. This can be recommended to similar projects aiming at change, as it represents a sense of completeness and unity in the design. To choose several participating organizations was both a challenge and an advantage to project leaders. The differences in the two groups involved more work and additional time for the project leaders as they had to adjust to different needs and processes. At the same time it proved to be very inspiring for the participating women to exchange experiences and discuss change initiatives in joint meetings. The design of the project demanded an open attitude to change during the meetings, which was both challenging and exciting for the project leaders. This is a lesson that should be taken into account when planning for resources in forms of time and energy. Moreover, the project leaders had to continuously learn how to live and embody the women as power resources approach in all interactions, which was inseparable from the overall results of the project.

REFERENCES

Acker, J. (1992), 'Gendering organizational theory', in A. Mills and P. Tancred (eds), *Gendering Organizational Analysis*, London: Sage.

Ahlbom, H. (2010, March 3), Männen håller makten. *NyTeknik*, retrieved from http://www.nyteknik.se/nyheter/karriarartiklar/article267887.ece.

Benschop, Y. and H. Dooreward (1998), 'Covered by equality: The gender subtext of organizations', *Organization Studies*, **19**(5), 787–805.

Calás, M. and L. Smircich (1991), 'Voicing seduction to silence leadership', *Organization Studies*, **12**(4), 567–601.

Cockburn, C. (1991), *In the Way of Women*, London: Macmillan.

Collinson, D. and J. Hearn (1994), 'Naming men as men: Implication for work, organization and management', *Gender, Work and Organization*, **1**(1), 2–22.

Dahlerup, D. (1988), 'From a small to a large minority: Women in Scandinavian politics', *Scandinavian Political Studies*, **11**(4), 275–98.

de Vries, I. (2010), *A realistic agenda? Women only programs as strategic interventions for building gender equitable workplaces*, Doctoral dissertation, University of Western Australia Business School.

Eduards, M. (1997), *Förbjuden Handling*, Malmö: Liber.

Eduards, M. (1998), 'Män – finns de?', *Kvinnovetenskaplig Tidskrift*, 3–4, 77–84.

Ely, R.J. and D.E Meyerson (2000), 'Theories of gender in organizations: A new approach to organizational analysis and change', *Research in Organizational Behavior*, **22**, 103–52.

Ferguson, K. (1984), *The Feminist Case against Bureaucracy*, Philadelphia: Temple University Press.

Gatenby, B. and M. Humphries (1999), 'Doing gender: Rolemodels, mentors and networks', *International Review of Women and Leadership*, **5**(1), 12–29.

Gherardi, S. (1995), *Gender, Symbolism and Organizational Cultures*, London: Sage.

Hagberg, J.-E., A. Nyberg and E. Sundin (1995), *Att göra landet jämställt*, Stockholm: Nerénius & Santérus.

Halford, S. and P. Leonard (2001), *Gender, Power and Organisations: An Introduction*, Basingstoke: Palgrave.

Halford, S., M. Savage and A. Witz (1997), *Gender, Careers and Organisations*, Basingstoke: Macmillan.

Hearn, J. and W. Parkin (2001), *Gender, Sexuality and Violence in Organisations*, London: Sage.

Holgersson, C. (2013), 'Recruiting managing directors – doing homosociality', *Gender, Work & Organization*, **20**(4), 454–466.

Höök, P. (2001), *Stridspiloter i vida kjolar. Om ledarutveckling och jämställdhet*, Stockholm: EFI.

Höök, P. (2003), 'Jämställdhet på hög nivå', in SOU 2003:16 *Mansdominans i förändring*, Stockholm: Fritzes.

Höök, P. (2006), 'Bakåt- och framåtblickande dialoger: Betydelsen av ett reflekterande förhållningssätt i jämställdhetsarbete', in U. Göransson and E. Sundin (eds), *Vad hände sedan?* Stockholm: VINNOVA.

Husu, L. and P. Koskinen (2010), 'Gendering excellence in technological research: A comparative European perspective', *Journal of Technology Management & Innovation*, **5**(1), 127–39.
Kanter, R.M. (1977), *Men and Women of the Corporation*, New York: Basic Books.
Marshall, J. (1984), *Women Managers: Travellers in a Male World*, Chichester: Wiley.
Meyerson, D. and M. Scully (1995), 'Tempered radicals and the politics of ambivalence and change', *Organization Science*, **6**(5), 585–600.
Rutherford, S. (2001), 'Equal opportunities: Making a difference', *Women in Management Review*, **14**(6), 212–19
Sheppard, D. (1992), 'Women managers' perceptions of gender and organizational life', *Gendering Organizational Analysis*, 151–66.
Snickare, L. (2012), *Makt utan magi: En studie av chefers yrkeskunnande*, Doctoral dissertation, KTH.
SOU 1994: 3 *Mäns föreställningar om kvinnor och chefskap*, Stockholm: Fritzes.
SOU 2003:16 *Mansdominans i förändring*, Stockholm: Fritzes.
Statistics Sweden (2011), *Higher education: Applicants and admitted to higher education at first and second cycle studies autumn term 2011 (UF46SM1101)*, Statistics Sweden. Retrieved from http://www.scb.se/Pages/Publishing CalendarViewInfo_259923.aspx?publobjid=15213.
Statistics Sweden (2012), *På tal om kvinnor och män. Lathund om jämställdhet 2012*, Örebro: Statistics Sweden.
Vinnicombe, S. and N. Colwill (1995), *The Essence of Women in Management*, London: Prentice Hall.
Wahl, A. (1992), *Könsstrukturer i organisationer: Kvinnliga civilekonomer och civilingenjörers karriärutveckling*, Stockholm: EFI.
Wahl, A. (1994), 'Att arbeta för förändring', in *SOU 1994:3 Mäns föreställningar om kvinnor och chefskap*, Stockholm: Fritzes.
Wahl, A. (1996), 'Företagsledning som konstruktion av manlighet', *Kvinnovetenskaplig Tidskrift*, **1**, 15–29.
Wahl, A. (1998), 'Deconstructing women and leadership', *International Review of Women and Leadership*, **4**(2).
Wahl, A. and P. Höök (2007), 'Changes in working with gender equality in management in Sweden', *Equal Opportunities International*, **26**(5), 435–48.
Wahl, A., C. Holgersson and P. Höök (2005), 'Irony as a feminist strategy for women managers', in Ulla Johansson and Jill Woodilla (ed), *Irony and Organizations: Epistemological Claims and Supporting Field Stories*, Malmö: Liber, pp. 109–25.
Wahl, A., C. Holgersson, P. Höök and S. Linghag (2001), *Det ordnar sig: Teorier om organisation och kön*, Lund: Studentlitteratur.
Wahl, A., M. Eduards, C. Holgersson, P. Höök, S. Linghag and M. Rönnblom (2008), *Motstånd och Fantasi. Historien om F*, Lund: Studentlitteratur.

8. Effective practices to increase women's participation, advancement and leadership in US academic STEM

Diana Bilimoria and Xiangfen Liang

Recent reports have highlighted the importance of the full participation of women in the science, technology, engineering and mathematics (STEM) workforce for the continued global leadership position of the United States in science and technology in the coming years and decades (National Academies, 2007a, 2007b; U.S. Department of Labor, 2007). Yet, even as women are increasingly holders of doctoral degrees in STEM fields, the proportion of women faculty in STEM in the nation's colleges and universities has remained slow to increase, particularly with low representation at the highest levels of the academic hierarchy. The leaky pipeline metaphor has been used to describe institutional level (cultural and structural) impediments to women's participation and advancement in academic STEM careers, describing the problems, barriers and resource inequities faced by women at each key transition point in the academic career pipeline (Bilimoria and Liang, 2012). The goal of this chapter is to describe effective initiatives to address gender equity issues and the leaky pipeline in academic STEM fields undertaken by the National Science Foundation's (NSF's) ADVANCE program in US colleges and universities.

For the purposes of our descriptions and evaluations, we draw on the findings of an earlier study conducted by us (Bilimoria and Liang, 2012). In the rest of this chapter, we first describe extant problems in the representation and experience of women faculty in academic STEM fields. Then, we address the NSF ADVANCE program and its emphasis on institutional transformation. Third, based on our earlier comprehensive evaluation of the NSF ADVANCE program, we summarize insights about effective practices in transforming higher education to become more gender equitable, including career pipeline and institutional culture initiatives. Here we describe the gender equity, diversity and inclusion initiatives that have worked best to increase the participation, advancement and leadership of women faculty in STEM fields.

WORKFORCE PARTICIPATION, EQUITY AND INCLUSION OF WOMEN IN ACADEMIC STEM

In this section we discuss two sets of issues relevant to the workforce participation, equity and inclusion of academic women in STEM fields: low participation and inhospitable treatment.

Low Participation of Women Faculty in Academic STEM Fields

In academic STEM fields, women hold a larger share of junior faculty positions than senior positions. According to Science and Engineering Indicators 2010 (National Science Foundation, 2010), women constituted 25 percent of full-time senior faculty (full and associate professors) and 42 percent of full-time junior faculty (assistant professors and lecturers) in 2006. Despite recent gains, women are significantly more likely to hold non-tenure track positions, are appointed to tenure track positions in most fields in far lower proportions than their representation in the candidate pool of doctoral degrees granted in the last decade, and are less likely to be tenured faculty than men, especially in doctoral institutions where "full-time women faculty are only half as likely as men to have tenure" (West and Curtis, 2006, p. 10). The percentage of underrepresented minority STEM doctorate holders in full professor positions has remained relatively flat, from 4.5 percent in 1999 to 5.7 percent in 2008 (National Science Foundation, 2011). Overall, women doctorate holders have made progress in occupying academic positions in recent years but they remain underrepresented in senior faculty positions and moderately represented in junior faculty positions in STEM.

Analyses of the workforce participation of women faculty reveal underrepresentation in several STEM fields. Leboy (2008) noted that close to half of the top ten National Institutes of Health-funded academic health centers in 2006 had no women among their junior tenure-track faculty in their biochemistry and cell biology departments, as a result a young woman might get the impression that her shot at a faculty position in these schools would be difficult, if not out of reach. In schools of engineering, women constituted about 13 percent of the tenured or tenure track faculty in 2009, including 22 percent of assistant professors, 15 percent of associate professors, and 8 percent of full professors (Gibbons,

2009). The percentage of women tenured or tenure track faculty ranged from 6 percent in mining engineering to 22 percent in environmental engineering (Gibbons, 2009). Academic chemistry exhibits very similar patterns of the under-representation of women, even though relatively more women complete doctoral degrees in chemistry. Women held only 12 percent of all tenure track faculty positions and only 21 percent of assistant professor positions at the top 50 chemistry departments (Nolan, Buckner, Kuck and Marzabadi, 2004).

The share of women faculty in mathematical sciences was also small, and varied considerably by subfield. According to Kirkman, Maxwell and Rose (2005), women comprised about 26 percent of full-time faculty in mathematical science. The share of full-time women faculty ranged from 12 percent for doctoral-granting departments in private institutions to 32 percent for master's granting departments. The share of tenured women faculty was highest in departments granting either a master's or a baccalaureate degree only (21 percent), and lowest in doctoral-granting departments (9 percent). The percentage of tenured/tenure track women faculty in mathematical sciences over the period 1998–2004 remained relatively stable (Kirkman et al., 2005).

In short, across academic STEM fields, women are less likely than men to be found in the full professor positions and more likely to be assistant professors (National Science Foundation, 2011; Nelson, 2007). Fewer differences in rank exist between male and female faculty in early career stages in STEM, but greater differences tend to appear between 15 and 20 years after receipt of the doctorate. Research also indicates that women are under-represented in senior academic ranks and faculty leadership positions such as presidents, chancellors, provosts, deans, and department chairs (Hollenshead, 2003). This may be related to the difficulties women faculty in STEM face in academic career advancement and the fact that they may not obtain the same levels of professional recognition for their scholarly work as do their male colleagues.

Inhospitable Climate and Culture in the Academic STEM

A variety of problems emerge from the lack of a critical mass of women and few women at the top of the academic hierarchy in STEM, particularly resource inequities, barriers, and problems related to differential treatment and evaluation at every level in the institution. A groundbreaking study conducted by the School of Science's Committee on Women Faulty at MIT (Massachusetts Institute of Technology, 1999) indicated the marginalization and exclusion of senior women faculty as academic colleagues, documenting their receipt of lower space, salary, and other resources, exclusion from informal and formal social gatherings, and exclusion from research and teaching collaborations. Other studies have documented a persistent gender gap in salaries (West and Curtis, 2006); female faculty members earn significantly less than male faculty members even after controlling for human capital, scholarly productivity, and personal characteristics (National Science Foundation, 2003). Additionally, women have less access to research assistance and funding than men (Creamer, 1998; Xie and Shauman, 1998), and they enter academic positions with more limited start-up packages, less office and lab space, and less graduate-student and support-staff assistance (Massachusetts Institute of Technology, 1999; Park, 1996).

Rosser (2004) reported that low numbers of women STEM faculty result in women feeling isolated, having limited access to role models and mentors, and having to work harder to gain credibility and respect from their male colleagues (see also Fox, 2010). With constrained access to key academic networks, women junior faculty are left on their own to learn how to navigate the promotion and tenure process in a male-dominated environment. Many women opt out of academic STEM, choosing private-sector positions because they become frustrated with the academic setting (Valian, 2004).

In two waves of early focus groups and interviews about the career experiences of women faculty members at a research university between 2001 and 2004, we found several important themes including: (1) an overall chilly climate and unwelcoming community for women described by participants as exclusionary, unfriendly, marginalizing, tough, isolating, male-dominated, and silencing; (2) a climate where "everything is negotiable", manifested in perceptions of side deals and of unequal application of procedures; (3) lack of transparency in university rules, policies, procedures and practices; (4) a pervasive lack of mentoring; (5) disproportionate service and teaching pressures faced by women faculty; and (6) unfair or unequal access to/allocation of resources, including purchase of library materials, assistance from teaching assistants, access to services from support staff, travel money, and protected research time (Case Western Reserve University, 2003). Other writings address the multiple dimensions of gender-based resource inequity in academia (Long, 1990, 1992; Evetts, 1996; Preston, 2004; Valian, 2004). For example, women faculty receive less office and lab space, have less access to graduate-student assistance, and get fewer services from support staff (Park, 1996).

The experiences of women faculty in STEM seem to derive from particular sets of beliefs held by (predominantly male) faculty and administrators. For example, participants in the focus groups mentioned above brought out the notion that leadership seems naturally male, and that masculinity appears to lead to power, manifested in conscious and unconscious ways at the university. Other beliefs regarding academia voiced by participants included that the academic enterprise requires complete dedication at the expense of everything else, especially in early career years, and that academia is essentially an individual profession, with individualized results and rewards.

These mindsets contribute directly and indirectly to the treatment and evaluation of women faculty. Similar other belief structures, detrimental to women in academia, have been identified by research from other institutions as well. For instance, Silver et al. (2006) summarize several factors that retarded the achievement of full professional equality at the University of Rhode Island. These factors included: demeaning and insulting statements and remarks made by the dean and faculty members toward women faculty; "window-dressing" efforts by the dean to support women in engineering programs rather than providing adequate funding for such efforts; public treatment of women faculty in a less respectful manner than male faculty; and commenting to women faculty on the perceived appropriateness of their clothing (Silver et al., 2006).

Prior research has described how the masculine image of science translates to the treatment and evaluation of women in the academic workforce. Van den Brink and Stobbe (2009, p. 451) note that "the most important factors (re)producing gender inequality at universities relate to the images of science, scientific practice and the ideal scientist". Research careers in STEM, in particular, are perceived to demand a single-minded, full-time focus on a specific topic, exclusive devotion to career, and aggressive self-promotion (Dean and Fleckenstein, 2007). A prevalent image is that of a scientist or engineer as a man hard at work in a laboratory during all hours of the night and weekends. The ideal worker concept (Acker, 1990, 1992) suggests that "the abstract worker is actually a man, and it is the man's body, its sexuality, minimal responsibility in procreation and conventional control of emotions that pervades work and organizational processes" (Acker, 1990, p. 152). Benschop and Brouns (2003) suggest that the image of the *ideal academic* represents a faculty member fully absorbed in his research program, and Bailyn (2003, p. 139) describes the *perfect academic* as someone who "gives total priority to work and has no outside interests or responsibilities". These powerful cultural images suggest that academic scientific research is exclusionary of women, contributing greatly to the negative experiences of women faculty. The chilly climate for STEM students also has been described previously (Hall and Sandler, 1984; Mills and Ayre, 2003).

Results of various interview and climate studies indicate the everyday experience of women faculty in STEM fields. In a cross-institutional study of 765 faculty conducted in eight research institutions during 2002–2004, Fox (2010) reported that women are less likely than men to report speaking daily about research and more likely than men to report speaking less than weekly. Women also gave significantly lower ratings of access to equipment and lower recognition from faculty colleagues in home units (e.g., departments), and were significantly less likely than men to characterize their home units as (a) informal (compared to formal), (b) exciting (compared to boring), (c) helpful (compared to unhelpful), (d) creative (compared to noncreative), and (e) inclusive (compared to noninclusive). In another climate study conducted at a large public university, in comparison with their male counterparts, STEM women faculty reported significantly lower equality of treatment, perceived the organizational climate as significantly less supportive, perceived lower support for family friendliness, reported more overt discrimination in areas such as salary, promotion, and access to resources, perceived that they undertook greater service involvement, and believed that their departments viewed them as less productive than their departmental averages (Blackwell, Snyder and Mavriplis, 2009).

Results from interviews with women and men faculty members at another research university indicated that female faculty were more likely to report negative interactions with colleagues, negative experiences with the process of evaluation, promotion and tenure, difficulty balancing work and family life, and overwhelming workloads (Hult, Callister and Sullivan, 2005). Several other climate studies conducted by universities indicate that male faculty experience more favorable interpersonal relations than women faculty. Tenure track women faculty often provide lower ratings than their men counterparts on items measuring institutional support, such as child care, career planning, teaching improvement, tenure-clock adjustments, and accruing resources. In addition, female faculty on the tenure track report lower satisfaction with their academic jobs than do male faculty (Bilimoria et al., 2006; Callister, 2006), and they are more likely to opt out of academic STEM (Valian, 2004).

A valuable concept from sociology addressing the experience of women faculty in STEM is the *accumulation of advantage and disadvantage*, which is the magnification of initial small differences into later large differences (cf. Merton, 1942/1973). The impact of accumulative disadvantage on the career outcomes of STEM women has been recognized. For example, the 2001 report *From Scarcity to Visibility: Gender Differences in the Careers of Doctoral Scientists and Engineers* noted that "while controlling for background differences eliminates much of the gender difference in salary, it does not eliminate it altogether [...] Further, with each progressive stage of the stratification process, it becomes more difficult to distinguish outcomes that are the result of individual differences between women and men from the result of men's cumulative advantage over women in science" (Long, 2001, pp. 216–17). A demonstration of the effects of accumulative disadvantage showed that very small differences in how individuals (or groups) are treated can result in very large disparities in career outcomes (Martell, Lane and Emrich, 1996).

INSTITUTIONAL TRANSFORMATION AND THE NSF ADVANCE PROGRAM

To address systematic gender inequality in academic STEM, that is, the overt, subtle, or hidden disparities in workforce opportunities between women and men faculty, and encourage the gender equity transformation of higher education, in recent years leading US federal research funding agencies have begun to seed institutional transformation through organizational change programs and research. For example, since 2001 the National Science Foundation (NSF) has established the ADVANCE awards to increase the participation and advancement of women in academic science and engineering careers and address structural impediments to women faculty's success in academic STEM (see http://nsf.gov/advance).

NSF is an independent US government agency created by the US Congress in 1950 to promote science and engineering through research programs and education projects. As described by Fox (2008), NSF has had a long history of funding initiatives to address the underrepresentation of women, through Career Advancement Awards and Visiting Professorships for Women in the 1980s, to Professional Opportunities for Women in Research and Education (POWRE) Awards in the 1990s; these earlier initiatives focused on awards made to individual women, principally for support of their research programs in science and engineering (Rosser and Lane, 2002).

In the 1990s, NSF began to focus on systemic initiatives, creating the Program for Women and Girls. The results of surveys of more than 400 awardees during the four years of the POWRE program drove an emerging awareness of the need to transition to a more institutional, systemic change program, to attempt to solve problems that cannot be addressed solely by supporting research projects of individual female scientists and engineers (Rosser and Lane, 2002). In 1999 an internal staff group was convened to address the issue of the significant underrepresentation of women in academic science and engineering. The committee concluded that to enable women's full participation, particularly at the senior level, it was imperative that the structures and cultures of their work settings be transformed (Sturm, 2006; Fox, 2008). Stemming from this, the NSF ADVANCE program was established in 2001 by the NSF's Office of the Director as an NSF-wide program, to catalyze the transformation of academic work environments in US higher education institutions in ways that enhance the participation and advancement of women in science and engineering.

Currently, NSF ADVANCE has three program components: Institutional Transformation (IT); IT-Catalyst; and Partnerships for Adaptation, Implementation, and Dissemination (PAID). The IT component has been in all program solicitations since 2001, and consists of five-year projects, funded in the range of $2 million to $5 million in total. These are comprehensive, institution-wide projects to transform the institutional practices, policies, climate, and culture of the university or college. ADVANCE IT projects are large-scale organizational development interventions composed of a diverse range of transformational initiatives, harnessing the synergies of partnering across multiple units within an institution. Between 2001 and 2008, four cohorts of ADVANCE IT grants were awarded to 37 higher-education institutions (hereafter ADVANCE universities or institutions) across the country.

IT-Catalyst (previously IT-Start) awards were piloted in a 2007 solicitation as two-year projects, in the $100,000–$200,000 range. Generally these are awarded for planning and assessment activities to prepare for transformational activities. Examples of project activities include climate surveys to establish baseline data, planning meetings with stakeholders, data collection and analysis, and research on potential strategies to eradicate gender bias. The third program component, PAID, consists of one- to five-year projects within or across institutions, with funding depending on the scope of the project. Some projects adapt, implement, and/or diffuse exemplary ADVANCE IT strategies to increase the participation of women in STEM academics, while others are social-science research proposals related to gender in STEM faculty and academic leadership positions. Examples of these projects include faculty climate surveys as well as training and leadership development programs aimed at accomplishing ADVANCE goals.

During 2001–2009, 111 different institutions of higher education were funded through the NSF ADVANCE initiative. Of these, 84 are public institutions and 27 are private. Several are minority-serving institutions, including seven Hispanic-serving institutions, six historically black colleges and universities (HBCUs), including one women's college, one Alaskan Native-serving institution, and one institution primarily serving persons with disabilities. Three institutions are women's colleges (including one HBCU). Nine professional and nonprofit STEM-related organizations have also been funded. The leaders of these ADVANCE projects have formed a unique and active community for the sharing of best practices, problem solving, and learning about gender equity and institutional transformation in higher education.

In sum, over the last decade NSF's ADVANCE program has become an increasingly widespread and influential national resource for systemic gender equity-related transformation of academic science and engineering across US universities and colleges. By focusing on the organizational level rather than the individual level of change, NSF ADVANCE encourages and disseminates comprehensive, innovative, and systemic initiatives to stimulate gender equity, diversity, and inclusion in academic STEM.

GENDER EQUITY INSTITUTIONAL TRANSFORMATION PRACTICES

Through our own systematic review of initiatives undertaken by the 19 universities constituting the first two cohorts of ADVANCE institutional transformation grant awardees (cf. Bilimoria and Liang, 2012), we identified two major clusters of ADVANCE initiatives aimed at improving gender equity, diversity and inclusion: (a) pipeline initiatives – initiatives to enhance the career trajectories of women and underrepresented minority (URM) faculty at every stage of the academic pipeline, and (b) cultural initiatives to improve extant institutional systems, policies, and climate.

Three types of **pipeline initiative** addressed improvements in the individual career trajectories of women and URM faculty at the ADVANCE institutions: (a) initiatives to increase the inflow of women into the pipeline; (b) initiatives to better equip women to successfully progress in the academic pipeline: and (c) initiatives to improve the institutional structures and processes related to key academic career transition points in the pipeline. Three ADVANCE initiatives were used most frequently *to increase inflow to the academic career pipeline*: small funding opportunities for doctoral students and non-tenure track faculty, workshops targeting graduate students and postdoctoral students, and mentoring of women graduate students. We also identified five most frequently used ADVANCE initiatives *to better equip women to succeed in the pipeline*, including faculty mentoring (including paired, group, panel, peer, and speed mentoring) initiatives, career development workshops for junior faculty and tenured faculty, small funding opportunities for research and professional development, leadership development initiatives especially for tenured women faculty, and networking initiatives.

The last set of pipeline initiatives addressed the improvement of *institutional structures, practices, and processes* involved in the recruitment, advancement, and retention of women faculty in STEM. Recruitment initiatives implemented across the ADVANCE sites included assisting search committees in identifying and meeting with candidates, training search committees on unconscious biases and effective recruitment practices, funding for targeted recruitment to diversify faculty bodies, updating and implementing dual-career hiring policies and practices, and providing tools and resources for search committees. Advancement initiatives, particularly initiatives to improve promotion and tenure (PandT) processes included unconscious bias training for PandT committees, information sessions for faculty to increase transparency in PandT criteria, special coaches and mentors for women at the tenure or promotion stage, and new or modified policies around tenure clock extensions. Retention initiatives also were undertaken at ADVANCE institutions, including salary-equity studies, start-up package and offer letter analyses, and cohort analyses. While faculty departure may be linked to many factors, resource inequities may provide the spark that catalyzes a productive scientist's departure. Ensuring resource equity may be an important way to improve climate perceptions (Bilimoria et al., 2006), as well as a significant means to retain both women and men scientists in academia.

A second set of initiatives employed at the ADVANCE institutions focused on **transforming the institutional culture**. Department climate was an area of focus for institutional transformation efforts. As individuals experience climate in their immediate workplace, perceptions about department climate are key determinants for faculty satisfaction and retention, and improving department climate is critical for the retention and advancement of women faculty (Fine, Williams and Callister, 2009). We identified four initiatives that were most frequently used to *improve the micro (departmental) climates* across ADVANCE universities: faculty climate surveys and feedback, small funding opportunities for departmental transformation, facilitated microclimate interventions, and leadership development and climate awareness training of department chairs. Faculty climate surveys were one of the most widely implemented strategies across ADVANCE sites. The core climate variables that were investigated in the climate surveys included treatment by colleagues/supervisors, recognition, respect, collegiality, expectations, sense of being valued, fit, exclusion, spousal employment, childcare responsibilities, job/career satisfaction, resource equity and access, service and teaching loads, and time allocation.

ADVANCE universities also focused on *improving the macro (school/college and university) climate*. These institutions worked on enhancing overall school/college- and campus-wide awareness of gender equity and institutional climate through establishing campus-wide advisory councils on women and minorities, bringing distinguished senior women scholars on visits to campus, undertaking gender equity awareness training for non-faculty campus constituencies such as students, holding climate awareness workshops for faculty and administrators through interactive theater presentations, instituting family-friendly and academic career flexibility policies, enacting child-care initiatives, and targeting the increase of women in administrative (department chair and dean) and faculty leadership (endowed chair) positions.

Figure 8.1 summarizes the variety of the initiatives employed at the ADVANCE universities. Our review reveals that the ADVANCE institutions implemented a dynamic portfolio of simultaneous, varied, and multilevel initiatives as recommended by Hogue and Lord (2007). Focusing on programs of change at the individual, unit and institutional levels, these initiatives targeted improvements in the career trajectories of women faculty in the academic pipeline as well as improvements in the institutional workplace climate. Clearly some initiatives worked better in certain environments, and some individual initiatives may have had more finite impact than others. Yet, we conclude from our review that a coordinated portfolio of organizational change initiatives consisting of simultaneously enacted and varied interventions targeted at multiple levels (individual, unit, and system-wide) in the institution are required to cumulatively effect gender equity institutional transformation. Many of these organizational change initiatives have been successfully adopted and advanced by subsequent NSF ADVANCE awardees, whether through Institutional Transformation (IT) awards, Partnerships for Adaptation, Implementation and Dissemination (PAID) awards, or IT-Catalyst awards, and by other higher education institutions in the US and other countries seeking improvements in gender equity, diversity, and inclusion.

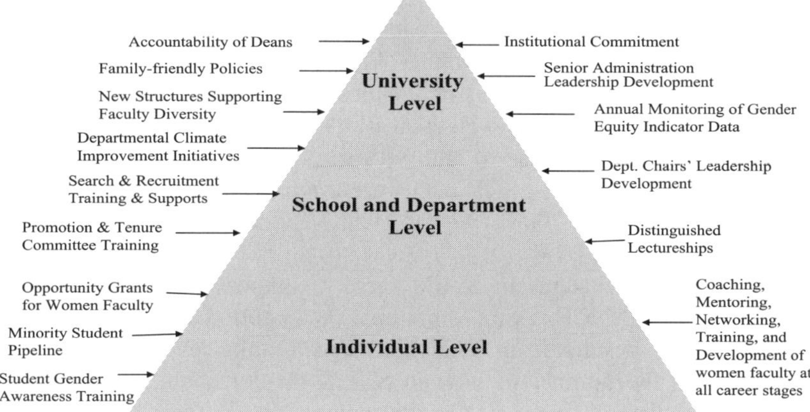

Source: Modified from Bilimoria and Liang (2012).

Figure 8.1 Summary of effective practices for gender equity transformation

INSTITUTIONAL TRANSFORMATION OUTCOMES

In this section, we summarize changes in STEM (science, technology, engineering and mathematics) faculty composition over the duration of ADVANCE programs originally reported in Bilimoria and Liang (2012). For the analyses of overall faculty in STEM, we obtained multiple years' data for all the 19 ADVANCE participating institutions. Pre-ADVANCE vs. post-ADVANCE analyses were conducted for the number of faculty by gender at each rank, and the percentage of women faculty within rank. To identify changes in the workforce participation of women faculty through ADVANCE, comparisons were made between the baseline year and the final year of each NSF award. A baseline year in general refers to the first NSF-funded year of an ADVANCE IT project. Similarly, a final year generally refers to the last NSF-funded year of an ADVANCE project, including any no-cost extension years.

In faculty composition trend analyses, we provide appropriate biannual comparisons with national reference groups using NSF's Survey of Doctorate Recipients (SDR, available at www.nsf.gov/statistics/doctoratework/). We obtained data about the composition of faculty at samples of four-year colleges and universities, as well as at very high and high research universities (RU/VH and RU/H) only, by field, sex, and rank in 2001, 2003, and 2006, respectively. Therefore, in our trend analyses, data drawn from SDR serve as national reference groups of STEM faculty at each rank and each discipline. We discuss trends in women's workforce participation at ADVANCE institutions relative to these national reference groups of samples of women faculty at four-year colleges and universities as well as at RU/VH and RU/H only, in STEM, engineering, natural sciences, and SBS disciplines, respectively. At the time of our data analysis, SDR data were available for three years (2001, 2003, and 2006). The 2008 SDR data, while collected, were not available for public use.

We examined changes in STEM faculty composition by gender and rank over ADVANCE award durations. As reported in Bilimoria and Liang (2012), results from Wilcoxon signed-ranks test of differences showed that the number of women STEM faculty at the assistant and professor ranks, as well as for all women at all (combined) ranks, increased significantly between the ADVANCE baseline year and the final year. However, the number of women associate professors did not increase significantly. Interestingly, changes in the number of men STEM faculty at all three levels and for combined ranks over the same time period were not statistically significant. These findings indicate that although the number of men STEM faculty at these universities increased modestly or remained the same during the ADVANCE award period, the number of women faculty increased significantly in these disciplines over the same time period. As there is clearly a coinciding period between the changes documented and ADVANCE IT award periods, we conclude that ADVANCE IT initiatives significantly facilitated an increase in the number of women faculty in STEM disciplines at these universities over their ADVANCE award periods.

Analyses of changes in the percentage of STEM women faculty at each of the 19 ADVANCE institutions over their award periods revealed that 18 out of 19 universities reported a percentage increase in the representation of women STEM faculty, with a 2–8 percent increase between the baseline year and the final year. The average change in the percentage of women STEM faculty experienced over the 19 institutions over their ADVANCE award periods was 3.5 percent. Over the ADVANCE IT awards, the average annual rate of increase was greater for women STEM faculty than for men STEM faculty at 18 out of the 19 institutions studied. In many of these universities, the average annual growth rate of men STEM faculty declined or improved only marginally. The average number of women STEM faculty at these 19 universities grew from 53 (15 percent of the total faculty) to 71 (18 percent of the total faculty) over their ADVANCE award periods, while the average number of men STEM faculty changed from 311 (85 percent of the total faculty) to 320 (82 percent of the total faculty) over the same time period. Across all 19 universities, the average annual growth rate for women faculty in STEM was 7.2 percent while the corresponding rate for men faculty in STEM was 0.6 percent. The average percentage growth rate over the total award periods across these 19 institutions was 39.7 percent for women faculty and 3.5 percent for men faculty in STEM; that is, the number of women STEM faculty at these 19 institutions increased on average over their ADVANCE award periods by almost 40 percent while the number of men STEM faculty increased on average by about 3.5 percent.

In comparison with national reference groups of women STEM faculty (all ranks) at four-year institutions and at research universities, ADVANCE Cohort 1 institutions started slightly higher and ADVANCE Cohort 2 institutions started slightly lower than the overall average percentage of women STEM faculty at the national sample of research universities. Both cohorts of ADVANCE universities showed increasing trends in the proportions (all ranks) of women STEM faculty, but exact comparisons could not be made since SDR data were not available for 2008. However, the findings indicate more rapid growth over the same time period in the overall representation of women STEM faculty (all ranks) at ADVANCE schools in comparison with national research universities.

Nationwide, women comprised 24–27 percent STEM assistant professors at research universities between 2001 and 2006. For the ADVANCE IT Cohort 1 research universities, women on average comprised 31 percent STEM assistant professors in 2007, up from 23 percent in 2002. For the ADVANCE IT Cohort 2 universities, women on average comprised 33 percent STEM assistant professors in 2008, up from 25 percent in 2004. Again, while exact comparisons are not possible due to the lack of 2008 SDR data, without question there have been increases in the percentages of women faculty at the assistant professor rank in STEM in both ADVANCE cohorts. These findings indicate more rapid growth over the same time period in the representation of women STEM assistant professors at ADVANCE institutions in comparison with national research universities.

Nationwide, women comprised 17–20 percent STEM associate professors at research universities between 2001 and 2006. For ADVANCE Cohort 1 four-year universities, the percentage of women associate professors ranged between 20 and 23 percent during AY 2002–07; for Cohort 1 research universities, the percentage of women associate professors ranged from 18–24 percent during AY 2002–07. For Cohort 2 universities, the percentage of women associate professors ranged between 16 and 19 percent during AY 2003–08. The percentage of women associate professors at ADVANCE Cohort 1 research universities showed an increasing trend from 2003 to 2007 in comparison with the national percentage of women associate professors, with a dip in 2003 from the previous year. The percentage of women associate professors in Cohort 2 lagged behind the national percentage of women associate professors. There was a sharp decrease in the percentage of women associate professors in 2008 for Cohort 2 universities. It is very possible that this trend is an artifact of the short time periods used to measure changes – it may be related to the increased number of women full professors (promoted from associate professors) in 2008.

Nationwide, women comprised only 7–9 percent STEM full professors at research universities between 2001 and 2006. Over the duration of the ADVANCE IT projects, an increasing trend was apparent for both cohorts. For ADVANCE Cohort 1 four-year institutions, women comprised 17 percent STEM full professors in 2007, up from 11 percent in 2002. For Cohort 1 research universities, women comprised 13 percent STEM full professors in 2007, up from 8 percent in 2002. The percentage of women full professors in ADVANCE Cohort 1 institutions was greater than the national level of women full professors in all research universities. For ADVANCE Cohort 2 universities, women comprised 10 percent of STEM full professors in 2008, up from 6 percent in 2004. As of 2006, the representation of women full professors in Cohort 2 lagged behind the national levels of women full professors at four-year institutions and research universities. The results thus indicate that ADVANCE Cohort 1 universities show a higher proportion of women STEM full professors than comparable national research universities, while Cohort 2 universities show a lower proportion.

In summary, from the findings presented in Bilimoria and Liang (2012) and summarized above, we conclude that overall the ADVANCE universities significantly increased the number of women faculty in STEM over the duration of their institutional transformation projects. The targeted efforts of ADVANCE universities to increase the number of women STEM faculty were successful; increases in the representation of women STEM faculty occurred during their institutional transformation award periods while lesser or no growth occurred in their numbers of men STEM faculty during the same periods. The 19 universities studied engendered a 7.18 percent average annual growth rate in the numbers of women STEM faculty over their ADVANCE award periods; that is, the average number of women STEM faculty at these 19 institutions increased over their ADVANCE award periods by almost 40 percent while the average number of men STEM faculty increased by about 3.5

percent over the same time period. ADVANCE universities were particularly successful in increasing the representation of women assistant and full professors in STEM areas. Comparisons with national samples of research universities from the SDR database suggest that ADVANCE universities generally led the pace in increasing the representation of women STEM faculty over the same time periods. However, the data also signaled that women faculty continue to be under-represented in the academic STEM workforce, particularly at the associate professor and professor ranks at the nation's research universities.

DISCUSSION

The study's findings indicate that targeted interventions through ADVANCE to increase the academic workforce participation, advancement and retention of women faculty in STEM disciplines were successful in bringing about significant changes. Results reported in Bilimoria and Liang (2012) showed that the workforce participation of women faculty overall and at the assistant and full professor ranks, in leadership, and across the three science and engineering disciplines studied (natural sciences, engineering, and social and behavioral sciences) improved significantly. Resource inequities and barriers to inclusion were systematically identified and reduced at these institutions. In comparisons with a national sample of research universities, the ADVANCE institutions generally led in increasing the workforce participation of women faculty in STEM. However, the nationwide composition of women faculty in STEM disciplines remains an important issue.

The findings show that the deployment of a portfolio of simultaneous, varied, and multi-level gender equity change practices can cumulatively transform organizations to become more diverse, equitable and inclusive. As Bilimoria and Liang (2012, p. 206) put it, "Simplistic, ad hoc, or piecemeal solutions cannot eradicate systematic, historical and widespread gender underrepresentation and inequities in the STEM academic workforce. To overcome existing barriers and inertia, wider and deeper change is needed in our universities and colleges. This requires greater reflexivity about everyday gender practices coupled with systematic actions to transform organizational structures, processes, work practices, mental models and workplace cultures – to enable equal employment, opportunities, treatment, evaluation, and valuing of women and men so that *all* employees can fully participate, contribute, and develop in their careers and enable their organizations to achieve their goals of effectiveness."

An ongoing issue of importance to organizational change efforts such as at these ADVANCE universities pertains to how to sustain the transformation engendered beyond the funding supports received from an external institution. The 19 universities studied utilized a number of different measures to institutionalize their projects, including by the (a) creation of new permanent positions, offices and structures to carry out successful initiatives, (b) implementation of new or modified policies around faculty work-life integration, (c) engagement of new and improved practices and processes of faculty diversity, equity, inclusion and development, and (d) obtaining new sources of internal and external funding for the continuation of effective programs.

In conclusion, for gender equity change to become institutionalized in organizations, an organization-wide transformational process must be utilized. Similar to other transformational efforts in organizations, such as the introduction of total quality management, process improvements, lean manufacturing, six sigma manufacturing, safety improvements, customer service improvements and others, gender equity improvements must also involve significant and cascading efforts to change the systems, processes, practices and culture of the organization. The success of such a transformational project is reflected not only by improving diversity, equity and inclusion within the finite period of the project but also by effectively sustaining and leveraging the results into the future by embedding the changes into the socio-cultural fabric of the organization. Hence, awareness creation, skill building, empowerment, leadership development, new practice experimentation, new policy creation, and structural changes need to occur simultaneously. The example of the ADVANCE initiative in US colleges and universities has shown that such efforts are likely to bear fruit even in times when faculty composition changes are difficult to engender.

REFERENCES

Acker, J. (1990), 'Hierarchies, jobs, bodies: A theory of gendered organizations', *Gender and Society*, **4**(2), 139–58.

Acker, J. (1992), 'Gendering organizational theory', in A.J. Mills and P. Tancred (eds), *Gendering Organizational Analysis*, Newbury Park, CA: Sage, pp. 248–60.

Bailyn, L. (2003), 'Academic careers and gender equity: Lessons learned from MIT', *Gender, Work, and Organizations*, **10**, 137–53.

Benschop, Y. and M. Brouns (2003), 'Crumbling ivory towers: Academic organizing and its gender effects', *Gender, Work and Organization*, **10**(2), 194–212.

Bilimoria, D. and X. Liang (2012), *Gender Equity in Science and Engineering: Advancing Change in Higher Education*, New York: Routledge.

Bilimoria, D., S. Perry, X. Liang, P. Higgins, E. Stoller and C. Taylor (2006), 'How do female and male faculty members construct job satisfaction? The roles of perceived institutional leadership and mentoring and their mediating processes', *Journal of Technology Transfer*, **32**(3), 355–65.

Blackwell, L.V., L.A. Snyder and C. Mavriplis (2009), 'Diverse faculty in STEM fields: Attitudes, performance, and fair treatment', *Journal of Diversity in Higher Education*, **2**, 195–205.

Callister, R.R. (2006), 'The impact of gender and department climate on job satisfaction and intentions to quit for faculty in science and engineering fields', *Journal of Technology Transfer*, **30**(3), 383–96.

Case Western Reserve University (2003), *Resource Equity at Case Western Reserve University: Results of Faculty Focus Groups Report*, accessed April 27, 2011, from http://www.cwru.edu/menu/president/resourcequity.doc.

Creamer, E. (1998), 'Assessing faculty publication productivity: Issues of equity', *ASHE-ERIC Higher Education Report*, **26**(2).

Dean, D.J. and A. Fleckenstein (2007), 'Keys to success for women in science', in R.J. Burke and M.C. Mattis (eds), *Women and Minorities in Science, Technology, Engineering and Mathematics*, Cheltenham, UK and Northampton, MA: Edward Elgar, pp. 28–46.

Evetts, J. (1996), *Gender and Career in Science and Engineering*, London: Taylor and Francis.

Fine, E., J. Williams and R. Callister (2009), *Managing Department Climate Change. Presentation at the ADVANCE Principal Investigators Meeting*, Washington, DC, accessed August 19, 2014, from http://www.portal.advance.vt.edu/Advance_2009_PI_Mtg/PiMtg2009_Climate_Change.pdf.

Fox, M.F. (2008), 'Institutional transformation and the advancement of women faculty: The case of academic science and engineering', in J.C. Smart (ed.), *Higher Education: Handbook of Theory and Research*, Dordrecht, Germany: Springer Science + Business Media B.V., pp. 73–103.

Fox, M.F. (2010), 'Women and men faculty in academic science and engineering: Social-organizational indicators and implications', *American Behavioral Scientist*, **53**(7), 997–1012.

Gibbons, M.T. (2009), 'Engineering by the numbers', accessed April 27, 2011, from http://www.asee.org/papers-and-publications/publications/collegeprofiles/2009-profi le-engineering-statistics.pdf.

Hall, R.M. and B.R. Sandler (1984), *Out of the Classroom: A Chilly Campus Climate for Women?*, Association of American Colleges, Washington, DC: Project on the Status and Education of Women.

Hollenshead, C. (2003), 'Women in the academy: Confronting barriers to equality', in L.S. Hornig (ed.), *Equal Rites, Unequal Outcomes: Women in American Research Universities*, New York: Kluwer Academic/Plenum Publishers, pp. 211–66.

Hogue, M. and R.G. Lord (2007), 'A multilevel, complexity theory approach to understanding gender bias in leadership', *Leadership Quarterly*, **18**(4), 370–390.

Hult, C., R. Callister and K. Sullivan (2005), 'Is there a global warming toward women in academia?', *Liberal Education*, **91**(3), 50–57.

Kirkman, E.E., J.W. Maxwell and C.A. Rose (2005), *2004 Annual Survey of the Mathematical Sciences (3rd Report)*, accessed April 27, 2011, from http://www.ams.org/profession/data/annual-survey/2005Survey-Third-Report.pdf.

Leboy, P. (2008), 'Fixing the leaky pipeline: Why aren't there many women in the top spots in academia?', *The Scientist*, **22**(1), 67, accessed October 15, 2010, from www.the-scientist.com/2008/01/1/67/1/.

Long, J.S. (1990), 'The origins of sex differences in science', *Social Forces*, **68**(4), 1297–316.

Long, J.S. (1992), 'Measures of sex differences in scientific productivity', *Social Forces*, **71**(1), 159–78.

Long, J.S. (ed.) (2001), *Scarcity to Visibility: Gender Differences in the Careers of Doctoral Scientists and Engineers*, Washington, DC: National Academies Press.

Martell, R.F., D.M. Lane and C. Emrich (1996), 'Male-female differences: A computer simulation', *American Psychologist*, **51**, 157–8.

Massachusetts Institute of Technology (1999), 'A study on the status of women faculty in science at MIT', *The MIT Faculty Newsletter*, **11**(4), accessed April 27, 2011, from http://web.mit.edu/fnl/women/women.html.

Merton, R.K. (1942/1973), *The Sociology of Science*, Chicago, IL: University of Chicago Press.

Monroe, K., S. Ozyurt, T. Wrigley and A. Alexander (2008), 'Gender equality in academia: Bad news from the trenches, and some possible solutions', *Perspectives on Politics*, **6**(2), 215–33.

National Academies (2007a), *Rising Above the Gathering Storm: Energizing and Employing America for a Brighter Economic Future*, Washington, DC: National Academies Press.

National Academies (2007b), *Beyond Bias and Barriers: Fulfilling the Potential of Women in Academic Science and Engineering*, Washington, DC: National Academies Press.

National Science Foundation (2003), *Gender Differences in the Careers of Academic Scientists and Engineers: A Literature Review*, NSF 03–322, Arlington, VA: Division of Science Resources Statistics.

National Science Foundation (2010), 'Science and engineering indicators 2010', accessed October 15, 2010, from www.nsf.gov/statistics/seind10/start.htm.

National Science Foundation (2011), 'Women, minorities, and persons with disabilities in science and engineering 2011', accessed April 27, 2011, from http://www.nsf.gov/statistics/wmpd/.

Nelson, D.J. (2007), 'National analysis of diversity in science and engineering faculties at research universities', accessed April 27, 2011, from http://chem.ou.edu/~djn/diversity/briefi ngs/Diversity percent20Report percent20Final.pdf.

Nolan, S.A., J.P. Buckner, V.J. Kuck and C.H. Marzabadi (2004), 'Analysis by gender of the doctoral and postdoctoral institutions of faculty members at the top-fifty ranked chemistry departments', *Journal of Chemical Education*, **81**(3), 356–63.

Park, S.M. (1996), 'Research, teaching, and service: Why shouldn't women's work count?', *Journal of Higher Education*, **67**(1), 46–84.

Preston, A.E. (2004), *Leaving Science: Occupational Exit from Scientific Careers*, New York: Russell Sage Foundation.
Rosser, S.V. (2004), *The Science Glass Ceiling: Academic Women Scientists and the Struggle to Succeed*, New York: Routledge.
Rosser, S.V. and E.O. Lane (2002), 'A history of funding for women's programs at the National Science Foundation', *Journal of Women and Minorities in Science and Engineering*, **8**, 327–46.
Silver, B., G. Boudreaux-Bartels, H. Mederer, L.C. Pasquerella, J. Peckham, M. Rivero-Hudec and K. Wishner (2006), 'A warmer climate for women in engineering at the University of Rhode Island', *2006 Annual Conference Proceedings Paper, American Society for Engineering Education*, accessed April 27, 2011, from http://www.uri.edu/advance/files/pdf/Papers percent 20and percent20Presentations/ASEE_Final_Draft.pdf.
Sturm, S. (2006), 'The architecture of inclusion: Advancing workplace equity in higher education', *Harvard Journal of Law and Gender*, **29**, 247–334.
U.S. Department of Labor (2007), 'The STEM Workforce Challenge: the Role of the Public Workforce System in a National Solution for a Competitive Science, Technology, Engineering, and Mathematics (STEM) Workforce', Washington, DC: Department of Labor, accessed October 15, 2010 from http://www.doleta.gov/Youth_services/pdf/STEM_Report_4 percent2007.pdf.
Valian, V. (2004), 'Beyond gender schemas: Improving the advancement of women in academia', *National Women's Studies Association Journal*, **16**, 207–20.
van den Brink, M. and L. Stobbe (2009), 'Doing gender in academic education: The paradox of visibility', *Gender, Work and Organization*, **16**(4), 451–70.
West, M.S. and J.W. Curtis (2006), 'AAUP faculty gender equity indicators 2006', accessed March 17, 2011, from http://www.aaup.org/AAUP/pubsres/research/geneq2006.
Xie, Y. and K.A. Shauman (1998), 'Sex differences in research productivity: New evidence about an old puzzle', *American Sociological Review*, **63**, 847–70.

9. Professional societies and gender equity in STEM

Erin L. Cadwalader, Joan M. Herbers and Alice B. Popejoy

INTRODUCTION

The flow of women through the STEM (science, technology, engineering and mathematics) pipeline to top positions in academia and industry is hampered by low volume and big, leaking cracks in the pipe itself. A strong push to ratchet up participation is currently underway in the United States, with an emphasis on attracting more girls and women to STEM fields and professions. The main assumption is that filling the pipeline will ultimately produce women in top positions, but this ignores the issue of chronic leakage in academia. Just as moving more water through a permeable pipe does not fix the leak, simply recruiting women and girls into STEM fields does not fix systemic problems that hinder women's advancement and result in gender disparate representation in the upper echelons of STEM fields.

The Association for Women in Science (AWIS) is actively working to identify reasons why women leak out of the STEM pipeline and to provide solutions through programs and advocacy to address the underlying leakage factors. The "chilly climate" for women in STEM, lagging promotion behind men to upper positions, a lack of policies that facilitate work–life accommodation, and implicit gender bias are key examples of inherent systemic factors contributing to the attrition of women from STEM fields (Blickenstaff, 2005; Morris and Daniel, 2008). In this chapter, we highlight gender disparity in scholarly recognition as a crucial element of the attrition process.

Scholarly awards are often given by scientific disciplinary and professional societies to recognize researchers for excellence in scholarly contributions to a field, and are important indicators as well as catalysts for professional development and career advancement. Through the Advancing Ways of Awarding Recognition in Disciplinary Societies

(AWARDS) Project, AWIS has investigated and found a significant, negative correlation between female gender and scholarly recognition (Lincoln, Pincus, Bandows Koster and Leboy, 2012; United States National Science Foundation, ADVANCE Grant #0930073). Subsequently, we developed a program to work with disciplinary societies on eliminating gender bias from their awards selection processes.

Scholarly Recognition Is Important

Scientists are often more motivated by curiosity and a desire for societal impact than by financial rewards and fame. Even so, scholars of organizational systems have shown repeatedly that employees value recognition, sometimes more than an increase in salary. Workplace satisfaction grows when people feel their contributions are valued, while dissatisfaction increases when they feel taken for granted. Scientists are no more immune to a desire to be appreciated than anyone else and most hope that their scholarly accomplishments will be valued, especially by peers (Frey, 2007). Such recognition can facilitate publication in top-ranked journals and potential funding from granting agencies.

For professionals in STEM, recognition can come from their workplace. Even more valued, however, is recognition from peers represented in disciplinary societies. Professional societies play crucial roles in the careers of STEM professionals: they provide grants and fellowships, publish journals, provide important opportunities for networking and professional development, and give awards for future research as well as recognition for past accomplishments. For many, loyalty to a professional society transcends changes in career status, employer, work sector, and geographic location. Societies are a constant throughout the arc of a STEM career, and recognition by one's disciplinary society carries considerable weight on a curriculum vitae. Such awards are listed prominently, and are considered during personnel actions.[1]

Scientific societies give awards for many reasons. Notably, they highlight the discipline by recognizing intellectual achievement and groundbreaking research. By giving awards, societies promote their fields of endeavor. Societies may also give awards to claim affiliation with thought leaders and to inspire younger generations. Awards may honor founders and pioneers; others thank members for service and commitment to advancing the field; some identify potential for greatness in rising stars. Others may be given simply because someone donated money to do so; thus giving awards in and of itself can be a fund-raising device. By giving awards for scholarly excellence, societies motivate others to achieve excellence as well.

Examining how professional societies create and bestow awards has provided insight into their implied value systems. If the demographics of awardees do not mirror the membership, the society is making a statement about which individuals are more highly valued. Recognizing women with awards shows that the society supports everyone's career, not just those of men. Giving awards to an array of individuals is an important signal that encourages diverse groups to engage with the organization as well. Societies that hope to attract more women and minorities are well advised to highlight the accomplishments of its members who are women and minorities. Societies that successfully engage a large pool of diverse members will incorporate more ideas and perspectives during its deliberations; following from a large body of literature on organizational effectiveness, such societies can expect to engage in better decision-making processes.

Some societies point out that they have awards reserved expressly for women. We applaud the intent of those programs, but suggest the practice is actually harmful. Setting aside certain awards for one demographic group implies that those individuals are not competitive enough to earn society-wide recognition. The paradoxical result is that women-only awards devalue women's accomplishments. Highlighting women's accomplishments carries the greatest impact when they receive awards alongside men. Our research shows that there are highly qualified women who deserve these awards, but whose accomplishments remain unrecognized. Ensuring that awards programs are equitable serves a society's mandate to serve its members objectively. Making sure that women's achievements are valued as much as men's and recognizing them appropriately is one way to patch the leaky pipeline, warm up the "chilly climate", and increase the retention of women in STEM professions.

THE AWARDS PROJECT AT AWIS

In the last few decades, the number of women earning doctoral degrees in STEM has increased dramatically, particularly in the life sciences and chemistry. Given this influx of women, one would expect a concomitant increase in the proportion of women being recognized for their scholarship in STEM fields, yet that did not appear to be the case.

In 2010, Dr. Phoebe S. Leboy, University of Pennsylvania Professor Emerita of Biochemistry, past president of AWIS, and passionate advocate for gender parity in STEM, began leading an effort to examine how scientific disciplinary societies recognize individuals for their scholarly achievements. This project was funded by the ADVANCE program of the National Science Foundation (NSF), which is designed to increase the representation and advancement of women in academic science and engineering careers. The two goals of the AWARDS Project (Advancing Ways of Awarding Recognition in Disciplinary Societies) were to assess the putative gender gap for scholarly recognition by societies, and then to work with disciplinary societies to achieve gender parity in their programs.

The first step was to solicit cooperation from scientific societies. Dr. Leboy enlisted seven "Pioneer Societies" (Table 9.1), encompassing a range of disciplines and having large memberships. Larger societies were targeted because they give more awards than small societies, which would allow richer data analysis. Furthermore, recognition from large societies tends to carry more weight and thus reaching gender parity for those societies would have substantial impact. The Pioneer Societies committed to provide data on their awards programs, and to participate in a workshop that would provide a platform for examining and possibly reforming their awards programs. Bolstered with those commitments, AWIS's proposal was successful in garnering external funding.

The first year of AWARDS was devoted to analyzing and gathering data. The results of those analyses confirmed that women were rewarded less frequently for scholarly achievements relative to men, and disproportionate to the available pool of senior women researchers (Lincoln, Pincus, Bandows Koster and Leboy, 2012). However, women appeared to be highly recognized for their "soft" contributions to a field, receiving more awards for service, mentoring, and teaching than would be expected given the proportion of women active in the field. In addition, Dr. Leboy examined the gender composition of leadership in the Pioneer Societies, and found that women were more likely to hold top leadership positions in the society than they were to earn scholarly awards. Table 9.1 below includes the number and proportion of women who received research and scholarly awards that are not gender specific between 2000 and 2010 (the database excluded both women-only awards and young investigator awards), relative to the proportion of women active in each respective discipline.

Table 9.1 Women researchers in AWARDS Pioneer Societies and scholarly awards

Society	Number of members	% of women members	Number of awards for scholarly excellence	% of women recipients for scholarly excellence (2000–2010)
American Chemical Society	164,000	21%	50	7.3%
American Geophysical Union	60,000	24%	10	11.9%
American Mathematical Society	30,000	24%	14	5.5%
American Statistical Association	18,000	33%	7	12.2%
Mathematics Association of America	20,000	23%	12	13.3%
Society for Industrial and Applied Mathematics	13,000	13%	12	4.7%
Society for Neuroscience	40,000	50%	7	36.4%

Source: Data published in Lincoln, Pincus, Bandows Koster and Leboy, 2012; Popejoy, Leboy, 2012.

The second phase of the AWARDS Project involved sharing data with the Pioneer Societies and urging them to assess their internal selection procedures for potential entry points of subjective evaluation and gender bias. AWIS hosted a workshop in 2010 to convene leaders from each of the seven Pioneer Societies (Table 9.1) and provided data as well as strategies for achieving equitable selection processes. During that workshop, role-playing and implicit association exercises helped participants understand the many issues surrounding gender parity in scholarly recognition (Greenwald, Nosek and Banaji, 2003). Each society was provided with the data for its own awards program, and ensuing discussions focused on best practices for mitigating the effects of implicit bias. Each society drew up a draft action plan for amending their procedures and sharing lessons learned with their colleagues.

In the following sections, we share major takeaway messages and best practices presented at the 2010 AWARDS workshop, outline the various action plans developed by society participants, and report on the ensuing results of their efforts.

BEST PRACTICES

Inoculate Selection Committee Members against Bias

The concept of implicit bias, which was developed over 50 years ago and is supported by decades of evidence, posits that regardless of the conscious ideas we espouse, we subconsciously hold notions about people that reflect the culture in which we were raised (Fazio, Sanbonmatsu, Powell and Kardes, 1986; Greenwald and Banaji, 1995; Greenwald, Nosek and Banaji, 2003). As social beings, all of us unconsciously categorize people into groups based upon stereotypes, as shortcuts to effective social interaction. Numerous studies have shown how implicit gender bias affects career progression. More women were admitted to symphony orchestras after screens were used to hide the identity of the musician auditioning from the selection committee (Goldin and Rouse, 2000). Studies in management have demonstrated that likeability and success are negatively correlated for women but not men (Ely, Ibarra and Kolb, 2011). Another study demonstrated that a company's initial public offering (IPO) is undervalued, and the CEO offered less executive compensation, when a woman is believed to be the CEO as opposed to a man (Bigelow, Lundmark, McLean Parks and Wuebker, 2011).

Most people are reluctant to accept that they are biased, and scientists in particular pride themselves on their impartiality. Yet scientists are humans raised in societies, and thus are subject to collective messages that suggest men are suited to science because they are independent and analytical whereas women are better suited to care-giving and co-operative enterprises. Using identical CVs but changing the name of the candidate to reflect either a man or woman, both men and women judged the "female" applicant for a psychology faculty position as less qualified than the "male" applicant (Steinpreis, Anders and Ritzke, 1999). Our own work with collaborators on the AWARDS Project has revealed that many scientists reject the idea that they are subject to such biases.

The significance of a recent study therefore cannot be overstated. Moss-Racusin et al. (2012) asked male and female science faculty in numerous disciplines and institutions to evaluate the résumé of a potential lab technician. Each rater was sent a résumé with identical credentials, and the résumés varied only in the assumed gender of the individual – half had male names and half had female names. Raters deemed the "female" candidate as less competent, a less desirable hire, less worthy of mentoring, and deserving of a lower starting salary than the "male" candidate. Most importantly, the implicit bias revealed in this study was observed for both male and female raters: we all have these subconscious biases. This study strongly implies that women are less likely to be supported in STEM careers owing to implicit bias from those in power.

Research also shows that when exposed to the concept of implicit bias, both men and women become "inoculated" and the effects of implicit bias are mitigated by their awareness of the issue (Abrams, Crisp, Marques, Fagg, Bedford and Provias, 2008). During our workshop for society leaders, we presented the evidence for implicit bias and then discussed strategies for mitigating its impact in awards programs. It is highly effective and beneficial to discuss the concept of implicit bias with members of awards selection committees before deliberation begins, to bring implicit (unconscious) bias out into the open and establish a goal of an objective review process.

Review and Update Awards Portfolio

Society leaders should think carefully about why they give awards, and whether their current portfolio of awards serves the goals and strategic plan of the society.

- **Names of awards**. Often societies name awards for pioneers and leaders in the discipline. We honor the intent to recognize such legacies, but named awards may give subtle cues that disadvantage women. For example, selection committee members might hesitate (subconsciously or consciously) to give an award that was named after a man to a female researcher.
- **Subdisciplinary awards**. Some awards, particularly those instituted several decades ago, may no longer reflect what is cutting-edge within the discipline, and some demographic segments of a

society's membership may not be eligible for such "relic" awards. Women tend to gravitate to newer and interdisciplinary specialties that may not have named awards. Thus reviewing the society's portfolio in light of shifting subdisciplinary trends can enhance recognition of diverse individuals.
- **Timing of awards**. Many awards attract very few nominations for various reasons, and societies should consider giving some awards less often to deepen the pool of candidates and increase the likelihood that award winners will reflect the demographics of the discipline.

Develop a Diverse Pool of Nominations to Reflect the Discipline

One critical step toward enhancing scholarly recognition of women is increasing the number and diversity of candidates from which committees select awardees. Having a large, diverse pool of nominations is crucial to achieve adequate representation of researchers in a discipline, and societies should be prepared to forego making awards if the pools are not sufficiently deep and diverse.

- Consider having a society-wide nomination or canvassing committee for all awards. This committee could be charged with identifying a diverse set of possible candidates, contacting senior members to encourage nominations, and developing criteria for acceptable candidate pool benchmarks that must be met before an awardee is selected.
- Use a variety of approaches to disseminate solicitations. Broad dissemination of awards programs is essential to develop a diverse pool. Historically, societies may have simply posted notices in print journals; today, however, online scientists are likely to miss such notices. Societies should employ dissemination strategies to reach those comfortable with online technology as well as those who prefer traditional methods of communication. Making sure multiple groups receive the solicitation is crucial.
- Use gender-neutral language. A subtle factor that can influence nominations is language. Small differences in how criteria are described can affect images of the ideal nominee. Words subconsciously associated with males include *exceptional*, *outstanding*, *brilliant* and *analytical* whereas words associated with female traits include *thorough*, *conscientious* and *methodical* (Schmader, Whitehead and Wysocki, 2007). Using a gender-neutral mix of words is likely to produce a more diverse pool of applicants. Committees

also should be alerted to the use of gendered language they may encounter in letters of recommendation.

- Define evaluation criteria explicitly before announcing the competition. Solicitation language should clearly reflect desired qualities the committee will evaluate, and also should delineate the components of a nomination package (CV, statements, nomination documents).
- Seek assistance from women's and minority committees and caucuses. Since one of the primary functions of these groups is to support career development, they can provide names of potential nominees, compile nomination packages, and contact well-respected senior colleagues to submit nominations.
- Carefully consider whether to allow carryover nominations. Some committees require fresh packages every year, while others allow nominations to carry over for a period of one to many years. The danger of allowing carryover nominations is that committees may be tempted to give awards for persistence rather than merit. We strongly recommend capping of the number of years an individual's dossier can be re-reviewed.

Evaluate Nominees Objectively

Selection committees are social organizations, and thus are subject to social influences. Acknowledging and possibly highlighting potentially biasing influences can produce more objective outcomes.

- **Committee diversity**. Having a diverse panel of individuals to solicit and review nominations may result in more diverse outcomes. We also recommend that societies have clear procedures for committee appointments, and make it easy for members to apply for such appointments. It is also worth mentioning that while it may be beneficial to have a diverse committee, some fields have particularly low numbers of women and minority researchers, whose time is already pressed by an overwhelming number of requests to sit on committees. It may be counterproductive to the careers of these individuals to participate in so much committee work. Therefore, the primary focus should be on training committee members to objectively evaluate nominees, regardless of who sits on a committee.
- **Define and prioritize desired qualities and qualifications**. When committees evaluate candidates, members should have a shared idea of what qualities are most important, and they should agree on the

weights of desired attributes before the nominations are evaluated. The committee must commit to consistently using their prioritized list of qualities, and we recommend a rubric with points assigned to those qualities.

- **Conflicts of interest**. Committee members should decide (or the society should provide guidancc) on what constitutes a conflict of interest (COI). Some that might trigger automatic recusals includes one's own student, postdoc, mentor, collaborators, and work colleagues. Other possible COIs can arise if the nominee has been trained or employed at the same institution as a committee member, if the committee member has reviewed manuscripts or proposals of the nominee, and others. Discussion of what constitutes a COI and how they should be handled is essential to ensure equitable outcomes, but most importantly a committee member with a determined conflict of interest should announce such conflicts to the entire committee and possibly be excluded from commenting or deliberation on that particular candidate.
- **Review of materials**. In some cases, a high volume of nominations may necessitate a division of labor for the review process. However, every nominee deserves to be evaluated by at least two committee members. Reviewers should fill out a standard rating sheet before the committee meeting commences to standardize the review process.
- **Planning for the committee meeting**. Many committees confer by phone or online rather than face to face. Although in-person deliberations would be ideal, situations where committee members meet remotely should incorporate mechanisms to allow visual cues (such as webcams). Additionally, it is crucial to allot adequate time for the deliberation, as rushed discussions rarely result in the best outcomes.
- **Committee interactions**. Committees are social groups, and social interactions affect group decisions. Agreeing upon a process to ensure that every member is heard promotes equitable outcomes, and generating a climate where everyone's opinion is heard and valued takes effort. The chair has an important responsibility to ensure that discussion focuses on accomplishments rather than personal qualities and institutional affiliations of the candidate, and for managing disruptive behavior, rudeness, or bullying among committee members. Repeatedly referring to standardized ratings of previously agreed-upon criteria can be especially helpful in directing an objective discussion.

- **Voting**. Anonymous voting encourages individual members to express their true preference rather than voting with the group, as influenced by political or social dynamics.

Equipped with this array of best practices, AWARDS Project Pioneer Societies evaluated their own awards programs and developed action plans to foster and fine-tune an objective selection process. AWIS continued to provide support and advice through the following 24 months to allow time for action plan implementation and a full annual cycle of awards. Throughout this time, we monitored their activities and invited all Pioneer Society representatives to return for a second workshop in 2012 to report on their reform efforts as well as outcomes of their most recent awards cycles.

OUTCOMES BY SOCIETY

American Chemical Society

The ACS is the largest scientific society in the world, and chemistry as a discipline has seen a dramatic increase in gender diversity: in 1982 only 16 percent of the PhDs in chemistry were given to women, while today that figure is over 40 percent. Between 2001 and 2010, women received 7 percent of scholarly awards given by the ACS.

The ACS action plan included broadening exposure of solicitations by publishing notices in society journals, as well as sending letters to technical divisions in industry, female chemists in the National Academy of Sciences, chemistry department chairs, and deans of science colleges. They also used their 2011 annual meeting as a platform to present information on the under-representation of women among nominees and awardees, and shared examples of letters with gender-neutral language. The ACS increased the proportion of women appointed to selection committees, partly by appealing to the membership for nominations of women. Selection committees were encouraged to learn about implicit bias and to review best practices, and were directed to emphasize the significance and impact of research during their discussions of candidates. Committee members were surveyed after their work to identify what selection criteria were used and how the discussions proceeded; they specifically were asked about the impact of candidate membership in the National Academy of Sciences (a highly coveted honor in the United States) on their decisions.

Results of the survey indicate that members of the National Academy had an edge in being selected for awards, but nominees with letters from National Academy members were not preferentially selected for awards. Most encouraging, in the 2011–2012 awards cycle, women constituted 7.7 percent of the nominees and 12 percent of the awardees.

American Geophysical Union

The AGU spans a number of disciplines, including meteorology, geology, and oceanography. The representation of women is highly variable across those disciplines, but overall women comprise 24 percent of the total membership. Winners of scholarly awards between 2000 and 2010 were 12 percent female.

The AGU action plan involved a major overhaul of their awards program to emphasize transparency. They changed or clarified several of their awards descriptions and categories to reflect current areas of research represented by the discipline. The AGU also developed and implemented conflict of interest policies, and required selection committee members to attend a two-hour training webinar. The webinar included screening of the AWIS-produced AWARDS Webcasts with information on implicit bias, as well as conflict of interest and best practices tips. To augment the pool of nominees, a canvassing committee was appointed and engaged in outreach to deans, department heads, and minority associations within their disciplines. The AGU also worked on a global evaluation rubric and analyzed potential networks of influence and connectivity between the committee members and nominees via the program UniPHY.

This ambitious action plan took more than a year to fully implement, and it may take several cycles of awards for its impact to become apparent. Indeed, the AGU leadership was disappointed that no woman won any scholarly, teaching, or service awards in 2011. However, the leadership itself is now highly diverse. More than half of the AGU Board of Directors is female, and the CEO, president-elect, and next-president-elect are all women. We remain optimistic that with commitment and support from these leaders, awards that the AGU bestows will become more equitable.

American Mathematical Society (AMS)

The AMS is a broad-based association encompassing every sub-discipline in mathematics. Women have historically been highly under-represented in mathematics, and now represent 24 percent of AMS members. Its leadership is now better balanced; nearly half of the Board of Directors is female, and women sit on both the Executive Committee and the Board of Trustees. Between 2001 and 2010 the AMS gave 5.5 percent of its scholarly awards to women.

Representatives from AMS forged an action plan for the society that included a diversity mandate on awards committees. The AMS developed a new prize oversight committee whose charge was to increase the number and diversity of nominations. Furthermore, the society created a Committee on Women in Mathematics to collect and disseminate data on recognition and to nominate outstanding women researchers for prizes.

Representatives reported that they experienced some resistance to the concept of implicit bias and many colleagues offered alternative explanations for the data showing underrepresentation of women among award-winners (e.g. motherhood, preference of women for teaching-intensive careers and service work over research). However, most were supportive of examining their awards selection processes for fairness.

At present, the AMS is considering appointing a canvassing committee to deepen nomination pools for their awards. They are also preparing a best practices handout for committee members, and they plan to revise web pages that describe the awards. Women constituted 6.3 percent of award winners in the most recent annual cycle, a slight increase from historical numbers.

American Statistical Association (ASA)

As the primary professional society for statisticians, the ASA has members working in industry, government, academia, and elsewhere. Women are well represented in the society at 33 percent, but only 12.1 percent of the ASA's scholarly awards went to women between 2001 and 2010. The ASA embraced the AWARDS program, and developed an action plan that included guidelines to increase transparency of the awards process. They also produced guidelines for awards committees about the significance of awards, composition of committees, strategies to diversify and deepen nomination pools, and training for committee members. These guidelines include best practices for selecting winners as well. They also updated the ASA website to provide greater access and bolster traffic to the awards solicitation page. Future plans include reviewing awards criteria for gender-biased language, and a review of the entire portfolio to ensure current awards reflect current scholarship.

In 2011, women won 18.2 percent of ASA's scholarly awards and a higher proportion of fellows were women in 2012. However, only one woman won a scholarly award in 2012, while all the mentoring and service awardees were female. These mixed results within a year of the workshop are not surprising, and continued monitoring will allow us to assess long-term impacts of the AWARDS program.

Mathematical Association of America (MAA)

The MAA has a primary emphasis on mathematics education. This society also stresses publication in its journals as a hallmark of excellence. With 25 percent women members, their awards have gone to only 12 percent women. The MAA was concerned that only 11percent of articles in their journals were senior-authored by women.

The MAA action plan was perhaps the most comprehensive of any Pioneer Society. They first appointed a task force to develop recommendations for committees. The Council on Prizes and Awards recommended that committee members be educated about implicit bias; clear guidelines and criteria be established and readily accessible on the MAA website; data on gender and ethnicity of awardees be reviewed regularly; and that procedures for evaluating nominees be reviewed. The task force developed a handout on implicit bias that is available online and distributed to all new committee members.

The MAA was particularly interested in gender parity for authors of papers published in their journals, because they view authorship as an important stepping-stone towards professional advancement and scholarly awards. They found that manuscripts senior-authored by women were less likely to be published, and thus the MAA has taken the bold step of instituting double-blind review for its journals,[2] because there is evidence that it reduces implicit bias against women (Budden, Tregenza, Aarssen, Koricheva, Leimu and Lortie, 2008). Thus, although only 7.1 percent of the scholarly awards went to women in 2012, we are optimistic that this change in the peer review process will have a significant impact over the long run.

Society for Industrial and Applied Mathematics (SIAM)

SIAM attracts membership from industry and academia; its members include mathematicians, engineers, and others who use mathematical approaches to applied problems. SIAM publishes 14 highly influential journals, and also has a prized Fellows program. At 13 percent of overall membership, women are poorly represented in these disciplines compared to other mathematical/statistical societies, and women have received only 5 percent of the scholarly awards from this society. Prior to 2012, 9.4 percent of the SIAM Fellows have been women.

SIAM responded to recommendations from the AWARDS workshop by reaching out to society leaders and publishing an article about the Project in their society newsletter. Topics concerning gender parity and the awards process were discussed at governing board meetings, and SIAM appointed a canvassing committee to increase the depth and diversity of nomination pools. They also provided guidance on diversity issues and implicit bias to selection committees.

Important changes in leadership ensued; women are now well represented among officer, board, and council positions, and they represent 15.6 percent of the editorial boards. Furthermore, the 2012 election cycle for SIAM fellows produced a nomination pool with 12 percent women, and the selected fellows were 20.1 percent women. Clearly, SIAM is closing in on gender parity in its awards programs as a result of their recent efforts.

Society for Neuroscience (SfN)

This large biomedical society has no dearth of women; indeed, women now earn half of the doctoral degrees in neuroscience. Even so, women were under-represented among the society's award winners: between 2001 and 2010 only 21 percent of SfN's scholarly awards went to women.

After attending the AWARDS workshop, SfN appointed a task force to develop recommendations for its action plan. One important action item was to ensure that selection committees have at least two women, a policy which is now firmly in place. Selection committees were asked to discuss the concept of implicit bias and were encouraged to show the AWIS AWARDS Webcasts to selection committee members. The society has also reviewed its solicitations to ensure gender-neutral language and published the identities of review committee members, which had previously been held in confidence. The task force emphasized their overall goal of increasing transparency and accountability, thereby convincing those skeptical of change.

These efforts clearly paid off. For the 2012 cycle, nominations for all awards shot up by 42 percent, and women were better represented in those pools. Furthermore, women won half of scholarly awards in 2011 and 42.9 percent in 2012.

AWARDS PROJECT EXPANSION

In 2011, AWIS invited additional scientific disciplinary societies to join the AWARDS Project, several of which approached AWIS because they were interested in improving their own awards parity. AWIS hosted a workshop in 2012 to introduce representatives from these new groups to the concept of implicit bias as well as to efforts undertaken by the Pioneer Societies. Data collection for this second cohort is ongoing and we will report longitudinal data from both cohorts in the coming years.

The second cohort of scientific societies involved in the AWARDS Project includes: American Astronomical Society (AAS), American Institute of Biological Sciences (AIBS), American Physical Society (APS), American Society of Plant Biology (ASPB), American Economic Association (AEA), Association of Psychological Sciences (APS), Botanical Society of America (BSA), Ecological Society of America (ESA), Entomological Society of America (ESA), Genetics Society of America (GSA), and Sigma Xi.

LESSONS LEARNED

Scientists are skeptical by nature, and require data to be convinced. Our work with disciplinary societies confirmed that in order to illustrate the concept of implicit bias, it was necessary to show society representatives data from *their* societies with relevant cohort data on availability pools. Some of the society representatives expressed difficulty convincing their colleagues who had not attended the workshop about the importance of these issues. Persistent messaging and strategic use of data-driven arguments are essential. It is also of note that society representatives were particularly receptive to messages about the science of implicit bias from AWIS, since the association has a strong relationship with the research community and a long history of advocacy for women's issues in STEM.

Working with professional societies presents special challenges for gender parity. Notable among those is turnover of key leaders. Most societies elect officers (who set policies) for one- to two-year terms; most of those officers with whom we originally worked on AWARDS rotated out of their positions during our project time frame. We had to expend considerable effort engaging new leaders in each society, and were not uniformly successful. Even so, we had engaged a cadre of members who were committed to gender parity and continue to work within their societies to further the goals of AWARDS.

FORWARD THINKING

The AWARDS Project is just a few years old so we do not yet have sufficient data to assess whether disciplinary society interventions have produced long-lasting change. Thus far, society leaders have expressed great appreciation for the project, and are enthusiastic about the potential of their action plans to promote gender parity and an objective selection process in their awards programs. Indeed, societies appear eager to learn from each other about best practices, and we think cultural transmission has high potential for achieving lasting change. To date, we have worked with a small number of large societies and hope that by vigorously disseminating information we can reach leaders of others societies as well. The AWARDS Project has some early successes in terms of changed procedures and policies, and we plan to disseminate those tools widely as well as expand the project to include many more societies in the coming years.

NOTES

1. This depends a great deal on work sector and employer. In general, such awards translate into other rewards in academic ranks and are less important in industry.
2. Most journals use single-blind reviews, in which reviewers know the identity of authors but authors do not know the identity of reviewers. A few journals use double-blind reviews in which author identity is removed prior to review.

DEDICATION

Dedicated in fond memory of Phoebe S. Leboy, PhD.

REFERENCES

Abrams, D., R.J. Crisp, S. Marques, E. Fagg, L. Bedford and D. Provias (2008), 'Threat inoculation: Experienced and imagined intergenerational contact prevents stereotype threat effects on older people's math performance', *Psychology and Aging*, **23**(4), 934–9.

Bigelow, L.S., L. Lundmark, J. McLean Parks and R. Wuebker (2011), 'Skirting the issues? Experimental evidence of gender bias in IPO Prospectus evaluations', *Journal of Management*, 42. Available at http://dx.doi.org/10.2139/ssrn.1556449.

Blickenstaff, J.C. (2005), 'Women and science careers: Leaky pipeline or gender filter?', *Gender and Education*, **17**(4), 369–86.

Budden, A.E., T. Tregenza, L.W. Aarssen, J. Koricheva, R. Leimu and C.J. Lortie (2008), 'Double-blind review favours increased representation of female authors', *Trends in Ecology and Evolution*, **23**(1), 4–6.

Ely, R.J., H. Ibarra and D.M. Kolb (2011), 'Taking gender into account: Theory and design for women's leadership development programs', *Academy of Management Learning & Education*, **10**(3), 474–93.

Fazio, R.H., D.M. Sanbonmatsu, M.C. Powell and F.R. Kardes (1986), 'On the automatic activation of attitudes', *Journal of Personality and Social Psychology*, **50**(2), 229–38.

Frey, B.S. (2007), 'Awards as compensation', *European Management Review*, **4**(8), 6–14.

Goldin, C. and C. Rouse (2000), 'Orchestrating impartiality: The impact of "blind" auditions on female musicians', *American Economic Review*, **90**(4), 715–41.

Greenwald, A.G. and M.R. Banaji (1995), 'Implicit social cognition: Attitudes, self-esteem, and stereotypes', *Psychological Review*, **102**(1), 4–27.

Greenwald, A.G., B.A. Nosek and M.R. Banaji (2003), 'Understanding and using the Implicit Association Test: I: An improved scoring algorithm', *Journal of Personality and Social Psychology*, **85**(2), 197–216.

Lincoln, A.E., S. Pincus, J. Bandows Koster and P.S. Leboy (2012), 'The Matilda effect in sciences: Awards and prizes in the US, 1990s and 2000s', *Social Studies of Science*, **42**(2), 307–20.

Morris, L.K. and L.G. Daniel (2008), 'Perceptions of a chilly climate: Differences in traditional and non-traditional majors for women', *Research in Higher Education*, **49**(3), 256–73.

Moss-Racusin, C.A., J.F. Dovidio, V.L. Brescoll, M.J. Graham and J. Handelsman (2012), 'Science faculty's subtle gender biases favor male students', *Proceedings of the National Academy of Sciences*, **109**, 16474–9.

Popejoy, A.B. and P.S. Leboy (2012), 'Is math still just a man's world?', *Journal of Mathematics and System Science*, **2**(5), 292–8.

Schmader, T., J. Whitehead and V.H. Wysocki (2007), 'A linguistic comparison of letters of recommendation for male and female chemistry and biochemistry job applicants', *Sex Roles*, **57**(7–8), 509–14.

Steinpreis, R.E., K.A. Anders and D. Ritzke (1999), 'The impact of gender on the review of the curricula vitae of job applicants and tenure candidates: A national empirical study', *Sex Roles*, **41**(7–8), 509–28.

PART III

Praxis: Changing extant discourse and practice about women in STEM careers

10. Gender equality interventions in the STEM fields: Perceptions, successes and dilemmas

Marieke van den Brink and Lineke Stobbe

INTRODUCTION

The under-representation of women in education and occupations in the STEM fields is a global phenomenon and is widely documented (Blickenstaff, 2005; Burke and Mattis 2007; Bystydzienski and Bird 2006; Etzkowitz, Kemelgor and Uzzi, 2000; Shen, 2013). Although some progress is made (Shen, 2013), women face challenges in almost all career phases and functions (EU, 2008; WOPI, 2011). Many explanations have been given, but less attention has been paid to studying the possibilities and activities towards changing this situation.

However, in recent years, the attention to evaluate gender equality interventions and programs has increased (Cronin and Roger 1999). Projects aiming at creating sustainable gender equality have proven complex (Acker, 2000; Benschop, Mills, Mills and Tienari, 2012; Bilimoria, Joy and Liang, 2008) and are accompanied by many dilemmas (Acker, 2000; Hearn, 2000; Nentwich, 2006). Although increasing numbers of governments, universities and research institutions seem convinced that gender equality policies are needed in order to increase the number of women in science, these policies continue to meet with open resistance, and they are considered highly controversial (Cockburn, 1991; Connell, 2006; Crosby et al., 2005; Hing et al., 2002; Van den Brink and Stobbe, 2014). Equality programs are often seen as the opposite of career policies based on merit and individual advancement (Bacchi, 1996; Noon, 2010; Tienari et al., 2009). Equality initiatives are then often framed in terms of dilemmas; with diversity, equal opportunities on the one hand, and merit and individual advancement on the other (Lamont, 2009). As a result, gender-equality programs are often received with ambivalence.

This study aims to advance the discussion on how gender interventions in organizations can become more effective by critically examining the discourses surrounding equality interventions in the STEM fields. The investigation of equality programs and the way in which they are perceived can develop our knowledge regarding the effectiveness (or lack of effectiveness) of such programs. These insights are urgently needed, particularly in light of the considerable effort and resources that contemporary organizations are channeling into gender equality programs, both in the Netherlands and worldwide (e.g. EU, 2008; MIT, 2011).

To illustrate the impact of perceptions on these programs, we draw upon empirical material on the evaluation of two formal gender equality programs in the Netherlands. The aim of these equality programs is to encourage women in the STEM fields to stay within the scientific community, and to increase the number of women professors. We begin by presenting the various ways that these efforts are perceived by academic men and women in the STEM fields, and will present three different and conflicting discourses: the "necessity" discourse, the "concern about quality" discourse, and the "stigmatization" discourse. These simultaneous discourses result in a dilemma in which equality programs are framed as helping women who are not able to make it on their own. However, in the discussion, we will show from a gender perspective that the support that men receive during their academic careers tends to be taken for granted, while women are expected to advance on their own in order to prove that they are sufficiently qualified. This double standard should be brought into the discussion to strengthen the legitimation of equality programs in academia.

EQUALITY MEASURES IN THE NETHERLANDS

Gender equality policies, interventions and measures are developed on an (supra-) national, institutional and departmental level. The most common measures to advance women in scientific careers are career training and development, stipends, scholarships and positions, networking and mentoring, and measures for life balance (Rees, 2002; Castano et al., 2010). A meta-analysis in Europe on policy measures distinguishes three areas where large-scale programs have been implemented over the last decade in Europe. First, career and professional development programs that involve all sorts of coaching and training activities that target the personal skill level of women in science. Then, a second bundle of measures offer stipends and position scholarships specifically geared to women in order to reach the next qualification level. And third, measures that include women support networks and mentoring. In this research, we will focus on the second bundle of measures.

The Dutch Context

In the Netherlands, the STEM disciplines are dominated by men, meaning that the upward mobility of women within the STEM fields is minimal (see Table 10.1). In science, women comprise a substantial proportion among PhD students (39 percent), but only 10 percent of all full professors are women (WOPI, 2012). In technology and engineering, the percentages are even lower.

Table 10.1 Percentage of women in the STEM fields

	PhDs	Postdocs	Assistant professors	Associate professors	Full professors
Science	39	32	23	14	10
Technology/ engineering	27	23	22	8	7

Source: WOPI 2012.

On a national and institutional level, several measures are introduced in the last ten years (2001–2011). In this article, I evaluate two gender equality measures.

FOM/f

The Foundation for Fundamental Research on Matter (FOM) promotes, coordinates, and finances fundamental physics research in the Netherlands. In 1999, the FOM/f program was initiated to encourage more women physicists to stay within the scientific community. The five-year program had a budget of over €4.5 million. In addition to providing financing and co-financing for research projects, academic positions, and prizes, the program aimed to increase the number of women in committees and boards and to facilitate the combination of work and care duties. In addition, a biennial workshop for women researchers was organized in order to provide an informal exchange of information and experiences. Since 2004, the program is not continued in the same way. FOM only funds a postdoc position for a maximum of three years spread over a period of at most five years. The condition is that the woman has organized a period of one to two years at a foreign institute in conjunction with this (not paid for by FOM).

Meervoud

This is a program from the Netherlands Organization for Scientific Research (NWO) that aims to increase the number of tenured positions held by women scientists in the earth and life sciences. The program is about creating temporary assistant professorship/lecturer positions linked to a guarantee for promotion to a permanent position as assistant professor within the university. The Netherlands Organization for Scientific Research provides a grant for staffing costs to cover a 0.6 FTE university position for a maximum of four years. They will also provide up to €6,000 a year in material costs. The program has been running since 2000, and was evaluated in 2010.

METHODS

To evaluate the programs, we draw on material from a research on the FOM/f program (Van den Brink and Stobbe, 2014). We used in-depth interviewing as the main source for our empirical data. In total, we interviewed 39 physicists: four policy-makers, 18 professors, six female postdocs and 11 female PhD students. We chose to interview only women postdocs and PhD students to discuss their experience with the FOM/f program. In the second program, Meervoud, we were also involved in the evaluation process and interviewed four beneficiaries and 12 academics in the earth and life sciences about the program (see Table 10.2).

Table 10.2 Summary of data collection methods

Program	Focus	Academic level	Discipline	Period	Data collection
FOM/f	Women only	All levels	Physics	1999–ongoing	Interviews, reports (Van den Brink and Stobbe 2014)
Meervoud	Women only	Postdoc to assistant prof	Earth and life sciences	2000–ongoing	Minutes of evaluation committee, interviews with women academics

Discourse Analysis

The technique of discourse analysis was employed to analyze the interview data (Fairclough and Wodak, 1997; Phillips and Hardy, 2002). This method enabled us to reveal the different discourses around the equality measures. My primary approach was to code and analyze our data into key categories of interest, themes and terms. We found that the general opinion about the program was positive, illustrated by the "necessity discourse". However, some male and female respondents showed ambivalent feelings about equality policies for women in general. They argued that hiring less qualified women would also be disadvantageous for the women themselves. In other words, both women and men highlighted the gender discrimination and gender segregation that such programs induce. Second, we looked for patterns of variation within the texts. This disrupts the apparent coherence of a piece of discourse, thereby allowing the analysis of two different processes at work: the text's internal inconsistencies and the way in which the discourse aims to combat alternative accounts (Tonkiss, 1998). We found that some interviewees were drawing on positive and critical discourses in the same interview. In other words, they were as well arguing for the program, and simultaneously arguing against the program. In dealing with and making sense of the inconsistencies in and between texts, we had to relate these three discourses to other dominant discourses within the Dutch (academic) society. This dimension gave me a way to identify a number of key discourses through which equality programs were constructed producing distinct perceptions. Gender equality programs were intertextually strongly related to the discourses of excellence, individualism, and merit. We will present and analyze these three discourses in the next section.

PERCEPTIONS OF GENDER EQUALITY POLICIES

In this section, we will analyze how men and women professors perceive the three gender equality programs and discuss the implications of these perceptions. We distinguish three discourses on the equality programs that are constructed in the function of existing academic practices and discourses about excellence, individualism and merit.

Necessity Discourse

The general opinion about the programs was positive: respondents believed that it was necessary to have special programs in order to encourage women to choose an academic career in the STEM fields. The respondents used in fact three lines of argumentation to underline why the programs were needed. Firstly and predominately, the respondents argued that the STEM community in the Netherlands neglects a great potential: *the labor potential argument*. Several respondents argued that a more balanced gender composition should be established within the STEM fields; it is not good for the field to neglect the potential of women and to have so few women faculty members. In addition, more women are needed to serve as examples that other women (older or younger) can follow. This observation reflects the role model argument. Appointing more women to academic functions was perceived as the only way to break the cycle of not having examples to imitate. Anna, a woman professor, stressed the importance of critical numbers and the visibility of women as potential candidates for professorships.

> I really stand behind the whole thing and I think they really made a difference. When this program started, I was the only woman physicist with a professor's title in the Netherlands and now there are like ten. In the first two years nothing happened so it is something of the last three years. What is also very good, I think, is that these women have become more visible. For example, there was a position for an associate professor and they hired a woman, and then she became more visible and suddenly she got a position as a full professor in Germany. If she hadn't received that position [as associate professor], she would probably never have received the [full] professorship (Anna, female professor).

Anna constructs accounts in which is argued that women are needed as role models in order to coach junior female academics and to teach them the academic culture and the rules of the game. In their view, female mentors can take into account the various career tracks that women might choose. Without a mentor who is encouraging and directive, she argues, women academics may find it hard to learn the strategies necessary to build an academic carrier (which men presumably already know).

The third line of argumentation stresses the different qualities that women bring to the workplace. Several respondents argued that women have a positive influence on the climate within the research group, and that women academics are "accurate", "systematic" and "hard working". This observation reflects the *difference* argument. Both men and women indicated that an environment with at least some women is not only more pleasant for women, but for most men as well. In their opinion, male-dominated environments are characterized by humor at the expense of women, by fierce internal and external competition, and by less social contact among colleagues. Adding more women would limit the prevalence of this culture. According to the respondents, it would make the workplace more friendly and collaborative, and therefore more attractive to both sexes.

The Concern about Quality Discourse

Several men, as well as a few women, argued that the equality programs were necessary, but, at the same time suggested that the programs might jeopardize the meritocratic values of their institutions or science as a whole.

> One should therefore always give priority to quality, in order to prevent less qualified women from getting positions that would otherwise have gone to men with better qualifications (Ben, male professor).

> Encouragement is okay, but I'm in favor of having equal quality requirements for both men and women. You just can't lower the standards for women. That would be disastrous for quality, as well as for the women we're talking about. If only two people apply – one man and one woman – and the man turns out to be the better candidate, you should just pick the man (Chris, male professor).

While convinced of the need to support special programs for women, both Ben and Chris were also critical towards the program, arguing that it might imply hiring or helping less qualified women, thereby lowering the quality standards within their institutions. They stressed that academic quality should be the first consideration when someone is hired, not gender. Although they acknowledged that it might be more difficult for women to build careers within the male-dominated STEM field, they considered that helping women during their careers could be unfair for men, or harmful for the quality of science. This meritocratic discourse was presented as a moral and normative standard that should be upheld and that it is closely related to the idea that everyone should be treated equally and should succeed on their own merit. They argued that everyone should conform to the objective quality standards and that women should earn their positions only according to their scientific excellence.

Within this quality discourse, gender is discursively practiced by considering the equality program as providing extra help to women who are unable to make progress on their own, in contrast to standard career trajectories, which they regard as meritocratic and gender-neutral (Bagilhole and Goode, 2001; Kvande and Rasmussen, 1994). In the STEM fields, there is a strong belief in objectivity and that research quality is easy to measure (Traweek, 1988, p. 162). Owing to this strong discourse of objectivity, measurement and neutrality, the influence of gender in scientific practice is often completely denied. Women are welcomed, but only when they conform to the existing image of the ideal scientist (Acker, 1992) and follow a strict career path that is translated into more than full-time devotion and willingness to spend long periods abroad (Van den Brink and Benschop, 2012a). The interviewees did not question the discourse of quality or excellence, nor did they address the masculine image of the ideal scientist or the ways in which they reinforced the masculine norm within their departments. Female faculty members were expected to be able to follow this masculine model with a little extra help, as provided through mentoring and coaching. The assumption was that women who follow this model will be as successful as their male colleagues. In this way, the different starting position of women is completely denied (Noon, 2010). The reluctance to consider gender as a relevant factor in career opportunities strengthens the notion that the university is an objective and gender-neutral institution in which meritocracy predominates.

The idea that equality programs are designed to help women in their scientific careers and that these programs can even be harmful for women persists among both men and women, will be discussed in the next section.

The "Stigmatization" Discourse

The perceptions that standards for the hiring and promotion of women faculty are lower than they are for male faculty were disquieting for women faculty members as well. Several women faculty members were somewhat reticent about the program and indicated that they had great difficulties with way in which they were being seen after having obtained special funds or chairs reserved for women.

> A special women's program will eventually turn against you. With these rules of promotion, you get dubious reactions. It is seen as an unjustified promotion of women. [...] Especially in case of a promotion, people easily conclude you were only promoted because you're a woman (Hester, female professor).

> Then other people will always use that as an argument to say that your research is not as good as the others (Inge, female professor).

These female interviewees expressed ambivalent feelings towards the equality program. Some women associated the equality programs primarily with unfairness and less as a way of rooting out the gender imbalance in the Dutch STEM field. They questioned whether they were hired because they were women, indicating that this tended to undermine their confidence. Others were hoping that people would eventually forget the source of their funding, so that they would lose the "stigma" that they had received upon being promoted through a special women's program. Other scholarly work confirmed that association with an affirmative action program can stigmatize beneficiaries (Heilman et al., 1997). For this reason, some of the respondents mentioned that they did not include the special funding in their résumés.

We also noticed that both women and men spoke very highly of women who had succeeded without special funds; in other words, they spoke highly of women who had done it on their own.

> A female staff member was appointed professor at the end of her career. I didn't believe that was completely just. She must have felt it wasn't completely due to her own efforts. With another female professor, it went more fairly. She is the icon of Dutch physics. She has reached this level completely on her own. So, whenever anyone tells me it is not possible for women faculty members to reach higher positions, she proves that it is (Johan, male professor).

The "Dutch icon" Johan is referring to, served as positive example to promote the scientific community's core belief of meritocracy. This woman who had not received help was showcased in order to demonstrate that women who were hard working and talented should be able to make it on their own. Female candidates who had managed to reach senior positions were scarce, however, and we noticed that the same names were mentioned repeatedly when interviewees related to "success stories". The exceptional position of these women within a male-dominated field attracts additional attention, and people tend to notice when they perform well. Benschop and Doorewaard (1998) introduced the concept of showpieces based on Kanter's token theory (1977). Showpieces are shown off, on the one hand to prove that there are equal chances and possibilities for women in the organization, and, on the other hand, to prove that women can be successful in top functions. Those who are included, but different from the male norm, become subject to hyper visibility (Essed, 2002; Van den Brink and Stobbe, 2009). These women are constantly used to show that gender equality exists and that women can make it on their own, as long they are qualified. Gender is practiced in this discourse as well, as equality programs are perceived as helping women who are deficient. Despite earlier considerations that women face barriers during their careers, the "best" female talents will rise anyway.

Therefore, they reinforce the ideal of the meritocracy and the norm that the best can make it on their own.

REFRAMING THE "GETTING HELP" DILEMMA

In this section, we will deconstruct the seemingly contradictory discourses surrounding the equality measures in the Netherlands, taking the dilemma as point of departure to reframe the contradictory connotations of equality programs. The central dilemma is that equality measures are seen as simultaneously necessary and harmful for science and scientific careers. It is necessary, as women need help in order to remain and build careers within the scientific community. It is harmful, as women who have received help also receive a "stamp" that can be quite difficult to lose. In addition, concerns were voiced that the program could result in hiring less qualified women. We call this situation the "getting help" dilemma in which equality programs are framed as helping women who are not able to make it on their own. This dilemma might restraint the universities, academic institutions and funding organizations from installing or continuing gender equality programs.

In our view, the "getting help" dilemma is caused by the normative discourse of meritocracy which is considered gender neutral. A meritocracy implies that only the merits of the individual scientist should count in the considerations regarding the hiring of new faculty members, not social identity categories as gender, race, class and age (Merton, 1973). In the views of both men and women academics, gender equality programs conflict with the ideals of the meritocracy (see also Deem, 2007; Lamont, 2009; Van den Brink and Benschop, 2012b). Reframing the "getting help dilemma" offers the possibility to nuance or even challenge the dominant and gender blind discourse of meritocracy. By highlighting the genderedness of scientific careers, we are able to illustrate the power structure under the dominant discourse of meritocracy by showing men's invisible support systems and the gendered construction of excellence.

Men's Support System

Members of the dominant group wish to preserve the impression of having earned their positions legitimately (Crosby et al., 2005). Male professors were most likely to believe that meritocracy operates in academia, and most tended to think that equality interventions undermine fair decisions. Male academics hardly ever acknowledged their privileged position and the structural advantages that they had received as a group. In two recent articles, we have argued that men also receive help during their academic careers, but this is hardly ever viewed as help (Van den Brink and Benschop, 2014; Van den Brink and Stobbe, 2014). Men give favors to each other and receive help through informal support systems. This is mostly observed by women.

> When men maintain their traditional mindset in which [they think] women are not so interested or they don't even think about it [the possibility of female candidates], they will take other men, because they have always known men in this profession. They know what men can do. Some day women will have children or whatever it is they think women do. If men do make a conscious effort to think 'she is a woman and she is equally good' or whatever, then I think that without thinking they would just take the man, because they think that they can rely more on the man – 'he is like me'. (Quote from female professor in STEM fields (Van den Brink and Benschop, 2014, p. 20).)

In this quote, the women professor argues that it is easier for men to identify with male faculty members and to provide them with additional support and encouragement. Several scholars have also documented that men tend to receive more encouragement to apply for positions through their male-support network (Bagilhole and Goode, 2001; Holgersson, 2013). The similar interests, shared communication styles, and the existing structure of informal networking create a strong support system (see also Katila and Merilainen, 1999, 2002). Men are helped, as they benefit from a "similar-to-me" effect, their similarity to "the proven success model" (Van den Brink and Benschop, 2014) as well as from the man-friendly work environment.

> Many committees exist of men only. Men might identify themselves easier with men. (Quote from male professor in the medical field (Van den Brink and Benschop, 2014, p. 50).)

In addition, Ibarra et al. (2010) found that women are less likely to receive sponsoring – in which the mentor goes beyond giving feedback and advice and uses his or her influence with senior members of the organization to advocate for the mentee. They argue that without sponsorship women are not only less likely than men to be appointed to top roles but may also be more reluctant to pursue a top position (p. 82). In our article (Van den Brink and Benschop, 2014), we argue that men academics support men candidates for professorial positions without much awareness that their support means the exclusion of women.

Women scientists thus have less scope within which to promote themselves, while we could assume that men support and assist other men in ways that advance their career goals. Women do not benefit from these support networks in the same way, so an equality program is installed to compensate for the structural disadvantage women encounter. Helping women by equality programs thus not automatically implies lowering the standards of excellence (see also Noon, 2010).

Academic Excellence as Gendered

The scientific standard of excellence has become objectified, and it is considered gender-neutral (Merton, 1973), especially in the context of natural sciences (Traweek, 1988). This was strongly voiced in the "concern about quality" discourse; in the end they favor "the best", and not "gender". Yet, our study supports the idea of feminist scholars that the definition of a good scientist implicitly favors men (Harding, 1986; Knights and Richards, 2003; Valian, 1998; Van den Brink and Benschop, 2012b). According to most respondents, a good scientist is highly motivated, a good communicator, and talented. At first glance, these characteristics appear to coincide with ideas about women (physicists). Although women are perceived as accurate, systematic, and hard working, they are also often seen as less confident. Some interviewees perceived women as better communicators, but also as less direct. At the same time, confidence and directness are needed to demonstrate high motivation and true skill in communication. According to the respondents, men perform better in this regard, although they are also characterized as lazier and more disorganized. Men make themselves visible by making noise and being self-confident, whereas women are not supposed to take center stage or exude self-confidence.

Studies on gender in academia show that the most important factors in the production (or reproduction) of gender inequality in universities and research institutes are related to the images of science, scientific practice, and the ideal scientist (Knights and Richards, 2003; Van den Brink and Benschop, 2012a). Particularly in male-dominated organizations (albeit not exclusively), hegemonic discourses are masculine discourses: discourses that assign higher value to men and masculinity. Several authors argue that science and (consequently) scientific institutions are overtly masculine, especially in those fields that are labeled as "hard" sciences, as in the case described in this study (Harding, 1986; Valian, 1998). In these contexts, masculinity and power are intertwined in such a way that men represent the standard; they naturally occupy the norm against which women's performance is measured. In other words, the attributes that are stereotypically labeled as masculine (e.g., technical ability, psychical strength, and goal-orientation) are valued more highly, and they are accepted as the natural norm. In real life, these attributes are perceived as innate, implying that they are perceived as inescapable and normal. As a result, Dutch women must be extremely talented and determined in order to pursue a career in the STEM fields. In summary, women are forced to fight certain images, while men do not. In fact, these images implicitly seem to favor men, as does the definition of quality that was discussed earlier. Although feminine qualities were valued by the interviewees, the image of the ideal scientist is still more geared towards men and masculinity. Again, the discourse of the meritocracy renders the masculine model of the ideal scientist invisible.

By showing men's support system and the gendered construction of excellence, we are able to reframe the "getting help" dilemma. Reframing the dilemma shows that the support that men receive during their academic careers tends to be taken for granted, while women are expected to advance on their own in order to prove that they are sufficiently qualified. In contrast, women's programs were visible and scrutinized, leading to the perception that women cannot succeed on their own merits.

CONCLUSION AND IMPLICATIONS

This chapter aimed to advance the discussion on how gender policies and interventions in organizations can become more effective by critically examining the seemingly contradictory discourses surrounding gender equality programs. We evaluated two formal gender equality measures in the Netherlands. When interviewing policy-makers and professors in depth about the program, a more complex picture emerged. Our respondents argued that it was necessary to have a special women's program in order to encourage women to pursue academic careers in the STEM fields, while simultaneously arguing that such a program might jeopardize the quality of research. Framing the results in terms of a "getting help" dilemma impedes the effectiveness of equality programs.

We identified an underlying gender practice that explains why the "getting help" dilemma exists for female academics, but not for their male counterparts. The support that men receive during their academic careers tends to be taken for granted, while women are expected to advance on their own in order to prove that they are sufficiently qualified. In contrast, women's programs were noticed, leading to the perception that women cannot succeed on their own merits. Scientists strongly relate to the discourse of the meritocracy, thereby overlooking the reality of a patriarchal support system, which helps men throughout their careers

(Bagilhole and Goode, 2001). Because neither men nor women question the fact that men receive continuous and frequent support and assistance throughout their careers, the situation remains unnoticed. One of the mechanisms of hegemony is the reduction of the socially constructed to the neutral and the normal. Men and women should realize that help and good quality can co-exist, as they obviously do for men. Moreover, special programs for women are based on the fact that women currently experience disadvantages in their scientific careers (Noon, 2010). Such programs are designed to compensate for the effects of those disadvantages; they could therefore be perceived as "getting even" instead of "getting help" (see also Noon, 2010). At this point, women need "help" and if we do not "help" them, their talent will be largely wasted.

In conclusion, the getting help dilemma could be a helpful "instrument" for interventions and training, as they allow us to reflect on current practices and to begin the process of questioning certain tacit rules and acting otherwise. Many universities in the Netherlands and beyond are captured by the dilemma of equality programs. They do want to increase gender equality in their departments, especially in the higher echelons, but are reticent because of the stigmatization and alleged quality loss of such programs. Training male and female senior academics to function as agents of change to overcome stereotypical thinking on gender interventions would provide a starting point. To increase the success chance of these programs, it is important that "champions" such as male and female research directors, deans, and policy-makers bring another discourse into the discussion – the invisible support of men and gender equality programs to counter the advantages men receive from this informal support. This could lead to a broader legitimation of equality programs in academia, also among recipients of these programs. Effective gender equality policies should therefore be informed by knowledge about these gender practices, and they should aim to display and change them.

REFERENCES

Acker, J. (1992), 'Gendering organizational theory', in A.J. Mills and P. Tancred (eds), *Gendering Organizational Analysis*, London: Sage, pp. 248–60.

Acker, J. (2000), 'Gendered contradictions in organizational equity projects', *Organization*, **7**(4), 625–32.

Bacchi, C.L. (1996), *The Politics of Affirmative Action: "Women", Equality and Category Politics*, London: Sage.

Bagilhole, B. and J. Goode (2001), 'The contradiction of the myth of individual merit, and the reality of a patriarchal support system in academic careers: A feminist investigation', *The European Journal of Women's Studies*, **8**(2), 161–80.

Benschop, Y. and H. Doorewaard (1998), 'Covered by equality: The gender subtext of organizations', *Organization Studies*, **19**(5), 787–805.

Benschop, Y., J.H. Mills, A. Mills and J. Tienari (2012), 'Editorial: Gendering change: The next step', *Gender, Work & Organization*, **19**(1), 1–9.

Bilimoria, D., S. Joy and X. Liang (2008), 'Breaking barriers and creating inclusiveness: Lessons of organizational transformation to advance women faculty in academic science and engineering', *Human Resource Management*, **47**(3), 423–41.

Blickenstaff, J.C. (2005), 'Women and science careers: Leaky pipeline or gender filter?', *Gender and Education*, **17**(4), 369–86.

Burke, R.J. and M.C. Mattis (2007), *Women and Minorities in Science, Technology, Engineering and Mathematics: Upping the Numbers*, Cheltenham, UK and Northampton, MA: Edward Elgar.

Bystydzienski, J.M. and S.R. Bird (2006), *Removing Barriers: Women in Academic Science, Technology, Engineering, and Mathematics*, Bloomington, IN: Indiana University Press.

Castaño, C., J. Martían, S. Vázquez and J.L. Martíanez (2010), 'Female executives and the Glass Ceiling in Spain' *International Labour Review*, **149**(3), 343–60.

Cockburn, C. (1991), *In the Way of Women: Men's Resistance to Sex Equality in Organizations*, Ithaca, NY: Cornell University Press.

Connell, R. (2006), 'The experience of gender change in public sector organizations', *Gender, Work & Organization*, **13**, 435–52.

Cronin, C. and A. Roger (1999), 'Theorizing progress: Women in science, engineering, and technology in higher education', *Journal of Research in Science Teaching*, **36**(6), 637–61.

Crosby, F.J., A. Iyer and S. Sincharoen (2005), 'Understanding affirmative action', *Annual Review of Psychology*, **57**, 585–611.

Deem, R. (2007), 'Managing a meritocracy or an equitable organization? Senior managers' and employees' views about equal opportunity policies in UK universities', *Journal of Education Policy*, **22**(6), 615–36.

Essed, P. (2002), 'Cloning cultural homogeneity while talking diversity: Old wine in new bottles in Dutch work organizations?', *Transforming Anthropology*, **11**(1), 2–12.

Etzkowitz, H., C. Kemelgor and B. Uzzi (2000), *Athena Unbound: The Advancement of Women in Science and Technology*, Cambridge: Cambridge University Press.

EU (2008), *Mapping the Maze: Getting More Women to the Top in Research*, Brussels: DG-Research, European Commission.

Fairclough, N. and R. Wodak (1997), 'Critical discourse analysis', in T. van Dijk (ed.) *Discourse Studies: A Multidisciplinary Introduction (Vol. 2. Discourse as Social Interaction)*, London: Sage, pp. 258–84.

Gersick, C.J.G., J.M. Bartunek and J.E. Dutton (2000), 'Learning from academia: The importance of relationships in professional life', *Academy of Management Journal*, **43**(6), 1026–44.

Harding, S. (1986), *The Science Question in Feminism*, Ithaca, NY: Cornell University Press.

Hearn, J. (2000), 'On the complexitiy of feminist intervention in organizations', *Organization*, **7**(4), 609–24.

Heilman, M.E., C.J. Block and P. Stathatos (1997), 'The affirmative action stigma of incompetence: Effects of performance information ambiguity', *Academy of Management Journal*, **40**, 603–25.

Hing, L.S.S., D.R. Bobocel and M.P. Zanna (2002), 'Meritocracy and opposition to affirmative action: Making concessions in the face of discrimination', *Journal of Personality and Social Psychology*, **83**(3), 493–509.

Holgersson, C. (2013), 'Recruiting managing directors: Doing homosociability', *Gender, Work & Organization*, **20**(4), 454–66.

Ibarra, H., N.M. Carter and C. Silva (2010), 'Why men still get more promotions than women', *Harvard Business Review*, **88**(9), 80–126.

Kanter, R.M. (1977), *Men and Women of the Corporation*, New York: Basic Books.

Katila, S. and S. Merilainen (1999), 'A serious researcher or just another nice girl? Doing gender in a male-dominated scientific community', *Gender, Work & Organization*, **6**(3), 163–73.

Katila, S. and S. Merilainen (2002), 'Metamorphosis: From "nice girls" to "nice bitches": Resisting patriarchal articulations of professional identity', *Gender, Work & Organization*, **9**(3), 336–54.

Kelan, E.K. (2009), 'Gender fatigue: The ideological dilemma of gender neutrality and discrimination in organizations', *Canadian Journal of Administrative Sciences/Revue Canadienne des Sciences de l'Administration*, **26**(3), 197–210.

Knights, D. and W. Richards (2003), 'Sex discrimination in UK academia', *Gender, Work & Organization*, **10**(2), 213–38.

Kvande, E. and B. Rasmussen (1994), 'Men in male-dominated organizations and their encounter with women intruders', *Scandinavian Journal of Management*, **10**(2), 163–73.

Lamont, M. (2009), *How Professors Think: Inside the Curious World of Academic Judgement*, Cambridge, MA: Harvard University Press.

Merton, R.C. (1973), *The Normative Structure of Science*, Chicago, IL: University of Chicago Press.

MIT (2011), *A Report on the Status of Women Faculty in the Schools of Science and Engineering at MIT, 2011*, retrieved from http://web.mit.edu/newsoffice/images/documents/women-report-2011.pdf.

Moss-Racusin, C.A., J.F. Dovidio, V.L. Brescoll, M.J. Graham and J. Handelsman (2012), *Science Faculty's Subtle Gender Biases Favor Male Students*. Proceedings of the National Academy of Sciences.

Nentwich, J. (2006), 'Changing gender: The discursive construction of equal opportunities', *Gender, Work & Organization*, **13**(6), 499–521.

Noon, M. (2010), 'The shackled runner: Time to rethink positive discrimination?', *Work, Employment & Society*, **24**(4), 728–39.

Phillips, N. and C. Hardy (2002), *Discourse Analysis: Investigating Processes of Social Construction*, Thousand Oaks, CA: Sage.

Rees (2002), *National Policies on Women and Science in Europe*, Office for Official Publications of the European Communities, European Commission: The Helsinki Group on Women and Science.

Shen, Helen (2013), 'Mind the gender gap', *Nature*, 495, 22–24.

Tienari, J., C. Holgersson, S. Meriläinen and P. Höök (2009), 'Gender, management and market discourse: The case of gender quotas in the Swedish and Finnish media', *Gender, Work & Organization*, **16**(4), 501–21.

Tonkiss, F. (1998), 'Analysing discourse', in C. Seale (ed.), *Researching Society and Culture*, London: Sage.

Traweek, S. (1988), *Beam Times and Life Times: The World of High Energy Physicists*, Cambridge, MA: Harvard University Press.

Valian, V. (1998), *Why So Slow: The Advancement of Women*, Cambridge, MA: MIT Press.

Van den Brink, M. and L. Stobbe (2009), 'Doing gender in academic education: The paradox of visibility', *Gender, Work & Organization*, **16**(4), 451–70.

Van den Brink, M. and L. Stobbe (2014), 'The support paradox: Overcoming dilemmas in gender equality programs', *Scandinavian Journal of Management*, **30** (2), 163–74.

Van den Brink, M. and Y. Benschop (2012a), 'Slaying the seven-headed dragon: The quest for gender change in academia', *Gender, Work & Organization*, **19**(1), 71–92.

Van den Brink, M. and Y. Benschop (2012b), 'Gender practices in the construction of academic excellence: Sheep with five legs', *Organization*, **19**(4), 507–24.

Van den Brink, M. and Y. Benschop (2014), 'Gender in academic networking: The role of gatekeepers in professorial recruitment', *Journal of Management Studies*, **51** (3), 460–92.

Van Eerd, A., N. Van der Marel, P. Rudolf and E. De Wolf (2009), *Women in Physics in the Netherlands: Recent Developments*, paper presented at the TIUPAP International Conference on Women in Physics.

WOPI (2012), *Numbers of University Staff*, retrieved 10.03.2013 from http://www.vsnu.nl/web/show/id=93919/langid=43/.

11. Dare to care: Negotiating organizational norms on combining career and care in an engineering faculty

Channah Herschberg, Claartje J. Vinkenburg, Inge L. Bleijenbergh and Marloes L. van Engen

The demands inherent to combining career and care responsibilities experienced by growing numbers of academics have been well documented (King, 2008; Schiebinger, Henderson and Gilmartin, 2008). The combination of an academic career and care is complicated by the notion of the ideal academic as "someone who gives total priority to work and has no outside interests and responsibilities" (Bailyn, 2003, p. 139), which still appears to be the existing norm within academia (e.g., Bleijenbergh, Van Engen and Vinkenburg, 2013). Academics are typically described as "committed solely to scientific discovery and, [...] in an androcentric manner, thought free from the requirements of self-care and the care of others" (Aulenbacher and Riegraf, 2010, p. 66).

Norms are an important component of organizational culture (Schein, 1990). We define them as manifestations of "shared, taken-for-granted implicit assumptions that a group holds and that determines how it perceives, thinks about, and reacts to its various environments" (Schein, 1996, p. 236). Norms influence organizational behavior as they take descriptive and prescriptive forms in determining "how we do things around here" (Sun, 2008), and enable organization members to anticipate each other's actions (Feldman, 1984). Members need to learn what the existing organizational norms are, usually by means of socialization (Wiener, 1982), and how to cope with them (Schein, 1990).

Poelmans (2012) developed a multilayered model or typology of different ways of dealing with organizational norms on combining career and care. The first type or intra-individual level of dealing with norms is to become aware of them so that one can decide how to confront them, referred to as norm nomination (Poelmans, 2012). Recognizing or becoming aware of norms is complicated, because norms often remain implicit and may have been internalized during organizational socialization (Ashforth and Mael, 1989). It may therefore require direct confrontation with individuals that do or think differently, or a change in family status (e.g., becoming a parent, getting divorced) for this type of intra-individual nomination to take place. The second type or inter-individual level as suggested by Poelmans (2012) is norm navigation, which means actively coping with norms. This process of coping can take different forms, such as conforming to, creatively and subtly moving around, or openly rebelling against norms (Schein, 1990). The final type or inter-group level of dealing with norms according to Poelmans' model (2012) is the development of new norms. Changing societal or organizational norms can take the form of the adoption of innovations, with early adopters openly navigating and creating new norms and laggards hanging on to the existing norm for as long as viable (Rogers, 1995).

Women, in academia and elsewhere, still predominantly bear the burden of care responsibilities. Once they have children, they face expectations of diminished career commitment, despite their growing presence in academic positions (King, 2008). Hence, the main focus of studies on combining academic careers with care responsibilities has been on women (e.g., Fletcher, Boden, Kent and Tinson, 2007), arguing that women are disadvantaged, especially those who have family involvements (Grant, Kennelly and Ward, 2000). Even though most scholarly attention goes to caring for children, we also mean care responsibilities to include the responsibility of caring for other (extended) family members and other dependants (Van Engen, Vinkenburg and Dikkers, 2012).

Owing to an increasing number of dual earner couples among academics (e.g., Schiebinger et al., 2008), the lived experiences of both men and women in academia may no longer match the ideal academic norm of having no care obligations. The rise of dual earners among academics matches current demographic developments common to industrialized nations, such as increasing female labor force participation, low fertility, and low mortality, which makes combining career and care an increasingly important social issue (Van Engen et al., 2012). This social issue concerns both men and women, as Fox, Fonseca and Bao (2011) found that both women and men scientists in nine US research universities reported work interfering with family. The masculine culture of academia also puts a burden on men who do not (want to) meet the androcentric characteristics of the ideal academic. Liebig (2010) presents one of the very few studies of fathers in academia, which clearly illustrates that active fathers struggle when trying to meet organizational norms. This struggle may be caused by the general expectation that men, in contrast to women, will remain dedicated to work even after the birth of a child. Fathers that do not adhere to these expectations (e.g., by asking for reduced hours) are more likely to be confronted with stigmatization and career penalties than mothers (Coltrane, Miller, DeHaan and Stewart, 2013, Williams, 2000).

Exploring the way men and women in academia cope with organizational norms on combining career and care is of importance in the domains of science, engineering, and technology (SET) as they are traditionally more tied to notions of masculinity than other domains such as arts, social sciences, and humanities (Barnard, Powell, Bagilhole and Dainty, 2010; Sagebiel and Vázquez-Cupeiro, 2010). In SET, the symbolic masculinity of the ideal academic is tied to the numerical dominance of men because of women's underrepresentation at all hierarchical levels (Britton, 2000), which renders combining career and care even more difficult than in other academic disciplines. Engineering is recognized traditionally as a scientific discipline that is practically devoid of connotations with femininity (Faulkner, 2000, 2007). In the context of academia, organizational norms are cross-cut by professional or occupational norms which may differ by academic discipline (Anderson, Ronning, De Vries and Martinson, 2010; Braxton, 1990). Since earlier research showed the norm of the ideal academic to be fluid between different disciplines (Bleijenbergh et al., 2013), the content of the organizational norms on combining career and care leaves room for exploration.

Moving beyond the issue of individual strategies for dealing with work–family conflict, in this chapter we explore organizational norms on combining career and care. Rather than considering work–family conflict as a given, we explore how academics in an engineering faculty relate to these norms by recognizing, debating, and challenging them. We inductively analyze transcripts of interviews and a focus group with academic staff in different hierarchical positions. We first illustrate how academics implicitly or explicitly address norms on combining career and care within the engineering faculty. Second, we explore how academics debate the nature and existence of the prevailing norms as well as try to figure out whether or not one can deviate from them. Third, we explore the conditions under which academics are able to navigate around these norms. Fourth, we show how a number of academics make a first step in changing the norms. Finally, we discuss how our analysis can advance theory building and research about organizational norms on combining career and care. In conclusion, we describe how our insights and our research approach can contribute to making academia a more inclusive workplace.

METHOD

Procedure

The study described in this chapter is part of an action research project conducted at two faculties of a technical university in the Netherlands (Van Engen, Bleijenbergh and Vinkenburg, 2010). We gained access to the organization because the executive board of the university commissioned the study of the representation of women and men academic staff at different hierarchical levels, and to gain insight in the recruitment, selection, performance evaluation, promotion, and retention processes that led to inequalities between women and men. We were explicitly invited to provide not only insights but also concrete suggestions for policy development and implementation, in order to support the executive board in meeting its goals for improvement in the representation of women at all hierarchical levels. The multi-method project entailed an analysis of data from the personnel information system, a survey, interviews, and focus groups. This chapter uses data from interviews and a focus group, as explained below.

The action research nature of this project materialized in a final series of three workshops organized for each faculty separately, with the dean, department chairs, and the HR director, i.e., the decision-makers. During these workshops, which were led by a professional facilitator, participants were first given the opportunity to confirm or alter the findings we presented. Next, all participants jointly deepened their insights into these findings and came up with possible intervention practices on which there was consensus among participants. These evidence-based recommendations were presented in a final written report (Van Engen et al., 2010) and an oral presentation to the executive board of the university, and are currently in various stages of implementation.

For this chapter, in order to analyze how academics relate to norms on combining career and care, we used data collected by interviews and a focus group at the faculty of engineering. In 2009, the faculty of engineering employed 684 academics of which 17.7 percent were women. Of the 55 full professors, 5.2 percent were women. The selection of the interviewees and focus group participants was made in cooperation with the HR departments of the faculties. Selection criteria reflected a small but strategic sample of women and men academics working at different hierarchical levels in the engineering faculty (the dean, full professors, associate professors, assistant professors, post doctoral researchers, and one academic that had recently left the university), both from Dutch and non-Dutch descent, from different ages, and with and without children. In alignment with the goal of the research project, women were purposefully oversampled.

Seven semi-structured interviews were conducted within this faculty by three of the authors in 2009 and 2010. The interviews addressed a wide range of issues related to the professional and personal lives of the academics. The interviews were conducted either in Dutch or in English (depending on the preference of the interviewee) and lasted approximately one and a half hours. To perform a member check of the preliminary findings, we performed a two-hour focus group with four other academics of the same strategic sample (three women and one man) in 2010. During the focus group meeting, we presented our preliminary findings in statements to the participants, which allowed them to confirm or alter the analysis we presented. The same researchers who performed the interviews also led the focus group. The interviews and the focus group were recorded on tape, transcribed verbatim, and inductively coded on the basis of sensitizing concepts (Corbin and Strauss, 2008) that were derived from the conceptual model of Poelmans (2012).

Framework of Analysis

As sensitizing concepts for our analysis we used the three types of coping with norms about combining career and care distinguished by Poelmans (2012): norm nomination, norm navigation, and new norm creation. These three concepts supported us in identifying different ways men and women related to the norms on combining career and care in the organization. In analyzing the data, we were struck by how the (previously implicit) norm of not talking about care was first recognized, then debated, and in some cases challenged over the course of an interview or the focus group. Especially the lively debate on the organizational norm in the member check focus group motivated us to scrutinize potential ways of dealing with organizational norms as well as possibilities for changing them. As a result of the different ways of coping with norms about career and care that we found in the data, we propose a refinement and adaptation to the existing typology. In addition to the types distinguished by Poelmans (2012), our study spurred an additional, mainly inter-individual type of dealing with norms, which we have labeled "norm negotiation". Norm negotiation implies debating the existence and nature of the norm, as well as possible room to deviate from it, which takes a different form than nomination or navigation.

RESULTS

1. Nominating Norms

The first theme we identified in our analysis was nominating norms: recognizing or naming the existing norm. Our data showed that academics are or became aware of the norm that care is not a topic of conversation within the engineering faculty. For some of them the norm was self-evident. When we asked a woman associate professor about the support she experienced from colleagues in combining career and care she replied: "It's none of their business I think" (Interviewee 1, woman). Others too recognized the norm as self-evident, but were able to identify these explicitly as "a norm". In the next excerpt a woman assistant professor actively reflects upon this experience. She becomes aware that the joint experience of combining work and care is not a topic to discuss:

> [...] I suppose that for each one of us, the partner is also working. So combining private life and work is an issue for everyone, I think. Um, so supposedly that should yes, in itself um, yes, be a kind of a connection between um all the members of staff, let's say it that way, however I haven't experienced it. [...] But I realize now, actually everyone has a partner who works, but that's never a topic.
>
> *Okay. You don't talk about it?*
>
> No, no.
>
> *Now I understand.*
>
> So the communication is mainly content based (Interviewee 2, woman).

Evidently, during the interview the academic realizes ("I realize now") how shared the experience of combing work and care in fact is ("that should yes, in itself um, yes, be a kind of connection between um all the members of staff"). At the same time she realizes the issue is not discussed at all ("that's never a topic"). Conversations by and large are based on the content of research. In the following excerpt a man assistant professor is aware of the organizational norm that a career in academia has primacy over all aspects of life. He explicitly states that deviating from the norm has a penalty and one should therefore be careful not to reveal if one personally does not support that norm. He literally calls that "stupid".

> *[...] so colleagues around you make different choices also?*
>
> Yes, I noticed that they often value a career more than I want to. Actually, yes however you should not say this out loud, a career is not of a very high importance to me, like I said, what do you expect? That, yes, you should enjoy it, it should give you satisfaction, a little appreciation of others is also nice. But that you are working in a harmonious team and that together you accomplish something and much less that um who will be, as quickly as possible, the boss of as many people as possible. Then I could have made different choices.
>
> *Yes, but you're also saying that you should never say it out loud, so that you think that is important. You have that in mind but you're not gonna say I think that is important, well maybe you will.*
>
> Yes, it is stupid in an organization like this to say out loud that you want to do something in moderation and um that it is not your highest goal. Well that is my impression (Interviewee 6, man).

When we disclosed our interpretation of the interview findings that care is not a conversation topic within the faculty, the focus group participants started to consider and discuss this norm. The next excerpt shows that one of the focus group participants immediately agreed with this interpretation whereas others asked for clarification before realizing that this is a norm that actually exists within the faculty.

> *Researchers: At [faculty], family is not a conversation topic amongst colleagues.*
>
> Participant (woman) B: I can agree on that.
>
> *Researcher A: [Name participant] can agree on that.*
>
> Participant (woman) C: You receive this feedback from people. So I wonder whether it is just a remark or is it a slight complaint they're making, or? That's why I wonder, is it an issue?
>
> *Researcher A: No, it is not a complaint. This is what we found very poignant.*
>
> *Researcher B: It struck us as interesting. That several people mentioned it. Well, they mentioned it, they observed it, so.*
>
> *Researcher A: They said things like "no, no we don't discuss that". And for us that was new.*
>
> Participant (man) A: Is it family or personal interest?

Researcher B: Family.

Researcher A: We have been discussing that. But we found that personal interests with regard to hobbies were discussed. So we thought we should call it family. Because it's about family relations; most often partners, children, or parents.

Participant (woman) C: Why did you find it striking? Sorry, we're now asking questions to you. Why did you find it striking?

Researcher A: Um because I'm also working at a university in [city]...

Participant (woman) C: And you discuss it?

Researcher A: and we discuss family um I think every lunch break.

Researcher B: At the coffee machine. Very often.

Participant (woman) C: So it is like a different culture or something?

Researcher A: That's right. So that's where the point of amazement began. So that's why of course also why we put it in a statement. So this is typically.

Participant (woman) B: I can agree on that because I also worked at an academic medical centre for a long time [...] for one day a week in [city], at the [organization] and I observed that there family is more often discussed than it is here.

Participant C first becomes aware of the existing norm when the researchers reveal their findings. She questions whether this is an issue at all and why the researchers experience the findings as striking. Apparently, the norm is so deeply embedded in the organization that to her not talking about family is not out of the ordinary.

These examples illustrate that in the dialogue with the researchers, academics become aware that even though nearly all academic staff combines career and care, it is not a topic of conversation in the workplace: they recognized and named the organizational norm.

2. Negotiating Norms

In the interviews some academics mentioned the existence of the organizational norm on combining career and care, subscribing to the implicit assumption that one does not talk about care. In their conversations with the interviewers and in the focus group, the participants explored the room for when is it allowed to talk about care and with whom.

There are instances when family issues can be discussed with colleagues, as in the example of two non-Dutch women researchers who share an office and both recently had a baby. As disclosed by one of the women:

> *And in your particular case, being a PhD student who is also a parent. Do you experience support there from your colleagues?*
>
> Yes, we're lucky, I'm sharing an office with a woman who is now postdoc and has a baby who is … She's not a baby any more, she's a [toddler]. She is one and a half years old. So she just went through everything and now she knows what, yes she can give me advice what to do. And she's also a foreigner so she, probably it's also helping because um for Dutch people many things are obvious and you, if you experience that for the first time, then it's a bit different (Interviewee 5, woman).

The woman academic expressed that she discusses family life with a colleague that has been in the same situation. Implicit is that the separate space for discussing the issue is the shared office. The same is the case for a man academic who experienced support from one man colleague in the same research group who was also in the same life phase:

> *And do you experience support from your colleagues? In your career?*
>
> From one direct colleague certainly. I am under the impression that we give each other that support, so to say. We are also about in the same phase, so that is possible. From others a bit less but I do not actively seek out for them, so um.
>
> *And the direct one, does this person work in your group too?*
>
> Yes.
>
> *Yes, he is a man as well?*
>
> Yes, he is a man as well (Interviewee 6, man).

These examples reaffirm the nominated norm that one does not talk about family issues, but also show that there is space for deviating from the dominant norms on combining career and care in the proximity of the same lab group or in the seclusion of a shared office for individual, yet shared deviations from the norm. The data also illustrates negotiations of the norm in relation to supervisors as the next quote reveals:

> *But do you also experience social-emotional support from them [two promoters]?*

> Yes. Because my professor, […] promoter, he knows that I'm alone here and also he knows that I don't have much friends here. So if I have any family problems as such, like once my father had a heart attack. So that time I went and I told him I could not work, because I was totally disturbed. Because I'm more attached to my family […] I could not work anymore. So he gave me holiday as such. […] So he's more supportive in my personal life (Interviewee 3, woman).

Noteworthy is the situation in which this academic asks for support in combining career and care. Her circumstances were quite extraordinary (living and working abroad, having a father living in another continent who had a heart attack) and in this extreme situation, family could be a topic of conversation. Again, in the separate space of an interaction between supervisor and subordinate and under extreme conditions, the issue of family life could be a conversation topic.

Interestingly, the focus group members too, once they had nominated the norm, started negotiating:

> Participant (woman) A: So then let me ask you whether you discuss your family with *all* of your colleagues or with some of them?
>
> *Researcher A: If I would think about it, everyone with whom I would have lunch will discuss his or her family. But I'm not lunching with all of them of course.*
>
> *Researcher B: No, but I would, I would. With the boss, with the dean. Yes.*
>
> *Researcher A: How is that to you?*
>
> Participant (woman) A: Because in my opinion it's normal that you cannot, you won't go around the whole faculty discussing your family with persons who might be your colleagues but you don't really know. But on the other hand there are some colleagues which, with whom you *will* discuss it.
>
> *Researcher A: And what's the difference between these colleagues with whom you discuss it and the others?*
>
> Participant (woman) A: Um some you better know simply.
>
> Participant (man) A: Yes, some you consider as friends and most of them are just colleagues. There is a difference.
>
> *Researcher A: So some colleagues you consider as friends and if you.*
>
> Participant (man) A: Yes, personally. […] So um, but but that I come back to more personal things, yeah. But that not with everybody. No, certainly not. And I don't feel the need for it either. But on the other hand, in our laboratory we have a procedure of drinking coffee two times a day as a group. So everybody sits together […] discusses a lot of things. But coming to think of it, family is not the hottest issue, no.

Researcher A: But it is an issue?

Participant (man) A: Sometimes yeah. Yes, but we have people, young fathers that discuss their children. If you call that discussing your family, yes. It's one-sided in a way because usually it goes about how they were kept awake all night.

(everyone laughs)

Researcher A: What is the hottest issue?

Participant (man) A: The hottest issue? Music.

Researcher A: Music?

Participant (man) A: Yes. Because there are a lot of people below 30, 35. Maybe I consider it the hottest issue because their choice of music is quite different than mine.

(everyone laughs)

The focus group members discussed the occasions when they talk about care with their colleagues and agreed that with colleagues who are considered as friends family can be a conversation topic. However, with colleagues who you do not know well, care responsibilities are not a topic of conversation and some "don't feel the need for it either". Interestingly, examples are given of young fathers who explicitly resisted this norm by talking in the larger group about their babies. Immediately after putting forward these deviations from the norm, these men are ridiculed. This may be because they mention babies only as examples of sleep deprivation – reinforcing the primacy of their work. However, it is also likely that this mockery, paradoxically, is a way for all involved to compensate for norm deviation and in doing so restoring or reproducing the norms about combining career and care.

The results show that the academics engage in negotiating the norm and find some room to deviate from the existing norm, but only in instances of major life changes (e.g., birth of a child, sickness of a parent), among close colleagues who are in a similar life phase (e.g., having young children), or with colleagues who are considered as friends. They do not see the need, or the opportunity, to change the existing organizational norms and adhere to the norm when they do not find themselves among colleagues they share a room or friendship with.

3. Navigating Norms

The interviews revealed that some academics found a way to cope with the existing organizational norms by navigating around them. By navigating the norm, they can possibly alter the masculine environment in which it is the norm not to talk about care obligations.

One man assistant professor had been working four days a week by using his parental leave to take care of his two young children one day a week. He tried not to "join the rat race" that comes with working in academia and tried to maintain his personal norms. At the time of the interview he was not entitled any longer to use parental leave but he used his vacation days to be able to take care of his kids one day a week. He wished for reduced hours and thus requested that by his supervisor. The next quote illustrates how he reflects upon the effect of care on his career, and at the same time challenges the existing norm in the faculty by considering care more important than his career:

> *Um what effect does your private life have on your career? Or did it have?*
>
> Um I hope an important effect in a way that it refrains me from giving work even more priority. Um it already is too much, but I refuse to, let's say, join the rat race to finish everything as good as possible and as quickly as possible. Even in the sense that my supervisors tell me 'actually you are fully qualified to make the next step', but I'm like I will continue proportionately but I have other priorities than um than those.
>
> *And um how do they look at that here?*
>
> With astonishment but with respect (Interviewee 6, man).

Even though he feels that his colleagues are astonished by the fact that he does not give total priority to work, this man academic refuses to entirely give in to the organizational norm and tells his supervisor and colleagues that he has other priorities besides his work. He used his right to paid parental leave to reserve time for care and now "buys time" by taking up vacation days.

In the situation of a temporary appointment buying time for care is more complicated. A woman PhD student had a baby during the first year of her PhD and requested extension to be compensated for the loss of time owing to her maternity leave.

> My [personnel] advisor. I did ask if in case I required it, would I get an extension to um change the four months maternity leave, to um, exchange for that [long term illness of supervisor]? And basically she said 'It's possible, but still whether or not the budget is there'. So it's not really ... *a right?*
>
> Yes. You don't really get, it's not, it's not definitive that you will always get it, I think.
>
> *[...] So you got an extension of how long?*

I got five months.

Five months' extension?

Yes.

But because your supervisor had been ill?

Yes. Yes.

Okay. But still the same extension.

Yes. Yes for me doesn't really make any difference. I mean um, maybe I'm the type of person who, who negotiates with my supervisor (Interviewee 4, woman).

This women academic altered her request when it turned out there was a chance of not getting an extension owing to a lack of budget, and ultimately got an extension owing to the illness of her supervisor. Note that in the Netherlands, contract extension on account of statutory maternity leave (16 weeks) is a legal right. Yet, executing this legal right is difficult when it concerns project-based, externally funded research. In this highly masculine environment, where maternity leave is not common, she managed to get an extension by amending the reason of her request. She found a way to deal with the organizational norms on combining career and care while still pursuing her goal.

The results show that, even though it is not really facilitated by the organization, academics sometimes creatively and subtly find their way around the norms on combining career and care: they manage to combine both worlds.

4. Creating New Norms

By not adhering to the prevailing organizational norm, some participants made a first step in changing the nominated norm. While acknowledging that working part time to care for children is much less common among (young) researchers than among administrative and technical support staff, one of our interviewees told us she does not think she is perceived differently for doing so. However, the jokes of her supervisor simultaneously show that her working pattern is present in the conversation as something that is deviating from the norm.

I just simply work less. So the output of each week is less than it could be.

But are you also viewed differently? Or in, more in general, is a person who works fewer hours viewed differently?

No, I don't think so.

No.

Yes, sometimes my supervisor said: 'Oh you're not working on Fridays, I would rather meet with you or do some stuff on Fridays, but you're not here'. But he's not, he's just joking mostly. It's not that he [is] um blaming me for something (Interviewee 5, woman).

In some cases, supervisors are more open about their own family situation and seem to accept and support the care responsibilities of their colleagues. When the next woman academic compares her case to others, she qualifies this situation as exceptional.

Um, um, well for my case I think people have been quite understanding. People around me. My supervisor has been quite understanding [...] Um so, for this, for my case I think it's okay. But I do know a couple of my friends who are not always that easily um combining their private lives [...].

Yes. Yes. So you were lucky?

Yes, in that sense I was lucky. I mean, I have a supervisor who understands family life. And [for] some of my other friends are [sic] not always the case.

Yes. *Um, how, you say 'my supervisor understands family life,' how does it come?*

Um, well he knows that I have a [child] and then he, he himself have [sic] children. And then I, I think in that sense he knows the obligations that I have to fulfill for my [child] and he doesn't push things beyond that, I think. Even if for example he wants me to go to a conference, he knows that I have to check my schedule with my husband's schedule. So both of us don't go to conferences at the same time (Interviewee 4, woman).

The next excerpt illustrates that by openly deviating from the existing norm, someone can become a trailblazer within the work environment.

Um and colleagues? To what extent do colleagues offer support in combining career and private life?

Um well sometimes by setting an example for instance when someone achieved something particular, for example that he works one day from home and then a precedent has been established that it um is thus possible.

Okay and were you actually the precedent or were there others before?

Um not in this case [working from home], no. With parental leave maybe, but yes that can be legally enforced so that actually doesn't count.

Yes, but to enforce it and to do it are two different things.

> Yes, well as a matter of fact I've made two people um aware of that possibility, especially people that um for example come from the United States. They are brought up in the rat race so they um explicitly ask if you won't be judged by that later on.
>
> *Oh they ask that?*
>
> Yes, like um how do people look at that and um is that even possible? (Interviewee 6, man).

This man academic explains he made other colleagues aware of the possibility to take parental leave to be able to care for children, as he did himself. Acting as a role model, he can create a snowball effect within the organization by recommending other academics with children to take up parental leave. In the long term, making it acceptable to talk about care may result in a change of the norm.

However, to really create new organizational norms it will take more than a few navigators, trailblazers, and role models to form a critical mass. As Poelmans (2012) stated: "We need the quiet leadership of courageous individuals who swim upstream and challenge the norms around parenting and career success" (p. 844).

DISCUSSION

In this chapter we have explored the way men and women at an engineering faculty relate to organizational norms on combining career and care. During the data collection we discovered that care is not considered a topic of conversation within the faculty, revealing a strong prescriptive norm of acceptable behavior. The interviews and focus group revealed that academics not only nominate or recognize this organizational norm on combining career and care, but also openly negotiate and sometimes even actively and publicly challenge it.

Poelmans' (2012) typology suggests different ways of dealing with organizational norms on combining career and care. He distinguishes between nominating norms at the intra-individual level, navigating norms at the inter-individual or individual-group level, and creating new norms at the inter-group level. In addition, Poelmans (2012) describes how these different ways and levels are phased, suggesting a development over time resulting in the creation of new norms. Based on our analysis, we propose to add the layer of "negotiating norms" to Poelmans' typology. Between norm nomination and norm navigation, we identified an intermediary form of actively negotiating norms, especially in the focus group. People engaging in this way of dealing with norms are openly debating the nature and existence of the norm, as well as trying to get a sense whether or not there is room to deviate from the existing norm. Furthermore, we propose that nominating, negotiating, and navigating are types or dimensions of dealing with norms rather than phases in time. Our interviews and focus group revealed that individuals can nominate, negotiate, and navigate at the same time, intra- as well as inter-individually. Academics do not go through different phases of confronting and dealing with organizational norms but rather vary between different ways of relating to the norm, depending on the situation.

Nominating norms (Poelmans, 2012) means recognizing and naming norms on combining career and care. Typically, "insiders are so thoroughly immersed in the culture that the normative system is invisible to them" (Anderson et al., 2010, p. 373). Indeed, Liebig (2010) in her study of fathers in academia finds that "male colleagues quite often do not know from each other if they have children. This situation reflects the power of a collective norm" (p. 167). Our interviewees and focus group participants become aware of what was previously invisible to them, and in doing so the implicit norm of not talking about care becomes explicit.

Norm negotiation, by debating the nature and existence of the norm as well as trying to figure out whether or not one can deviate from the norm, appears to be possible. Talking about care appears to be possible under extreme circumstances or in secluded spaces, among colleagues who are friends or who are in a similar life stage. According to Feldman (1984), groups "establish norms that discourage topics of conversation" (p. 49) in order to prevent damage to the self-image of a group member. Indeed, disclosing personal information may not be without risks (Phillips, Rothbard and Dumas, 2009), especially for low status group members. The negotiated conditions under which it is possible to talk about care provide some room within the existing masculine culture to deviate from the norm, without openly challenging or changing it. The mockery of young fathers, when talking about sleepless nights over coffee, in the focus group becomes a normalization account – the norm is in fact not challenged but reinforced. The norm is used as a mechanism of informal social control (Braxton, 1990), and by making fun, the self-image of fathers is preserved.

Navigating norms, by actively and openly coping with the norm, is quite remarkable under such circumstances. Some academics proactively confront the norm, by taking up parental leave or by requesting compensation for maternity leave. Some academics go even further, in working reduced hours, in taking care responsibilities into account when scheduling conferences, and by promoting parental leave to new colleagues. Talking openly about these care-related decisions with supervisors or colleagues means that these academics are publicly demonstrating they dare to care. These academics act as trailblazers in contributing to the development of new norms and in creating more room for care in academia.

Even if creating new norms is hard to achieve and not (yet) common, in line with Braxton's (1990) finding that "norms of science are not absolutes but are relative" (p. 474), these early signs of change are promising. In this sense, the negotiation and navigation of existing norms may precede the creation of new norms. With the addition of active negotiation of organizational norms to the Poelmans (2012) typology, we identify a research space for studying incremental change in scientific organization cultures.

Practical Implications

Our study suggests that care issues are important for both men and women academics working at an engineering faculty. Our data also illustrate that care as a public conversation topic is a taboo, except for occasional complaining about sleepless nights – a confirmation of the prevalence of work over care. Maintaining and reproducing this norm in a changing demographic context causes inertia for academics with care responsibilities.

The engineering faculty we studied offers various statutory arrangements for paid maternity and parental leave. However, the possible use of these arrangements is hindered because their existence and utilization are not openly discussed. As long as those academics taking up maternity or parental leave remain largely invisible, others will not consider it a viable option, especially those coming from abroad. Similarly, the apparent lack of compensation for taking up maternity leave during a temporary appointment such as a PhD project or postdoc thus remains largely unchallenged. Under such conditions, taking up maternity or parental leave has negative consequences for performance evaluations, as academics who do so are held against the same standard as those who did not take leave.

Our analysis suggests that universities in general, and this faculty of engineering in particular, can facilitate the combination of career and care if they would actively and openly compensate for "time to care" (e.g., maternity and parental leave) in promotion criteria and research time allocation. Furthermore, these compensation policies should be communicated as a regular labor condition. In such manner, the burden of responsibility of requesting compensation is moved away from the individual (Brescoll, Glass and Sedlovskaya, 2013). This is one way to explicitly make care a topic of conversation. We indeed recommended introducing compensation of maternity and parental leave in output norms, which was adopted by the university board.

Another way to facilitate the combination of career and care is to introduce role models, preferably in senior positions, who "dare to care". One way to support this is to abolish the prohibition of part-time or compressed work weeks for managerial positions. The university board, based on our recommendations indeed decided to allow compressed workweeks (e.g., 4 x 9 hours) and large part-time positions (32 hours) for managerial positions. Finally, we advised the board that the universities HRM policies should assume that each employee is part of a dual career couple. As a consequence the university needs to offer childcare on campus, dual hiring streams for international employees and leave facilities. These measures help to expand the notion of the ideal academic to incorporate the combination of career and care (Van Engen et al., 2012).

In the light of demographic changes, it becomes increasingly important to promote sustainability in combining career and care in academia (Van Engen et al., 2012). With most, if not all, academics having to combine career and care responsibilities, universities need to facilitate this combination. When universities become more open and inclusive towards academics who dare to care, they will be better able to utilize all academic talent, both women and men. As argued by Liebig (2010):

> Actively parenting men and changing gender relations challenge the structural premises and rationalities of academic life. [...] Higher education should get prepared for men and women, who start from a new societal understanding of parenthood, far away from stereotypes such as the 'male breadwinner', or 'male achiever' and want to make use of paternity leave, part-time work or other family friendly policies (p. 169).

Strengths and Limitations

Anderson, Ronning, De Vries and Martinson (2010) suggested the use of focus groups: "discussions with scientists using the format of focus groups to elicit both individual and group assertions and reactions concerning scientific norms [...] used specifically and deliberately to investigate the normative structure of science" (p. 373). Taking this approach has provided us with the opportunity to uncover the existing norm of not talking about care in the faculty of engineering, as well as witness an active negotiation of that norm. A limitation of our study, however, is that we examine this organizational norm on the basis of a single case. Case study research is a suitable research strategy to understand organizational norms in their context, but the validity of the results would be improved by systematically comparing our case with other cases at a technical university (George and Bennett, 2004). Are comparable processes of nominating, negotiating, navigating, and creating norms to be found in technical universities in different countries? For future research we suggest comparative case study research in technical universities, especially in settings with more women academics. In addition, a carefully designed intervention study in order to uncover, challenge, and change organizational norms on combining career and care in academia would provide an opportunity for both external generalization and a quantitative test of predictions derived from this explorative study.

As a final point, we want to emphasize that we describe our case explicitly as action research. Indeed, being involved in the research process as researchers with a feminist perspective, helped to put the existing organizational culture on the research agenda. The active debate in the focus group on organizational norms on career and care in comparison to those at other universities helped us realize how much organizational cultures differ and to become more aware of our own assumptions. The fact that the three researchers performing the interviews and focus groups were senior researchers in the ranks of associate and assistant professor helped us to be conversation partners on an equal academic level to the academics working at the engineering faculty. As previous research suggests that decision makers, especially in their role as supervisors, play an important role in facilitating the combination of career and care (King, 2008), we involved them in various stages of this action research project. Proponents of the dominant "inclusive excellence" approach in promoting diversity in academia, according to Danowitz and Bendl (2010) recognize "the importance of deep organizational cultural change, although it gives only minimal attention to the power of faculty norms and cultures and the difficulty of changing them" (p. 358). We hope to have overcome some of the difficulties inherent to this approach by involving decision makers, by exposing them to the existing organizational norm, by exploring how academics differentially relate to this norm, and by challenging their own norms about combining career and care. Their continued involvement in implementing the suggested recommendations is of crucial importance in making this technical university a more inclusive employer for those who dare to care.

REFERENCES

Anderson, M.S., E.A. Ronning, R. De Vries and B.C. Martinson (2010), 'Extending the mertonian norms: Scientists' subscription to norms of research', *Journal of Higher Education*, **81**(3), 366–93.

Ashforth, B.E. and F. Mael (1989), 'Social identity theory and the organization', *The Academy of Management Review*, **14**(1), 20–39.

Aulenbacher, B. and B. Riegraf (2010), 'The new entrepreneurship in science and changing gender arrangements: Approaches and perspectives', in B. Riegraf, B. Aulenbacher, E. Kirsch-Auwärter and U. Müller (eds), *Gender Change in Academia*, Wiesbaden: VS Verlag für Sozialwissenschaften, pp. 61–73.

Bailyn, L. (2003), 'Academic careers and gender equity: Lessons learned from MIT', *Gender, Work & Organization*, **10**(2), 137–53.

Barnard, S., A. Powell, B. Bagilhole and A. Dainty (2010), 'Researching UK women professionals in SET: A critical review of current approaches', *International Journal of Gender, Science and Technology*, **2**(3), 361–81.

Bleijenbergh, I., M.L. Van Engen and C.J. Vinkenburg (2013), 'Othering women: Fluid images of the ideal academic', *Equality, Diversity and Inclusion*, **32**(1).

Braxton, J. (1990), 'Deviancy from the norms of science: A test of control theory', *Research in Higher Education*, **31**(5), 461–76.

Brescoll, V.L., J. Glass and A. Sedlovskaya (2013), 'Ask and ye shall receive? The dynamics of employer-provided flexible work options and the need for public policy', *Journal of Social Issues*, **69**(2), 367–88.

Britton, D.M. (2000), 'The epistemology of the gendered organization', *Gender & Society*, **14**(3), 418–34.

Coltrane, S., E.C. Miller, T. DeHaan and L. Stewart (2013), 'Fathers and the flexibility stigma', *Journal of Social Issues*, **69**(2), 279–302.

Corbin, J. and A. Strauss (2008), *Basics of Qualitative Research: Techniques and Procedures for Developing Grounded Theory*, Los Angeles: SAGE.

Danowitz, M. and R. Bendl (2010), 'Gender mainstreaming, diversity management and inclusive excellence: From similarities and differences to new possibilities', in B. Riegraf, B. Aulenbacher, E. Kirsch-Auwärter and U. Müller (eds), *Gender Change in Academia: Re-mapping the Fields of Work, Knowledge, and Politics from a Gender Perspective*, Wiesbaden: VS Verlag für Sozialwissenschaften, pp. 351–62.

Faulkner, W. (2000), 'Dualisms, hierarchies and gender in engineering', *Social Studies of Science*, **30**(5), 759–92.

Faulkner, W. (2007), 'Nuts and bolts and people: Gender-troubled engineering identities', *Social Studies of Science*, **37**(3), 331–56.

Feldman, D.C. (1984), 'The development and enforcement of group norms', *The Academy of Management Review*, **9**(1), 47–53.

Fletcher, C., R. Boden, J. Kent and J. Tinson (2007), 'Performing women: The gendered dimensions of the UK new research economy', *Gender, Work and Organization*, **14**(5), 433–53.

Fox, M.F., C. Fonseca and J. Bao (2011), 'Work and family conflict in academic science: Patterns and predictors among women and men in research universities', *Social Studies of Science*, **41**(5), 715–35.

George, A.L. and A. Bennett (2004), *Case Studies and Theory Development in the Social Sciences*, Cambridge, MA: MIT Press.

Grant, L., I. Kennelly and K.B. Ward (2000), 'Revisiting the gender, marriage, and parenthood puzzle in scientific careers', *Women's Studies Quarterly*, **28**, 62–85.

King, E.B. (2008), 'The effect of bias on the advancement of working mothers: Disentangling legitimate concerns from inaccurate stereotypes as predictors of advancement in academe', *Human Relations*, **61**(12), 1677–711.

Liebig, B. (2010), 'Academic life and gender relations: The case of fathers in professorship', in B. Riegraf, B. Aulenbacher, E. Kirsch-Auwärter and U. Müller (eds), *Gender Change in Academia*, Wiesbaden: VS Verlag für Sozialwissenschaften, pp. 161–71.

Phillips, K.W., N.P. Rothbard and T.L. Dumas (2009), 'To disclose or not to disclose? Status distance and self disclosure in diverse environments', *The Academy of Management Review*, **34**(4), 710–32.

Poelmans, S. (2012), 'The "Triple-N" model: Changing normative beliefs about parenting and career success', *Journal of Social Issues*, **68**(4).

Rogers, E.M. (1995), *Diffusion of Innovations* (Vol. 4), New York: The Free Press.

Sagebiel, F. and S. Vázquez-Cupeiro (2010), *Stereotypes and Identity: Meta-analysis of Gender and Science Research: Topic Report*, European Commission.

Schein, E.H. (1990), 'Organizational culture', *American Psychologist*, **45**(2), 109–19.

Schein, E.H. (1996), 'Culture: The missing concept in organization studies', *Administrative Science Quarterly*, **41**(2), 229–40.

Schiebinger, L., A. Henderson and S.K. Gilmartin (2008), *Dual-Career Academic Couples: What Universities Need to Know*, Michelle R. Clayman Institute for Gender Research, Stanford University.

Sun, S. (2008), 'Organizational culture and its themes', *International Journal of Business and Management*, **3**(12), 137–41.

Van Engen, M.L., I. Bleijenbergh and C.J. Vinkenburg (2010), *Structurele en culturele belemmeringen in de doorstroom van vrouwen naar hogere functies binnen de TU Delft*, Delft: Technical University Delft.

Van Engen, M.L., C.J. Vinkenburg and J.S.E. Dikkers (2012), 'Sustainability in combining career and care: Challenging normative beliefs about parenting', *Journal of Social Issues*, **68**(4).

Wiener, Y. (1982), 'Commitment in organizations: A normative view', *The Academy of Management Review*, **7**(3), 418–28.

Williams, J.C. (2000), *Unbending Gender: Why Family and Work Conflict and What to Do about It*, New York: Oxford University Press.

12. 'Engineering is gendered' is a threshold concept

Sally Male

INTRODUCTION

Despite dramatic increases over the twentieth century in the representation of women in professions such as law, medicine, and veterinary science, engineering remains a profession in which women are under-represented in Australia, New Zealand, the US and Western Europe including Ireland and the UK. Many initiatives have been implemented in these countries over the most recent three decades, yet women remain under-represented among engineering students and even more under-represented among practising engineers.

In Australia, female percentages of domestic professional engineering degree completions decreased from a modest peak of 16.9 per cent in 2001 to 12.9 per cent in 2010 (Kaspura, 2012, p. 54). Female engineering students in Australia have had higher success rates than male engineering students (King, 2008). However, after graduation women leave the profession at higher rates than men and the percentage of women in the engineering profession in Australia is even lower than indicated by female student participation rates. Only 11.8 per cent of the supply of engineers in Australia was female at the last census (Kaspura, 2013, p. 1).

Addressing the problems arising from under-representation of women in engineering is a greater imperative than one of achieving equal opportunity, strength in diversity, or increasing the talent pool. There is evidence that the dominance of men in engineering has shaped engineering practice, the identities of engineers, understanding of engineering practice and consequently design and implementation of engineering curricula. Understanding this is critical to improving engineering practice and will be difficult to achieve chiefly because the concept is foreign to many engineers.

Problems arising from the under-representation of women in engineering influence women, members of the profession, and society. It is easy to recognise the problems that arise directly from the low numbers of women in the profession. For example, the under-representation of women in engineering means that talented women are missing opportunities in the profession.

For the profession and society, the under-representation of women in engineering is problematic because it is an indicator of potential talent lost. The diversity of perspectives within the profession is limited by unnecessary restriction to a more homogenous pool than should be available. Consequently the range of ideas, knowledge and styles within engineering teams is unnecessarily narrow.

For society, a limitation on the quality of the engineering profession is a disadvantage. Engineers have the potential to shape people's lives. They influence the availability of resources and tools that people use to meet their needs and wants.

The above direct problems with low representation of women in the engineering profession are not the only concerns. The corollary of low representation of women is male dominance in the engineering profession, which can shape aspects of engineering practice, engineering education, and cultures within the profession. I refer to this as the concept that engineering is gendered. Evidence of this masculine influence on engineering is described below under the heading 'The threshold concept that engineering is gendered'. This is not intended as an 'essentialist' view, dichotomising engineering and women such as Barnard, Powell, Bagilhole, and Dainty (2010, p. 363) classify much research on women in science, engineering and technology. Certainly it does not imply that engineering is better suited to men than women or that women are better suited to some engineering roles than others. Instead I mean that engineering practice, culture and education are influenced by often subconscious assumptions that prioritise *stereotypically* masculine attributes, characteristics and actions over those that are *stereotypically* feminine. Many researchers have described engineering as gendered masculine in this way (e.g. Faulkner, 2009; Fletcher, 1999; Gill, Sharp, Mills, & Franzway, 2008; Hacker, 1981; Robinson & McIlwee, 1991).

In this chapter I argue that in addition to the problems already identified, the masculine nature of engineering culture can directly limit the effectiveness of engineering education and engineering practice and the inclusivity of the profession. Furthermore, most engineers, both men and women, are generally unaware of the influences. Yet, it is only with understanding of the concept that engineering is gendered that engineers will be able to recognise the masculine influence in practices and assumptions they take for granted, and identify changes to improve engineering practice, and the inclusivity of the profession. Thus indeed it is problematic if engineering is gendered, and it is important that engineers are aware of the possibility that some aspects of the profession that engineers take for granted might be unnecessarily shaped by masculine culture.

In this chapter I draw on a study in which I identified threshold concepts in a foundation engineering curriculum. By focusing on the concept that engineering is gendered within the framework of a higher education theory I unearth the imperative for dismantling the gendered aspects of engineering, and propose critical understanding necessary to achieve this. Additionally, by considering troublesome features of the concept that engineering is gendered I identify approaches to help members of the profession understand the concept and hence separate masculine assumptions and values from engineering practice.

THRESHOLD CONCEPT THEORY

Threshold concept theory originated in higher education and has been used in disciplines including engineering and computer science. Meyer and Land (2003) proposed that many disciplines of study have concepts that are experienced as thresholds by many students of the discipline. These concepts are ontologically and epistemologically transformative. Through the often lengthy process of struggling with and eventually understanding and feeling comfortable with such concepts, people experience significant changes in their perceptions of valid knowledge and significant repositioning of their identities. When a person comes to understand a threshold concept, she or he becomes capable of new ways of thinking and understanding not previously possible.

In this chapter the term 'student' is not restricted to higher education students. I apply threshold concept theory to all members of the engineering profession: students, academics and professionals, considering all to be lifelong learners.

Owing to the transformative nature of threshold concepts and sometimes additional factors such as curriculum structures and teaching approaches, most threshold concepts are not only transformative but also troublesome for many students. Threshold concept theory includes examples of types of troublesome knowledge, many of which were originally identified by Perkins (1999, 2006). One relevant type of troublesome knowledge is 'foreign' knowledge (Perkins, 2006, p. 40). Foreign knowledge is troublesome because it is understood only when a student takes a perspective that is different from the perspective she or he usually takes. Identifying how a concept is troublesome can help in developing approaches to help students overcome the concept.

A concept is threshold in a discipline if it is critical to students' progress – for future learning or for effective practice in the discipline. Engineering threshold concepts are critical to learning in engineering or to practising engineering. Threshold concept theory has been found to be valuable for focusing curricula (Cousin, 2010). By identifying threshold concepts as part of curriculum design, education programmes can be designed such that students' and teachers' time is focused on the concepts that are most critical and for which students require the most effort and support.

In threshold concept theory, Meyer and Land (2003) describe threshold concepts as helping students to think and act like people in their disciplines. However, in this chapter rather than identifying a concept that students must understand in order to think like an engineer, I propose a concept that all engineers should, rather than do, understand.

Within the framework of threshold concept theory are listed common features of threshold concepts. Threshold concepts are frequently 'irreversible', 'integrative' and 'discursive' (Meyer & Land, 2003, pp. 4-5). Understanding of an irreversible concept is not generally lost once achieved. Understanding an integrative concept integrates concepts that were previously unconnected for the student. Understanding a discursive concept improves a student's use of language.

A potential benefit of identifying threshold concepts as part of curriculum design is the possibility of identifying concepts that are critical and yet would not otherwise appear in the curriculum. A contemporary engineering curriculum in Australia is likely to include engineering science and learning outcomes such as communication skills, teamwork skills, understanding of ethics, and sustainable design skills (Bradley, 2008). In identifying threshold concepts, a curriculum designer considers students' experiences of barriers to progress. The process can reveal hurdles for students that experts would not usually recognise, such as tacit knowledge.

The threshold concept that engineering is gendered is not only troublesome for students but also for practitioners. Therefore literature was more important in identifying the threshold concept than it would be in identifying other threshold concepts. As discussed below, approaches to identifying threshold concepts have included student consultation or observation, and teacher consultation. However, these approaches were not fruitful regarding the concept that engineering is gendered.

In threshold concept theory, the state a student experiences between when a threshold concept comes into view and when the student understands and accepts the concept is described as the 'liminal space' (Meyer & Land, 2003, p. 10). While in this space, a student finds the threshold concept troublesome. The liminal space can be short in duration or take years to traverse. Schwartzman (2010) found that students experience anxiety and can respond defensively or reflectively to inconsistency between their understanding and a new experience. This can occur when students are in the liminal space and struggling with a troublesome threshold concept.

It is tempting to imagine that for many engineering students and engineers the threshold concept that engineering is gendered has come into view and the liminal space for this concept has been entered. Engineering students are aware that men occupy the majority of places in engineering. However, this is not the same as the suggestion that the dominance of men influences how engineering practice is performed, understood and taught, and that other alternatives might be possible. Unlike most other threshold concepts, the threshold concept that engineering is gendered is not part of engineering discourse. A desire to attract and retain more women in the profession is articulated widely but the concept that engineering could be gendered is rarely part of the discussion.

PROCESS OF IDENTIFYING THE THRESHOLD CONCEPT

When threshold concept theory is used in the development of a curriculum, an early step is to identify the threshold concepts experienced by students of the discipline. Educators have achieved this in many ways. Kabo and Baillie (2009) and Zander et al. (2008) used interviews and phenomenographic analysis to identify levels along dimensions of understanding in engineering and computer science respectively. Carstensen and Bernhard (2008) observed engineering students in laboratories. Harlow, Scott, Peter, and Cowie (2011) observed engineering students in laboratories and conducted interviews. Holloway, Alpay, and Bull (2010), also in computer science and engineering, included quantitative students surveys.

The threshold concept that engineering is gendered was identified in a two-year project that identified threshold concepts in an engineering foundation course – the first two years of an engineering science major leading to any discipline of engineering at the University of Western Australia (Male, 2012a). In this chapter the project is called the 'engineering threshold concepts project'. Potential threshold concepts were identified in interviews with engineering academics, and focus groups with student tutors, and focus groups with students. Participants were asked to identify potential threshold concepts and provide evidence, based on their experience, that the concepts were transformative and troublesome (Quinlan et al., 2013). Sample interview questions for academics are below (Male, 2012b, p. 19).

1. Can you think of any possible thresholds in this or similar previous units [the academic has taught]?
2. [For each,] why is this threshold significant: what is the new way of thinking and for what is it used?
3. [For concepts identified,] can you describe the particular transformative way of thinking that students have trouble with? (Possible probe: what makes you think this? (questions from students, assignments scripts, exam scripts, laboratory performance).)
4. Can you identify causes of the thresholds identified? (Possible probes: types of troublesomeness, programme structure, teaching method, learning opportunities, students' backgrounds?)
5. Are the threshold concepts taught earlier in the course or do they rely on concepts taught in other units?
6. Are there ways you have found useful to help students understand each identified concept?

Academics identified potential threshold concepts based on their experiences observing students, students' questions and students' assessments. Below is an example of a quote from an academic referring to his experience of students finding the concept of modelling troublesome.

> Intuition in one domain does not apply in another domain … Trouble comes in the form of baggage they carry from one domain to another. For example, impedance is only defined in the frequency domain and not in the time domain … Students do not appreciate that abstraction puts you in a new world and baggage from other worlds must not be used. (academic) (Male & Baillie, 2014, p. 396)

Academics also volunteered potential threshold concepts based on their own experiences. Tutors identified potential threshold concepts based on their experiences, their interactions with students, and students' difficulties in assessments the tutors had marked. Students identified potential threshold concepts based on their experiences and their peers' experiences.

Identified potential threshold concepts were negotiated in interdisciplinary and inter-university workshops around Australia. Workshops were also held in New Zealand and Europe. As the main researcher for the engineering threshold concepts project, I proposed only one of the potential threshold concepts that were then negotiated at interdisciplinary workshops. This was the concept that engineering is gendered. It was the only concept, among those listed in the final inventory of engineering threshold concepts, that had been identified on the basis of literature and not by participants in the project (Male, 2012b, p. 17).

Two other engineering academics agreed that the concept that engineering is gendered is a threshold concept. One suggested the more generic concept that engineering was influenced by culture as an alternative concept. Six interdisciplinary workshops were held around Australia to negotiate potential threshold concepts, and no other participants chose to negotiate the threshold concept of 'engineering as gendered'. Each workshop involved 12 to 40 participants. Twice an explanation of the concept was requested. Workshop participants then avoided discussing it further. Perhaps they did not agree with the concept, or perhaps they required further explanation. Or again, perhaps it was a concept they found too sensitive to discuss in groups. In the discussion below on how the concept is troublesome it should become apparent that all of these are plausible explanations.

THE THRESHOLD CONCEPT THAT ENGINEERING IS GENDERED

A growing literature on women in engineering provides strong evidence for the concept that engineering is gendered. Here I refer to studies that together provide evidence that engineering is gendered and that the concept is threshold for many engineering students, and for engineers working in universities and elsewhere. Although many of the studies have not been designed to create generalisable knowledge, the widespread consistency across studies is strong evidence that engineering is gendered. To demonstrate the threshold nature of the concept, I describe how the concept is transformative in that it provides a new way of thinking and understanding that helps people to think and act in a way that would not previously have been possible.

Before focusing specifically on engineering, it is necessary to clarify that any profession can be gendered. It is convenient to conceptualise an organisation and expand the concept to the engineering profession by considering people in many engineering organisations interacting in teams. Acker (1990) described a theory of gendered organisations. These reinforce a gendered hierarchy in which men and women occupy separate roles. People in such organisations unwittingly adopt a culture in which it is assumed that all of the characteristics associated with the dominant gender, including for example, communication styles, leadership styles and family responsibilities, are normal and ideal. Within this framework, in engineering organisations where women are under-represented, men and women can adopt a culture in which they subconsciously assume that stereotypically masculine characteristics and activities such as technical engineering are of higher status than stereotypically feminine characteristics and activities such as caring for others.

The impact of gendered values and assumptions on how people in an organisation judge and relate to one another is significant. Ridgeway (2009) explains that people are framed as masculine or feminine as the first part of interaction, even at the start of a virtual or paper interaction. This framing interacts with gendered aspects of the profession. Furthermore, the scope of gendered assumptions is not limited to men being more appropriate for certain roles, segregation of all roles (engineering and other roles), and subconscious bias. The dominance of men in the profession is also thought to influence the status of activities and characteristics within the culture of the profession. For example, Hacker (1981, p. 341) found the patriarchal culture among faculty in an engineering institute in the US as 'subordinating sexuality and the body and elevating scientific abstraction'.

Gendered Culture in Engineering Faculties

Findings consistent with gendered cultures in engineering faculties have been made in multiple countries. Hacker (1981) found practices consistent with an overtly gendered culture among academics in an engineering faculty in the US. Godfrey and Parker (2010) found features consistent with a gendered culture in an engineering faculty in New Zealand. In her participatory study, Tonso (2007) observed actions consistent with a gendered culture within an engineering faculty in the US.

Focusing on the most recent of these studies, Tonso observed female students in team projects being ignored by their peers as if their ideas had not been heard, questioned as if they had no technical credibility, and exploited in that a woman who did much of the work was not acknowledged. Tonso also observed a female student having greater difficulty gaining access to equipment than male students, in the university and in an engineering workplace. The concept that engineering is gendered helps to explain these observations.

Godfrey and Parker conducted an ethnographic case study of the cultural dimensions of an engineering faculty in New Zealand. Several aspects were consistent with a gendered culture among the engineering academics and students. Students and academics identified with the degree being 'hard' and a female graduate was quoted remarking that this conflicted with a 'soft' feminine identity (pp. 12–13).They reported that although learning outcomes that were not purely technical such as professional skills, communication, management and social and environmental responsibilities had long been taught at the university, they were marginalised to separate units rather than integrated into mainstream units. Both of these findings are consistent with Hacker's observation that the gendered culture includes marginalisation of anything stereotypically feminine especially related to people.

Godfrey and Parker found that 'female students often encountered (and resisted) gendered expectation' (p. 13), quoting a female student relating frustration that students in her team had not listened to her technical advice. Female students were 'other' than the male norm that was required to belong among the engineering students. For female academics (seven among over 100), acceptance was a slow process over several years. These features are also consistent with a gendered culture.

Conflict between 'hard' engineering technical competencies and feminine characteristics as noted by Godfrey and Parker, was found to support identity conflict for female students of electrical and electronic engineering in a Danish university in a study by Du (2006). Similarly, identity conflict owing to the gendered nature of engineering was found in Powell, Dainty and Bagilhole's (2012) mixed methods study of engineering and technology students at a university in the UK. Although in a male-dominated discipline, the female students had not considered how they performed gender. Many of the students in their study harboured conflicting assumptions: a belief that gender constraints no longer existed, which conflicted with subconsciously assumed gender stereotypes about engineering.

The above examples reveal that potential impacts of a gendered culture in engineering education include:

- low status, within the curriculum, for learning that is not purely technical;
- identity conflict for students who do not fit the male norm;
- lack of acceptance for academics (male and female) who do not fit the male norm;
- experiences that would restrict opportunities to learn such as lack of access to equipment;
- experiences that could harm self-efficacy such as lack of respect from team-members.

My fear is not that the above potential impacts of a gendered culture in engineering faculties will cause female students to fail or withdraw. As noted in the introduction, female engineering students in Australia have had higher academic success rates than male engineering students (King, 2008). The problem is that female and male engineering students' preparation for engineering practice is compromised by the gendered culture in engineering faculties. While at university, students build attitudes, identity and self-efficacy (Du, 2006). Students in a gendered faculty are likely to learn gendered practices as the norm and take these into the workplace. They will not be prepared to recognise and avoid or minimise discrimination or harassment or other gendered practices. Additionally, men and women's development of competencies other than purely technical could be compromised owing to marginalisation of these aspects of curricula. Furthermore, owing to learning to identify with the 'hard' skills, students are likely to find the socio technical reality of engineering practice unexpected. Just as worrying, female students' self-efficacy and opportunities to experience operating equipment could be compromised.

Gill, Mills, Sharp, and Franzway (2005) called for engineering education to prepare students for engineering workplaces. Understanding that engineering faculties are gendered would be transformative for engineering students and academics. It would allow them to reflect on whether gender influenced their decisions and actions and those of others and ask whether a different action would be better. Understanding that gendered culture in the faculty is likely to be the cause could also influence their responses to actions they recognise as potentially gendered and how they internalise gendered encounters that could influence their identities.

Gendered Cultures in Engineering Workplaces

Findings consistent with gendered cultures in engineering workplaces abound. I refer to studies in the US, Australia and the UK. In the US, Fletcher (1999, p37) found in a 'major high-technology company' that interactions that enhanced and maintained team cohesion, such as recognising the contribution of a team member, were marginalised within the culture by both male and female engineers. Nevertheless these activities were specifically intended to ensure success of the engineering project, and were critical to this success. Fletcher referred to these activities as 'relational practice' (pp. 47–87). Relational practice was marginalised in that it occurred on the edges of formal spaces and time periods: before or after a meeting, perhaps in a passage or tearoom, verbally rather than formally and privately rather than publicly. Similarly, relational practice was not recognised as an essential competency or achievement, i.e. a valid part of engineering practice. Fletcher noted that both the male and female engineers used feminine terms when referring to relational practice. It was regarded as associated with mothering and caring and consequently of low status, just as Hacker had observed gendering of engineering among academics.

Fletcher's finding that relational practice was critical to engineering projects in her study is consistent with more recent findings that engineers spend much time coordinating the work of people over whom they have no official authority, and that engineers rely heavily on others for knowledge and skills (Trevelyan, 2007). If the engineers in the organisation studied by Fletcher had been aware of how gendered culture can marginalise an important aspect of engineering practice, they might have paid greater attention to relational practice as part of engineering practice, and ensured that it was among criteria for recruitment and promotion. Furthermore, this could have improved the success of the organisation's engineering projects.

Similarly, in the UK, in an ethnographic study of building design engineering, Faulkner (2007) found that male and female engineers could experience identity conflict between: technical engineering identities, their unexpected experience of engineering work as both technical and social, and for women their gender identities. Faulkner concludes that there are diverse masculinities and femininities, and that engineering is diverse and should be understood as more than pure technical work. Faulkner found that female engineers, unlike male engineers, faced the problem that they were invisible as engineers in the workplace because it was assumed that a competent engineer would be masculine. At the same time, female engineers found that they were visible as women despite being invisible as engineers in the workplace. Consequently female engineers frequently had to demonstrate their credibility as engineers in a way their male counterparts did not because their credibility was assumed.

Hatmaker (2012) found further evidence that engineering workplaces can affect engineers' identities. She interviewed female engineers in the US, asking about their workplace personal interactions, how they responded, and how the interactions influenced their identities. Two of the identified ways that interactions marginalised participants' professional identity were by 'imposing gendered expectations', for example when participants were asked to take notes, or by 'amplifying their gender identity', by drawing attention to them being female or a wife or mother over being an engineer (p. 5). In response to these two types of interaction the women either blocked the interaction with a blunt reply or rationalised it by deciding to tolerate it and explaining a justification for this to themselves. The ability to recognise the interaction as arising from a gendered culture and label the interaction as gendered could be valuable in both responses. Hatmaker reported that one consequence of the interactions was feeling devalued. Having an explanation that confirms the interaction as systemic rather than individual is likely to be important for protecting self-efficacy.

The above finding by Faulkner and Hatmaker that women experienced visibility as women and invisibility as engineers was also experienced by the female engineering students in Godfrey and Parker's study. Additionally, the finding was dominant in the Australian mixed method study of engineers by Gill et al. (2008). This is of course consistent with engineering being a gendered profession.

Engineering workplaces in Australia have unacceptable levels of harassment and discrimination. In 2010 the median salary of female engineers with five to ten years of experience was 8.5 per cent less than that of male engineers with the same years of experience (Association of Professional Engineers Scientists & Managers Australia, 2010). In the second Australian Career Review of Engineering Women survey (Mills, Mehrtens, Smith, & Adams, 2008) 22 per cent of respondents reported they had been sexually harassed. In a 2009–2010 Women's Survey Report (Association of Professional Engineers Scientists & Managers Australia, 2010) more than 20 per cent of female engineering respondents reported that they had been sexually harassed. The second Career Review of Engineering Women reported that female participants had fewer children (0.37 on average) than women in other professions (1.7 on average) or male participants (with 1.99 children on average). This suggests that there are barriers to women in engineering with children. With these statistics, it is not surprising that women leave the profession at higher rates than men (Mills et al., 2008; Tilli & Trevelyan, 2010) and are generally less satisfied than male engineers (Kaspura, 2013). The statistics are again strong evidence of a gendered profession.

HOW THE CONCEPT IS TROUBLESOME

The threshold concept that engineering is gendered is both foreign and hidden for many engineers and engineering students. These are features recognised in threshold concept theory as reasons why knowledge can be troublesome.

The concept that engineers' judgements could be affected by culture conflicts with the tendency of engineers to identify themselves as logical objective thinkers. The concept is therefore a foreign concept for many engineers. Godfrey and Parker (2010, p. 12) in their study in a university in New Zealand found the following.

> Throughout the study there was an unquestioned assumption by faculty that the knowledge, mathematical procedures and scientific processes, and the laws on which solutions were based were race and gender free.

From the above quote it is clear that for the academics in Godfrey and Parker's study the concept that engineering could be gendered would be foreign.

In addition to the above troublesome foreign feature of the concept that engineering is gendered, the concept is hidden. It is difficult for people who belong or have assimilated to a culture to be aware of aspects of that culture and the assumptions arising from it (Ihsen, 2005). Therefore the concept that engineering is gendered is hidden to members of the engineering profession.

Final additions to the above troublesome features of understanding the concept that engineering is gendered are features that could make members of the engineering profession uneasy about accepting the concept. Men and women who have already succeeded in a gendered culture could be threatened by a suggestion that the status quo should be dismantled. More significantly, it is dangerous to a student's or an engineer's ability to belong in a cultural group if they declare the culture of the group to be flawed (Powell, Bagilhole, & Dainty, 2009). Engineering students work closely together over long hours. Similarly engineers work in teams within and across organisations (Gill et al., 2008; Godfrey & Parker, 2010). Therefore, for engineering students and engineers it is important to belong to, and hence not take any risk and question, the dominant culture.

It has been found to be common for female engineering students and engineers to outwardly condone the masculine culture, to be unsupportive of women, and to display masculinity in order to belong (Jolly, 1996; Powell et al., 2009). They thereby avoid any risk of being associated with disrupting the masculine culture. Short-term survival trumps long-term cultural change.

A problem with proactively demonstrating support for a masculine culture and fitting into this culture arises when a woman can no longer fit, such as when she has children, or discovers she has experienced discrimination. People who are aware of gendered cultures in engineering have a responsibility to share their understanding with other members of the profession to help them make informed decisions about their responses to the culture.

HOW THE CONCEPT IS TRANSFORMATIVE

In the introduction to this chapter I promised an argument for changing engineering culture beyond the opportunity to improve gender inclusivity. Potential benefits of wider understanding of the concept that engineering is gendered lie in three areas. Benefits to gender inclusivity in engineering, engineering education, and engineering practice are all possible as a result of helping engineering students, academics and engineers to understand the concept that engineering is gendered. Understanding the concept opens up new ways of thinking and understanding that can empower all three groups of stakeholders.

Hacker (1981) noted that students learn a culture from faculty members and that engineering students become the managers leading workplaces of the future. Consequently the culture modelled by academics, and adopted by engineering students while at university, is significant, and helping engineering academics and students to be aware of the concept that engineering is gendered is important.

The transformative feature of threshold concepts means that once a student understands and accepts the concept, she or he gains a new capability to think and understand, learn, or do something he or she previously could not. Achievements possible for engineering students, academics and professionals in industry owing to the transformative feature of the concept that engineering is gendered are listed below.

IMPROVING GENDER INCLUSIVITY IN UNIVERSITIES AND WORKPLACES

In universities and in workplaces students, academics, and engineers with an understanding of how engineering is gendered should be better prepared than otherwise to survive, thrive, and change culture and practice to improve inclusivity. Examples of such possibilities are listed below.

Recognising Gendered Actions, such as Interpersonal Interactions and Role Segregation, as Gendered rather than Normal or Individual

The first step in reducing gendered actions is to recognise that they occur. As discussed, this is difficult for anyone central to the dominant culture, including male and female engineers who have learnt to assimilate to the culture of engineering faculties (Ihsen, 2005). Awareness of how engineering is gendered is necessary for recognising gendered actions.

Making Informed Decisions about Responses to Gendered Actions

As discussed, people often condone a masculine culture in order to belong. They must understand how engineering is gendered in order to recognise when they experience or observe gendered actions and make an informed decision about their responses.

Recognising Discrimination and Harassment

If it is not understood that women and men are likely to be influenced by unconscious bias and that organisational structures are likely to be gendered, then it is easy to take part or suffer from the consequences before it is too late to recover. Only when people identify discrimination and harassment, can they address it.

Discrimination is pervasive and not always easy to recognise. It is important that people assume unconscious bias is present in their organisations. One of the reasons people criticise initiatives such as scholarships to support female engineers is that they do not realise that engineering is gendered. Members of the engineering profession should realise that practices are unlikely to be equitable and diversity management only starts to level the field.

Revealing Limitations of the Deficit Model

Planning to manage gender by supporting women to fit into current cultures and systems without critically analysing these to reveal any gendered features is flawed. Understanding that engineering is gendered reveals the flaw.

IMPROVING ENGINEERING EDUCATION

Improving the Status of Socio-Technical Competencies among Academics and Students

Students and academics who understand how engineering is gendered should be aware of the risk of marginalising competencies that are stereotypically feminine, for instance teamwork and communication. When faculty members or students unwittingly undermine social aspects of the socio-technical curriculum, people present should be able to name the accident as an example of the gendered culture of engineering.

Recognising Unconscious Bias and Discrimination and Proactively Minimising It

Teamwork is increasingly part of engineering education in Australia, being more authentic than individual work, and teamwork is a stipulated learning outcome for programme accreditation. Peer assessment is often a component of the assessment for team projects. In this circumstance it is essential that students and academics are aware of the high likelihood of unconscious bias among all students and academics. Understanding the concept that engineering is gendered should help academics and students to be alert to minimising unconscious bias.

Broadening the Scope for Future Engineering Education

It is likely that if more engineers and engineering educators understood that engineering is gendered they would identify gaps in our understanding of engineering practice that have arisen from the gendered nature of engineering. Trevelyan's (2007) finding that engineering practice is socio-technical has not been understood until recently. With the covers removed from stereotypically feminine aspects of engineering practice, further important dimensions of practice that should be part of a university engineering education might be recognised.

IMPROVING ENGINEERING PRACTICE

Improving the Status and Recognition of Socio-Technical Competencies in the Profession

Fletcher revealed that, in the firm she studied, personal interactions that kept the team cohesive were critical to the success of engineering projects. This is an example of engineering practice being socio-technical. Fletcher noted that it is important to ensure this activity is valued.

OTHER THRESHOLD FEATURES OF THE CONCEPT

In addition to being transformative and troublesome, two of the other common features of threshold concepts are being irreversible and discursive. The concept that engineering is gendered is irreversible. Once understood it is not forgotten because it is extremely transformative and incidents that can be explained by the concept are frequent in an engineer's work.

The concept is discursive because once an engineering student or an engineer understands the concept they have language to describe and explain phenomena and incidents that they experience or observe. This is powerful because naming a practice can help to alter it.

RECOMMENDATIONS FOR TEACHING THE THRESHOLD CONCEPT

Engineering educators have a responsibility to society, and especially to female students in engineering, to take steps to ensure that women and men in engineering understand the threshold concept that engineering is gendered.

Based on threshold concept theory, any initiative to help members of the profession understand that engineering is gendered should accommodate sufficient time for people to pass through the liminal space. Similarly, some defensiveness should be expected.

Any effort to teach the concept must be designed to tackle the troublesome features. For engineering students and engineers the concept is foreign, hidden, threatening and hazardous.

Because the concept is foreign, students and engineers must be taken outside their normal modes of thinking for the concept to come into view. Role-play in workshops can be valuable. In the early 2000s I developed scenarios as prompts for discussions on harassment and discrimination and rights and responsibilities among engineering students at Curtin University (Lawrance & Male, 2001). The scenarios were based in the university. Academics participated in panel discussions with the students, and consequently both academics and students learned from the experience. Aligning an assessment with the topic and involving engineering academics ensured that the workshop was taken seriously. A video of the scenarios was later used in classes with engineering students at the University of South Australia and the University of Melbourne. I also adapted the scenarios for engineering workplaces and used them in workshops with engineers.

Because the concept that engineering is gendered is hidden, it must be revealed. As noted in the above discussion on gendered culture in engineering faculties, it was normal for female engineering students in Powell, Dainty and Bagilhole's (2012) study not even to have considered how they performed gender. Educational structures to support reflective practice are likely to at least encourage students and engineers to think about how they perform gender. Reflective practice is already recommended as part of accredited engineering programs in Australia (Bradley, 2008). Reflective practice is recognised as supporting effective learning from experiences such as exposure to engineering practice (Billett, 2011; Kelly & Dansie, 2012). Shared reflective practice such as discussion about experiences on internships and vacation employment would provide opportunities to consider whether a gendered culture was experienced and the alternative responses. This could also minimise harmful influences on self-efficacy such as experienced by some women in Hatmaker's study. It could be an opportunity to ensure that students consciously think about their responses and potential short- and long-term advantages and disadvantages of these. In a male-dominated discipline students ought to be encouraged to consider in their reflective writing how gender is performed. The concept that engineering is gendered can be threatening. Therefore it must be introduced sensitively without any students or professionals being humiliated or being made to feel they stand out.

CONCLUSIONS

By identifying the concept that engineering is gendered as threshold, I have identified this as potentially powerful in improving gender inclusivity in engineering faculties and workplaces and improving engineering practice and engineering education. The concept should be taught to engineering students, academics, and engineers in industry. However, the concept has troublesome features. It is likely to be hidden from most members of the profession because features of a culture are often hidden from those who share the culture. The concept will be foreign to many members of the profession as it conflicts with the assumption that engineering practice is objective. Acceptance of the concept is threatening to those already successful in the profession and condoning the threshold concept is hazardous to belonging in the profession. In conclusion, the concept that engineering is gendered is critical for all engineers, yet teaching it will be a difficult and slow process as engineers pass through the liminal space towards understanding and using the concept. I recommend role-play and reflective practice.

ACKNOWLEDGEMENTS

This chapter was developed from a short piece for the Women in Science Enquiry Network (Male, 2010).

The engineering threshold concepts project was supported by a grant from the Australian Government Office for Learning and Teaching. The study was led by Caroline Baillie and undertaken by me supported by a team at The University of Western Australia. I am grateful to Caroline, Erik Meyer, members of the team and the students and educators who participated.

I sincerely thank Peta Muller for valuable suggestions.

REFERENCES

Acker, J. (1990). Hierarchies, jobs, bodies: A theory of gendered organizations. *Gender and Society, 4*(2), 139–158.

Association of Professional Engineers Scientists & Managers Australia. (2010). Women in the Professions: The State of Play 2009-10 Executive Summary of the APESMA Women in the Professions Survey Report. Melbourne: Association of Professional Engineers Scientists & Managers Australia.

Barnard, S., Powell, A., Bagilhole, B., & Dainty, A. (2010). Researching UK Women Professionals in SET: A Critical Review of Current Approaches. *International Journal of Gender Science, and Technology, 2*(3), 362–381.

Billett, S. (2011). Final Report Curriculum and pedagogic bases for effectively integrating practice-based experiences. Strawberry Hills NSW: Australian Learning and Teaching Council.

Bradley, A. (2008). Accreditation Criteria Guidelines Document G02 Rev 2 (Engineers Australia Accreditation Board, Trans.) *Accreditation Management Systems Education Programs at the Level of Professional Engineer*. Barton, ACT: Institution of Engineers Australia.

Carstensen, A.-K., & Bernhard, J. (2008). Threshold concepts and keys to the portal of understanding: Some Examples from Electrical Engineering. In R. Land, J. H. F. Meyer & J. Smith (Eds.), *Threshold Concepts within the Disciplines* (pp. 143–154). Rotterdam: Sense Publishers.

Cousin, G. (2010). Neither teacher-centred nor student-centred: threshold concepts and research partnerships. *Journal of Learning Development in Higher Education, 1*(2).

Du, X.-Y. (2006). Gendered practices of constructing an engineering identity in a problem-based learning environment. *European Journal of Engineering Education, 31*(1), 35–42.

Faulkner, W. (2007). 'Nuts and Bolts and People': Gender-Troubled Engineering Identities. *Social Studies of Science, 37*(3), 331–356.

Faulkner, W. (2009). Doing gender in engineering workplace cultures. I. Observations from the field. *Engineering Studies, 1*(1), 3–18.

Fletcher, J.K. (1999). *Disappearing acts: gender, power and relational practice at work*. Cambridge, MA: MIT Press.

Gill, J., Mills, J., Sharp, R., & Franzway, S. (2005). *Education Beyond Technical Competence: Gender Issues in the Working Lives of Engineers*. Paper presented at the 4th ASEE / AaeE Global Colloquium on Engineering Education, Sydney.

Gill, J., Sharp, R., Mills, J., & Franzway, S. (2008). I still wanna be an engineer! Women, education and the engineering profession *European Journal of Engineering Education, 33*(4), 391–402.

Godfrey, E., & Parker, L. (2010). Mapping the Cultural Landscape in Engineering Education. *Journal of Engineering Education, 99*(1), 5–22.

Hacker, S. (1981). The culture of engineering: Woman, workplace and machine. *Women, Technology and Innovation, 4*(3), 341–353.

Harlow, A., Scott, J., Peter, M., & Cowie, B. (2011). 'Getting stuck' in analogue electronics: threshold concepts as an explanatory model. *European Journal for Engineering Education, 36*(5), 435–447.

Hatmaker, D.M. (2012). Engineering Identity: Gender and Professional Identity Negotiation among Women Engineers. *Gender, Work & Organization, online first*, no-no. doi: 10.1111/j.1468-0432.2012.00589.x

Holloway, M., Alpay, E., & Bull, A. (2010). *A Quantitative Approach to identifying Threshold concepts in Engineering Education*. Paper presented at the Engineering Education 2010 (EE2010) Inspiring the next generation of engineers, 6–8 July, Aston University.

Ihsen, S. (2005). Special Gender Studies for Engineering? *European Journal of Engineering Education, 30*(4), 487–494.

Jolly, L. (1996). *An ethnographic investigation of the first year engineering student experience*. Paper presented at the The Third Australasian Women in Engineering Forum, Finding the challenge in change: choices for women in engineering, University of Technology, Sydney.

Kabo, J., & Baillie, C. (2009). Seeing through the lens of social justice: a threshold for engineering. *European Journal of Engineering Education, 34*(4), 317–325.

Kaspura, A. (2012). The Engineering Profession: a Statistical Overview (9th ed.). Barton, ACT: Institution of Engineers Australia.

Kaspura, A. (2013). The Engineers Australia Survey of Working Environment and Engineering Careers, 2012. Barton ACT: Institution of Engineers Australia.

Kelly, P., & Dansie, B. (2012). S_2P Student to Practice, Hubs and Spokes Project Report.

King, R. (2008). Addressing the Supply and Quality of Engineering Graduates for the New Century. Surrey Hills NSW: Carrick Institute for Learning and Teaching in Higher Education.

Lawrance, W.B., & Male, S.A. (2001). *Introduction of Rights and Responsibilities in the University Environment to First Year Engineering Students*. Paper presented at the 12th Australasian Association for Engineering Education Conference, Queensland University of Technology.

Male, S.A. (2010). The Threshold Concept That Science and Engineering are Gendered. *Women in Science Enquiry Network Journal, 83*, 15–16.

Male, S.A. (2012a). Engineering Thresholds: an Approach to Curriculum Renewal Final Report. Sydney: Australian Government Office for Learning and Teaching.

Male, S.A. (2012b). Integrated Engineering Foundation Threshold Concept Inventory. Sydney: Australian Government Office for Learning and Teaching.

Male, S.A., & Baillie, C.A. (2014). Research guided teaching practices: Engineering thresholds; an approach to curriculum renewal. In A. Johri & B. Olds (Eds.), *Cambridge Handbook of Engineering Education Research* (pp. 393–408): Cambridge University Press.

Meyer, J.H.F., & Land, R. (2003). Enhancing Teaching-Learning Environments in Undergraduate Courses Occasional Report 4 Retrieved 31 May 2010, from http://www.etl.tla.ed.ac.uk/docs/ETLreport4.pdf

Mills, J.E., Mehrtens, V., Smith, E.J., & Adams, V. (2008). CREW revisited in 2007 the Year of Women in Engineering: An Update on Women's Progress in the Australian Engineering Workforce. Canberra: Engineers Australia.

Perkins, D. (1999). The many faces of constructivism. *Educational Leadership, 57*(3), 6–11.

Perkins, D. (2006). Constructivism and troublesome knowledge. In J.H.F. Meyer & R. Land (Eds.), *Overcoming Barriers to Student Understanding: Threshold concepts and troublesome knowledge* (pp. 33–47). London and New York: Routledge.

Powell, A., Bagilhole, B., & Dainty, A. (2009). How Women Engineers Do and Undo Gender: Consequences for Gender Equality. *Gender, Work & Organization, 16*(4), 411–428.

Powell, A., Dainty, A., & Bagilhole, B. (2012). Gender stereotypes among women engineering and technology students in the UK: lessons from career choice narratives. *European Journal of Engineering Education, 37*(6), 541–556. doi: 10.1080/03043797.2012.724052

Quinlan, K.M., Male, S.A., Baillie, C.A., Stamboulis, A., Fill, J., & Jaffer, Z. (2013). Methodological Challenges in Researching Threshold Concepts: A Comparative Analysis of Three Projects. *Higher Education, 66*(5), 585–601. doi: 10.1007/s10734-013-9623-y

Ridgeway, C. L. (2009). Framed Before We Know It: How Gender Shapes Social Relations. *Gender and Society, 23*(2), 145–160.

Robinson, J. G., & McIlwee, J. S. (1991). Men, Women, and the Culture of Engineering. *The Sociological Quarterly, 32*(3), 403–421.

Schwartzman, L. (2010). Transcending disciplinary boundaries: a proposed theoretical foundation for threshold concepts. In J. H. F. Meyer, R. Land & C. A. Baillie (Eds.), *Threshold Concepts and Transformational Learning* (pp. 21–44). Rotterdam: Sense Publishers.

Tilli, S., & Trevelyan, J.P. (2010). Labour Force Outcomes for Engineering Graduates in Australia. *Australasian Journal of Engineering Education, 16*(2), 101–122.

Tonso, K.L. (2007). *On the Outskirts of Engineering*. Rotterdam: Sense Publishers.

Trevelyan, J.P. (2007). Technical Coordination in Engineering Practice. *Journal of Engineering Education, 96*(3), 191–204.

Zander, C., Boustedt, J., Eckerdal, A., McCartney, R., Mostrom, J. E., Ratcliffe, M., & Sanders, K. (2008). Threshold concepts in computer science: a multi-national empirical investigation. In R. Land, J. H. F. Meyer & J. Smith (Eds.), *Threshold Concepts within the Disciplines* (pp. 105–118). Rotterdam & Tapei: Sense Publishers.

Index